Annotated Legal Documents on Islam in Europe: France

Annotated Legal Documents on Islam in Europe

VOLUME 10

The titles published in this series are listed at *brill.com/ldie*

Annotated Legal Documents on Islam in Europe:

France

Compiled and Annotated by

Anne Fornerod

BRILL

LEIDEN | BOSTON

Library of Congress Cataloging-in-Publication Data

Names: Fornerod, Anne, 1975- compiler.
Title: Annotated legal documents on Islam in Europe. France / compiled and annotated by Anne Fornerod.
Description: Leiden : Brill, 2016. | Series: Annotated legal documents on islam in europe ; volume 10 |
Includes bibliographical references and index.
Identifiers: LCCN 2016004921 | ISBN 9789004316348 (pbk. : alk. paper)
Subjects: LCSH: Muslims–Legal status, laws, etc.–France.
Classification: LCC KJV4207.M56 A2 2016 | DDC 342.4408/5297–dc23
LC record available at http://lccn.loc.gov/2016004921

Typeface for the Latin, Greek, and Cyrillic scripts: "Brill". See and download: brill.com/brill-typeface.

ISSN 2214-1340
ISBN 978-90-04-31634-8 (paperback)

This book is printed on acid-free paper and produced in a sustainable manner.

Printed by Printforce, the Netherlands

Contents

Foreword by the Editors

This is the tenth volume in the series *Annotated Legal Documents on Islam in Europe*. The publication of this series reflects the growing concern with the status of Islam in Europe which has been expressed in recent years. This has most obviously been the case in political discourse, something which can be traced back to the early 1990s. But the concern has also moved into the legal field, most markedly, of course, with limitations on Muslim female dress enacted in France and Belgium and the ban on building minarets on mosques in Switzerland. The atrocities committed mostly by European Muslim extremists in Paris in January and November 2015, and the huge number of Muslim refugees coming into the EU have certainly intensified the debate on the legal status of Muslims in Europe as a whole. The discussions provoked by these events have often reflected a general ignorance about the religious status and rights of Muslims in the various European countries, status and rights which can differ significantly. A closer look at the legislation quickly shows how different it can be from one country to another and, in some cases, how far back in time such legislation can go. Despite the common legal and political foundations constructed since 1945 in instruments such as the European Convention on Human Rights and the more recently accumulated legislation of the European Union, this closer look reveals how difficult it can be to talk of the 'European practice' in this field. In some countries Islam has an officially recognised status which in several cases originates in the first half of the 20th century, so it is not new. In other countries no such recognition of any religion is available even if informal ways of favouring one religion over another may exist. Since 1990 especially, European courts have moved to equalise the status of Islam with that of other religions in the practical exercise of religious freedom in various countries. Particular practices regarded as core religious obligations—in the case of Islam practices such as male circumcision, access to correctly slaughtered meat and otherwise *halal* food, free time for the main periods of worship and religious festivals, and the right to build mosques—can be controversial in some countries while less so in others. Children's access to Islamic religious instruction can be achieved in cooperation with the state education systems in some countries, while in others the community must rely on its own arrangements. All of these multitudinous issues are reflected variously in the national legislation.

The aim of this series is to make this legislation available to both the interested researcher and the practising lawyer. Altogether the series is expected to comprise 32 volumes, one for each of the 28 countries of the European Union plus Norway and Switzerland, and a volume each dealing with the European Union (treaties, directives and decisions of the Court of Justice of the European Communities) and the European Court of Human Rights. Excerpts of relevant legislation will be introduced and summarised by the volume compiler, and where court cases have provided significant interpretation of the law they will also be referred to. The legislation itself is reproduced in the original language, as the editors and the publisher agreed early on in the preparation of the series that any attempt to translate legislation into English would be unsatisfactory and could be misleading. The annotation by the compiler should give sufficient guidance to users to allow a decision as to whether to arrange a translation for their specific purposes.

While there is in many countries legislation explicitly referring to aspects of Islam, most often regarding official recognition or to do with education, in other countries there is none. France is often presented as the model of the separation of state and religion, expressed in the term *laïcism* for which 'secularism' is an unsatisfactory translation. As the detailed study which this volume facilitates shows, the situation is not as clear-cut as is often assumed.

An attempt has been made to ensure that the volumes are structured in as similar a manner as possible. The starting point for this has been the thematic organisation of the first six volumes of the *Yearbook of Muslims in Europe* which Brill has published annually since 2009 (the *Yearbook* has been restructured from vol. 7 published in 2015). But it has only been a starting point, and in each volume the compiler and the editors have agreed on the structure which makes most sense for the legislation of the country concerned. Normally one member of the editorial group takes responsibility for discussing the structure and compilation of each volume with the compiler: in this instance it is Prof. Marie-Claire Foblets, Max Planck Institute for Soocial Anthropology, Halle, Germany, who has undertaken this task. We are also grateful to Kate Elliott for the care shown in copy editing the volume. The idea for this project came from the publisher, where Nicolette van der Hoek and Nienke Brienen-Moolenaar have played an invaluable role in ensuring that the project has maintained its momentum. As editors, we appreciate how much their expertise contributes to ensuring that a project like this can run smoothly.

It is in the nature of such a project that each volume, if left as it stands, will gradually become out of date as new legislation and cases appear. It is the intention of the editors and publishers in due course to make the contents available on-line in a form which will permit regular updating.

The Editors
December 2015

General Introduction

In June 2014, the French Council for the Muslim Faith (*Conseil Français du Culte Musulman*) published a document entitled the 'Citizens' Convention of Muslims in France for living together' by which it intended to clarify its place and role in French society and to assert the willingness of the citizens of Muslim faith to adhere to Republican values and principles. In particular, this text states that 'Islam is perfectly compatible with the laws of the Republic. No need for new law, legal adaptation or jurisprudential evolution: Islam finds its marks in the common law'.[1] At first sight, such a statement would make any further investigation of relations between Islam and French law seem superfluous. In other words, would the challenge consisting in integrating the now second-ranking religion in France into the legal framework be achieved? It has, however, also been argued that public authorities' attitude towards Islam relies *de facto* on management and includes 'important areas of legal uncertainty, or areas outside law'.[2] With regard to the years of focus on Islam-related issues in media, social and political spheres, the question arises as to how these issues are addressed in the legal field. It is hardly conceivable that a religion—with institutions and practices—would stand apart from and outside the legal framework designed for religious groups and practices. The question is then not so much to know whether but how and where the law applicable to Islam shows variations and differences, in comparison with other faith groups.

Historically, France is known as the 'elder daughter' of the Catholic Church. This refers to the baptism of the Merovingian king Clovis, the first king ever baptised in Europe at the very end of the sixth century. This tradition was interrupted following the 1789 Revolution which put an end to the monarchy by divine right, and where state and religious authorities were separated. Since then and until 1905, France experienced two types of relation between state and religious institutions: a strict separation between state and religion in the years from 1790 was succeeded by the Napoleonic system of recognised faith groups. This system was based on a close relationship between faith groups and public authorities, whereby the latter gained control over the former. It was further characterised by a registration of faith groups, which applied at that time to

1 Full text available at: http://www.lecfcm.fr/wp-content/uploads/2014/06/cfcm_texte_convention_version_finalisee2.pdf.

2 Messner, Francis, Prélot, Pierre-Henri and Woehrling, Jean-Marie, *Traité de droit français des religions*, no. 696.

the Catholic, Lutheran, Reformed and Jewish faiths. Moreover, the Napoleonic system of recognised faiths resulted in the public funding of mainly religious ministers and places of worship. The Act of 9 December 1905 on separation between Church and State meant the end of such an organisation but is still in force in Alsace-Moselle.[3]

The 1905 Act still provides a fundamental legal basis for the religion-state relationship. Today France embodies a system of strict separation between public authorities and religious groups that would entail very limited, if any, relation between state and religion. A detailed examination of the legal regulation of religious beliefs and practices reveals a much more complex situation, if only because religious practices and activities call for a legal framework like all other social phenomena. Contrary to received wisdom, the French system shares legal principles applicable to the regulation of religious groups with other European countries, like state neutrality and freedom of religion and the related right to practise.

It is, however, equally true that, irrespective of the faith group concerned, this legal system is influenced by a dual approach of *laïcité*[4] that is rooted in French history. Along with the implementation of *laïcité* as a legal principle synonymous with neutrality, equality and freedom of religion, the legal framework for religious groups and activities is occasionally subject to the influence of another conception of *laïcité* which tends to obscure the social role of religion or simply its presence in the public sphere.[5] *Laïcité* as a core Republican value inherited from the somewhat idealised time of the political regime of the Third Republic (1870–1940) undeniably weighs on the applicable law and is reflected in the normative level of the texts aimed at regulating religious issues.

As the 1905 Act is part of a Republican pact fundamental to the cohesion of French society, public authorities resort to more limited and targeted texts in order to tackle the unavoidable task of regulating religious issues. The need for the regulation of religious practice calls for a certain pragmatism, which would explain the importance by volume and contents of administrative circulars on the fringe of the 1905 Act, while they have a limited normative value. It follows that French legislation on religions offers a specific legal structure as it relies

---

3 On this point see below *1.2 Specific situation in Alsace-Moselle* and, in general, *Traité de droit français des religions*, no. 464 et seq.

4 This duality is analysed by Alessandro Ferrari in his paper 'De la politique à la technique: laïcité narrative et laïcité du droit. Pour une comparaison France/Italie', in Brigitte Basdevant-Gaudemet, François Jankowiak (eds), *Le droit ecclésiastique de la fin du XVIIIe au milieu du XXe siècle en Europe*, Leuven, Peeters.

5 On this point see the analysis of David Koussens (2011).

on few parliamentary Acts but countless regulatory provisions. These include decrees (issued by the President of the Republic or by the Prime Minister exercising regulatory powers pursuant to Article 21 of the Constitution) and numerous circulars, defined as instructions on the substance or the procedure of the public services. Most of these circulars are issued by the Ministry of Home Affairs, in charge of matters pertaining to religious groups and activities.

As a result, providing a complete view of the law applying where individuals—and groups—act as Muslims leads us to consider a much larger set of rules than those entrenched in the 1905 Act. In this regard, applicable legislation can be divided into three 'categories'. The first one corresponds to general legislation applicable irrespective of religion, in that religious context or status has no influence on its adoption or implementation. This is the case, for example, of the 1901 Act on associations (see below *1.1. Religious communities as associations*) or non-discrimination law. Due to the general character of most legislation, passed even without the aim of regulating religion, case law references will serve as an illustration.

The second category entails legislation explicitly applicable to all religious groups, although its adoption may implicitly be designed for Islam. This is how the Act of 15 March 2004 prohibiting the conspicuous wearing of religious symbols in public schools was interpreted (see below *12.2.2 Prohibition of religious dress for pupils*).

The third category includes legislation expressly referring to aspects of Islam (like, for example, a reference to Aïd El Kebir[6]). Even in this case, the legislation shows no specificity beyond its object, Islam.

Finally, France undoubtedly falls within the countries in which legislation very limitedly refers to aspects of Islam. As a result, case law plays an unusually central role. On the one hand, and as in other countries, it indicates how general legislation applies to Islam in practice. On the other hand, it is worth emphasising that French case law traditionally occupies a central place in the regulation of religion by often filling the regulatory or legislative gaps in this field. Definitions of principles as important as *laïcité* for example are enshrined neither in legislative texts, nor in constitutional texts, but, rather, are dealt with in case law.

6 'Id al-Kabir; the spelling of this and other Arabic/Islamic terms has been retained as they exist in French practice.

CHAPTER 1

Status of Religious Communities

1.1 Religious Communities as Associations

Since the Act of 9 December 1905, the French legal system of relations between state and religious communities has been characterised by separation. The result is that the state does not recognise any religious groups. This principle of 'non-recognition' of faith groups should be read in the light of the former applicable legislation. Indeed, the Act of 1905 above all aims at bringing to an end the Napoleonic system of recognised religious groups, which accordingly were publicly funded and controlled by the state. Henceforth, religious groups are submitted to a regime of private law. However, the 1905 legislation introduces a specific type of association: the religious association (*association cultuelle*), whose regime is mainly defined in Articles 4, 18 and 19.[1] At the time of the separation, these associations were meant to replace the former Napoleonic religious institutions responsible for managing properties for worship and then to take over the ownership of these properties (Article 4 of the 1905 Act).[2] However, due to the refusal of the Catholic Church to create such associations,[3] the government adapted the law and the Act of 2 January 1907 on public worship was passed. This provides that religious associations can be replaced by 1901 Act associations (Article 4 of the 1907 Act).

In any case, the regime of the religious associations of the 1905 Act, which is still applicable to religious groups other than Catholic ones is partly based on the Act of 1 July 1901 on associations which, for example, regulates their creation. Pursuant to Article 5, a preliminary declaration must be filed with the prefecture.

---

1 For various reasons, the Catholic Church refused to create such religious associations. An agreement was reached between Rome and the French Government in the 1920s, leading to another type of religious association (*association diocésaine*), whose status is similar to that of the 1905 Act religious associations. See Messner F., Prélot, P.H., Woehrling, J.M., *Traité de droit français des religions*, no. 1966 et seq.

2 In a sense, this status specifically designed for religious associations in itself goes against the idea of a strict separation between state and religion.

3 The main reason for this refusal was that the religious associations brought together the religious leaders and the faithful on an equal basis, contrary to the hierarchical structure of the Catholic Church.

Religious associations are above all characterised by their purpose, which must be exclusively religious according to Article 19 of the 1905 Act. Article 19 provides that religious activities should be strictly understood as relating to worship only. In the event that a religious group does not meet this legal condition, it will be organised according to the 1901 Act regime. The 1905 association status is advantageous from a tax point of view (see below *3.3 Tax exemptions*) while the 1901 association status is more flexible especially as regards the creation of the association and its object. As stated by the European Court of Human Rights, 'there is no definition of the religious association and the recognition or not of the status of religious association is not done at the time of declaration, but when the association gets government approval to benefit from certain tax or property arrangements'.[4] The French Council of State has defined the criteria of such recognition and the religious purpose covers the celebration of ceremonies and worship-related activities such as buying, renting or building places of worship or training and paying religious leaders (see below case 1).

All these provisions apply to both religious groups existing in 1905 and those created or developed later, such as Islam. Regarding Islam specifically, it is worth stressing that a reform adopted in 1981 and partly revising the 1901 Act proved to be favourable for Muslim groups willing to create 1901 associations. Indeed, the Act of 9 October 1981 made it easier to create such associations as it repealed the decree of 12 April 1939 on the creation of foreign associations, which required prior administrative authorisation.[5]

However, the restrictive purpose of religious associations (1905 Act) and the enlarged role of the mosque in the life of the Muslim community often make it necessary to create two types of associations.[6] So as to allow religious groups to choose the most appropriate legal structure for their internal functioning, the Ministry of Home Affairs issued an administrative circular on 23 June 2010 on

---

4 European Court of Human Rights, 30 June 2011, no. 8916/05, *Association Les Témoins de Jéhovah c/ France*, § 33.

5 Associations were deemed foreign when a quarter of their members were foreigners. On this issue see Janine Ponty, 'Les étrangers et le droit d'association au xxe siècle', *Matériaux pour l'histoire de notre temps*. 2003, no. 69, pp. 24–25.

6 See Hervé Maurey, *Les collectivités territoriales et le financement des lieux de culte*, Rapport d'information n° 345 (2014–2015), Sénat, pp. 25 and 53. Available at http://www.senat.fr/rap/r14-345/r14-345.html. This difficulty had already been pointed out by a previous report of 2006: see Jean-Pierre Machelon, *Les relations des cultes avec les pouvoirs publics: rapport au ministre de l'Intérieur*, Paris, La Documentation française, 2006, p. 39.

both categories of associations. This text provides an updated overview of the applicable law, taking case law into account.

Loi du 1er juillet 1901 relative au contrat d'association

Article 2: Les associations de personnes pourront se former librement sans autorisation ni déclaration préalable, mais elles ne jouiront de la capacité juridique que si elles se sont conformées aux dispositions de l'article 5.

Article 3: Toute association fondée sur une cause ou en vue d'un objet illicite, contraire aux lois, aux bonnes mœurs, ou qui aurait pour but de porter atteinte à l'intégrité du territoire national et à la forme républicaine du gouvernement, est nulle et de nul effet.

Article 5: Toute association qui voudra obtenir la capacité juridique prévue par l'article 6 devra être rendue publique par les soins de ses fondateurs.
La déclaration préalable en sera faite à la préfecture du département ou à la sous-préfecture de l'arrondissement où l'association aura son siège social. Elle fera connaître le titre et l'objet de l'association, le siège de ses établissements et les noms, professions et domiciles et nationalités de ceux qui, à un titre quelconque, sont chargés de son administration. Un exemplaire des statuts est joint à la déclaration. Il sera donné récépissé de celle-ci dans le délai de cinq jours.
Lorsque l'association aura son siège social à l'étranger, la déclaration préalable prévue à l'alinéa précédent sera faite à la préfecture du département où est situé le siège de son principal établissement.
L'association n'est rendue publique que par une insertion au Journal officiel, sur production de ce récépissé.
Les associations sont tenues de faire connaître, dans les trois mois, tous les changements survenus dans leur administration, ainsi que toutes les modifications apportées à leurs statuts.
Ces modifications et changements ne sont opposables aux tiers qu'à partir du jour où ils auront été déclarés.
Les modifications et changements seront en outre consignés sur un registre spécial qui devra être présenté aux autorités administratives ou judiciaires chaque fois qu'elles en feront la demande.

Article 6: Toute association régulièrement déclarée peut, sans aucune autorisation spéciale, ester en justice, recevoir des dons manuels ainsi que des dons d'établissements d'utilité publique, acquérir à titre onéreux, posséder

et administrer, en dehors des subventions de l'État, des régions, des départements, des communes et de leurs établissements publics:
1° Les cotisations de ses membres;
2° Le local destiné à l'administration de l'association et à la réunion de ses membres;
3° Les immeubles strictement nécessaires à l'accomplissement du but qu'elle se propose.
Les associations déclarées qui ont pour but exclusif l'assistance, la bienfaisance, la recherche scientifique ou médicale peuvent accepter les libéralités entre vifs ou testamentaires dans des conditions fixées par décret en Conseil d'État.

Article 7: En cas de nullité prévue par l'article 3, la dissolution de l'association est prononcée par le tribunal de grande instance, soit à la requête de tout intéressé, soit à la diligence du ministère public. Celui-ci peut assigner à jour fixe et le tribunal, sous les sanctions prévues à l'article 8, ordonner par provision et nonobstant toute voie de recours, la fermeture des locaux et l'interdiction de toute réunion des membres de l'association.

Loi du 9 décembre 1905 concernant la séparation des Églises et de l'État

Article 4: Dans le délai d'un an, à partir de la promulgation de la présente loi, les biens mobiliers et immobiliers des menses, fabriques, conseils presbytéraux, consistoires et autres établissements publics du culte seront, avec toutes les charges et obligations qui les grèvent et avec leur affectation spéciale, transférés par les représentants légaux de ces établissements aux associations qui, en se conformant aux règles d'organisation générale du culte dont elles se proposent d'assurer l'exercice, se seront légalement formées, suivant les prescriptions de l'article 19, pour l'exercice de ce culte dans les anciennes circonscriptions desdits établissements.

Titre IV: Des associations pour l'exercice des cultes
Article 18: Les associations formées pour subvenir aux frais, à l'entretien et à l'exercice public d'un culte devront être constituées conformément aux articles 5 et suivants du titre Ier de la loi du 1er juillet 1901. Elles seront, en outre, soumises aux prescriptions de la présente loi.

Article 19: Ces associations devront avoir exclusivement pour objet l'exercice d'un culte et être composés au moins:
Dans les communes de moins de 1,000 habitants, de sept personnes;

Dans les communes de 1,000 à 20,000 habitants, de quinze personnes;
Dans les communes dont le nombre des habitants est supérieur à 20,000, de vingt-cinq personnes majeures, domiciliées ou résidant dans la circonscription religieuse.
Chacun de leurs membres pourra s'en retirer en tout temps, après payement des cotisations échues et de celles de l'année courante, nonobstant toute clause contraire.
Nonobstant toute clause contraire des statuts, les actes de gestion financière et d'administration légale des biens accomplis par les directeurs ou administrateurs seront, chaque année au moins présentés au contrôle de l'assemblée générale des membres de l'association et soumis à son approbation.
Les associations pourront recevoir, en outre, des cotisations prévues par l'article 6 de la loi du 1er juillet 1901, le produit des quêtes et collectes pour les frais du culte, percevoir des rétributions: pour les cérémonies et services religieux même par fondation; pour la location des bancs et sièges; pour la fourniture des objets destinés au service des funérailles dans les édifices religieux et à la décoration de ces édifices.
Les associations cultuelles pourront recevoir, dans les conditions prévues par le deuxième alinéa de l'article 910 du code civil, les libéralités testamentaires et entre vifs destinées à l'accomplissement de leur objet ou grevées de charges pieuses ou cultuelles.
Elles pourront verser, sans donner lieu à perception de droits, le surplus de leurs recettes à d'autres associations constituées pour le même objet.
Elles ne pourront, sous quelque forme que ce soit, recevoir des subventions de l'État, des départements et des communes. Ne sont pas considérées comme subventions les sommes allouées pour réparations aux édifices affectés au culte public, qu'ils soient ou non classés monuments historiques.

Article 20: Ces associations peuvent, dans les formes déterminées par l'article 7 du décret du 16 août 1901, constituer des unions ayant une administration ou une direction centrale; ces unions seront réglées par l'article 18 et par les cinq derniers paragraphes de l'article 19 de la présente loi.

Loi du 2 janvier 1907 concernant l'exercice public des cultes

Article 4: Indépendamment des associations soumises aux dispositions du titre IV de la loi du 9 décembre 1905, l'exercice public d'un culte peut être assuré tant au moyen d'associations régies par la loi du 1er juillet 1901 (1, 2, 3, 4, 5, 6, 7, 8, 9, 12 et 17) que par voie de réunions tenues sur initiatives individuelles en vertu de la loi du 30 juin 1881 et selon les prescriptions de l'article 25 de la loi du 9 décembre 1905.

Circulaire du 23 juin 2010, le support institutionnel de l'exercice du culte: les associations cutuelles régies par la loi du 9 décembre 1905 et les associations exerçant un culte sous le régime de la loi du 1er juillet 1901, NOR: IOCD1016585C (excerpt)[7]

Après avoir constaté le profond changement du paysage religieux intervenu au cours du siècle dernier sur le territoire de la République, avec l'apparition de nouvelles religions aux côtés des quatre cultes reconnus jusqu'en 1905 (catholicisme, protestantismes réformé et luthérien, judaïsme), la commission de réflexion juridique sur les relations des cultes avec les pouvoirs publics, présidés par le professeur Jean-Pierre machelon, a notamment étudié la question du support institutionnel de l'exercie du culte dans son rapport remis au ministre de l'intérieur le 20 septembre 2006. Les auditions auxquelles elle a procédé ont montré que les différences entre le régime juridique des associations régies par la loi du 1er juillet 1901 relative au contrat d'association et celui des associations cultuelles régies par la loi du 9 décembre 1905 concernant la séparation des Églises et de l'État ne sont pas toujours distinctement perçues par les responsables de groupes religieux, notamment au sein des confessions qui ne jouissent pas d'une implantation ancienne sur le territoire. Il n'est pas rare que le choix de tel ou tel support juridique apparaisse danvatage comme le fruit du hasard que comme le produit d'une réflexion mûrie.

Un groupe de travail a été mis en place pour étudier les suites qui pourraient être données aux préconisations en restant dans le cadre juridique fixé par la loi du 9 décembre 1905. Il a estimé qu'une meilleure conaissance du droit des associations dans le domaine cultuel était de nature à permettre à chaque culte de choisir la structure juridique la plus appropriée à son fonctionnement interne, les uns préférant exercer leurs activités strictement cultuelles au sein d'une association placée sous le régime juridique de la loi du 9 décembre 1905, les autres choisissant de pratiquer leurs activités cultuelles et leurs activités annexes au sein d'une association régie par la loi du 1er juillet 1901. Les deux régimes juridiques découlant de ce choix diffèrent sensiblement tant en ce qui concerne les obligations que doivent respecter les associations que les avantages liés au statut juridique choisi. La présente circulaire a pour objet de présenter ces deux régimes juridiques, à la lumière de la jurisprudence.

7 The full text of the circular (31 pages) is available at http://circulaires.legifrance.gouv.fr/pdf/2010/06/cir_31326.pdf.

Case Law

Case 1: An association can be considered a religious association within the meaning of the 1905 Act only if its purpose is exclusively religious and provided that its activities are not contrary to public order. Within the meaning of Article 19 of the 1905 Act, a religious purpose corresponds to the celebration of ceremonies for the performance of rites and practices by people united by a common religious belief. A religious association can carry out only activities related to its religious purpose i.e. buying, renting or building places of worship or training and paying religious leaders (*Council of State, Opinion, 24-10-1997, no. 187122, Association locale pour le culte des témoins de Jéhovah de Riom*).

1.2 Specific Situation in Alsace-Moselle

The specificity of the three *départements* of Eastern France comes from the fact that the law on recognised religions is still applicable, due to historical circumstances. Indeed, at the time the Act of 9 December 1905 and the Act of 1901 on associations were passed, the three *départements* were still part of the Second German Reich, as they had been annexed in 1871 after the Franco-Prussian war. However, once they had been returned to France following World War I, the local law was maintained, including that regarding religious institutions and activities. This applies to four religious groups: the Catholic Church, the Reformed Church, the Lutheran Church, and Jews. This local law mainly rests on the Act of 18 Germinal year X, which brings together the Concordat of 1801 signed between the Holy See and the French government and the Organic Articles unilaterally adopted by the latter. The Jewish denomination is regulated by decrees of 17 March 1808.

Unlike those four recognised religious groups, Islam is regulated by some provisions of general local law applicable to non-recognised religious denominations. Pursuant to Article 21ff. of the Local Civil Code,[8] religious groups can freely organise themselves as associations provided that they enroll in the register of associations held by the local court. No distinction is drawn between associations having a religious purpose and others. Furthermore, associations in local law with a religious purpose, like the 1905 Act associations, benefit from certain tax advantages even if this purpose is not exclusively religious.[9] Despite the non-applicability of the 1905 Act in those three *départements*, the admin-

8 Available at http://www.idl-am.org/.

9 See *Traité de droit français des religions*, no. 2125.

istrative court of Strasbourg has held, however, that an association in local law should have an exclusively religious object in order to benefit from certain tax advantages available in the 1905 Act on religious associations (*Administrative Court of Strasbourg, 30-12-1998, Église Néo-Apostolique de France*, no. 952542) (see below *3.3 Tax exemptions*).

Code civil local

Article 21: Les associations peuvent se former librement.
Une association acquiert la capacité juridique par l'inscription au registre des associations du tribunal d'instance compétent.

CHAPTER 2

Relations between the State and Islam

In the French system of relations between public authorities and religions there is no recognition of any religions (Article 2 of the 1905 Act). The result is that there is no specific legal tool applicable to religious groups enabling them to organise their relations with the state. Since 1905, religious groups have been able to choose between two kinds of association: the general status of 1901 Act associations or the specific status of 1905 Act associations designed only for religious practice (see above *1. Status of religious communities*). The French Council for the Muslim Faith (*Conseil Français du Culte Musulman*, hereinafter CFCM), which is the representative body of Islam in France, is organised as a 1901 Act association. As a result, there is no legal but, instead, political recognition. The limited legal basis available for organising the representation of Muslims in France does not, however, reflect the difficult and complex process that led to the setting up of the present CFCM.

2.1 The French Council for the Muslim Faith

The organisation of a representative body for the Islamic community of France has a long history and has been a particular focus of attention for several years. The first attempt to set up representation for Islam in France led to the creation of the association entitled the Muslim Institute Committee of Paris, created in 1915, some years before the building of the Great Mosque of Paris and aimed at offering an independent intellectual centre for Muslims living in France.[1] The present structure, however, has its roots in more recent times. Indeed, due to the growing importance of the Islamic community in France, the need has arisen for public authorities to have a Muslim representative body likely to address and discuss the main aspects of Muslim religious practice. Indeed, unlike other main religious groups, which inherited their own representative body from the recognised faiths system in force until 1905, the Muslim faith lacked such a body.

1 Chems-Eddine Hafiz, Gilles Devers, *Droit et religion musulmane* (Paris: Dalloz, 2005), pp. 80–81.

The creation of the CFCM and of the various Regional Councils for the Muslim Faith (*Conseils Régionaux du Culte Musulman*, hereinafter CRCMs) is the outcome of years of negotiations and efforts initiated in 1990 by the then Minister of Home Affairs to set up a unique representative body for Islam.[2] The turning point was in 1999 when the Ministry of Home Affairs managed to bring together the members of the various groups representing Islam in France for a consultation process called *al istichâra*. This consultation started with the signing of one common text entitled *Legal principles and basis governing relations between the government and the Muslim Faith in France* in October 2000, which is, however, devoid of legal effect. Two years later all the participants in the consultation process agreed a set of election procedures by signing a framework agreement.

The creation of the CFCM and of the CRCMs results from elections, which took place in April 2003.[3] The members of the general assembly of the CFCM were elected by several thousand delegates designated by representatives of approximately 900 places of worship.[4] The CFCM includes several internal commissions aimed at dealing with various aspects of religious practice such as the building of places of worship, burial grounds, ritual slaughtering, pilgrimages to Mecca and imam training. The CFCM and the CRCMs are organised in associations, whose purpose, revised in 2012, consists in 'promoting dialogue between its members in order to develop mutual exchanges and reflection on common issues concerning the Muslim Faith in France; ensure the representation of Muslim places of worship with national and public authorities; supporting the dignity and the interests of Muslim faith in France through all legal means and in particular before courts; to implement joint projects likely to promote the progress and image of the Muslim faith; to foster dialogue with all parts of civil society and other religions.'[5]

The principle of separation explains why public authorities could monitor the election process but were not entitled to be part of it. Indeed, in 2003, at the time of the election of the first CFCM, several members of parliament wondered to what extent local public authorities could have been more closely involved in this election process.[6] The association remains the legal form of

2 See, among others, Alain Boyer, *Le droit des religions en France* (Paris: PUF, 1993), p. 229.

3 Two other elections have followed since then, in 2008 and 2013.

4 The number of delegates is calculated from the surface area of places of worship.

5 Text available at http://www.lecfcm.fr/wp-content/uploads/2009/02/statuts-approuves-age-paraphes.pdf.

6 See for example parliamentary question no. 14743 of 24 March 2003, available at http://questions.assemblee-nationale.fr/q12/12-14743QE.htm.

organisation of religious groups but it does not reflect the complex net of relations and informal ways of communication between the state and Muslim representatives.[7] A specific structure deserves to be mentioned here. The operation of the foundation for Islamic charities (*Fondation des œuvres de l'Islam de France*) was created by the decree of 25 July 2005 under the common legal status of public interest organisation with the aim of improving conditions for religious practice and providing a framework for fundraising and management.[8] Its main purpose consists in centralising funds for the building of places of worship. It was, however, soon paralysed by quarrels, but the CFCM has recently expressed the wish to reactivate this major tool needed to finance religious buildings.[9]

2.2 A National Forum for Dialogue

As the Minister of Home Affairs observed in 2003, the purpose of the CFCM is to represent the diversity of Muslim religious practices and tackle the various issues pertaining to such practices but not to embody all the structures active in Muslim non-ritual activities.[10] From the beginning of this process the question was raised of its representativeness, as not all tendencies and forces among Muslims recognise themselves as part of the CFCM.[11] The internal discord among the various groups has prevented the solution of still pending issues like the funding of places of worship or imam training. Consequently, in February 2015, the Minister of Home Affairs declared his intention to launch

7 See Malika Zeghal, 'La constitution du Conseil Français du Culte Musulman: reconnaissance politique d'un Islam français?', *Archives de sciences sociales des religions*, no. 129, 2005, 97–113, available at http://assr.revues.org/1113.

8 See Hervé Maurey, *Les collectivités territoriales et le financement des lieux de culte*, Rapport d'information n° 345 (2014–2015), Sénat, pp. 25 and 53. Available at http://www.senat.fr/rap/r14-345/r14-345.html.

9 Ibid. p. 28. See also the parliamentary question, *Journal Officiel*, Sénat, 14-10-2010, p. 2658 and ministerial response, *Journal Officiel*, Sénat, 01-12-2010, p. 11103, available at http://www.senat.fr/questions/base/2010/qSEQ10101055S.html.

10 Parliamentary question no. 12645, *Journal Officiel*, Assemblée nationale, 24 February 2003, p. 1340; Ministerial response, *Journal Officiel*, Assemblée nationale, 9 June 2003, p. 4554. Available online at http://questions.assemblee-nationale.fr/q12/12-12645QE.htm.

11 See Malika Zeghal, 'La constitution du Conseil Français du Culte Musulman: reconnaissance politique d'un Islam français?', *Archives de sciences sociales des religions*, no. 129, 2005, pp. 97–113, available at http://assr.revues.org/1113.

a reform in this field. The CFCM—and the CRCMs—will not be demoted but, along the lines of what exists for the Catholic Church, a forum for dialogue will additionally take place twice a year, including the Prime Minister, to discuss very specific questions in all areas of concern for French Muslims.[12] The administrative circular of 18 March 2015[13] on the organisation of consultations with representatives of French Muslims in *départements* for the establishment of a national forum for dialogue explains that this forum is intended to strengthen dialogue between the Government and the Muslims of France by providing concrete answers to their expectations about worship or related topics. The forum will bring together in the presence of the Prime Minister the members of the CFCM, imams, and representatives of mosques and of civil society. In order to establish the list of issues to be addressed by the forum for dialogue, regions and *département* prefects will first organise consultation locally, involving local Muslim associations, but also members of the business world, of universities, city stakeholders and all people willing to get involved in such issues. The first meeting of this forum took place 15 June 2015 and addressed the following issues: the safety of places of worship and the image of Islam; the building and managing of places of worship; the training and status of chaplains and religious leaders; and ritual practices.[14]

Loi du 1er juillet 1901 relative au contrat d'association

Article 1: L'association est la convention par laquelle deux ou plusieurs personnes mettent en commun, d'une façon permanente, leurs connaissances ou leur activité dans un but autre que de partager des bénéfices. Elle est régie, quant à sa validité, par les principes généraux du droit applicables aux contrats et obligations.

Article 2: Les associations de personnes pourront se former librement sans autorisation ni déclaration préalable, mais elles ne jouiront de la capacité juridique que si elles se sont conformées aux dispositions de l'article 5.

12 See the official statement of the Minister available at http://www.interieur.gouv.fr/Actualites/L-actu-du-Ministere/Dialogue-avec-l-Islam-de-France.

13 Available at http://circulaires.legifrance.gouv.fr/pdf/2015/03/cir_39347.pdf.

14 See the agenda of this first meeting at http://www.interieur.gouv.fr/Actualites/L-actu-du-Ministere/Premiere-instance-de-dialogue-avec-l-islam-de-France.

Loi du 9 décembre 1905 concernant la séparation des Églises et de l'État

Article 2: La République ne reconnaît, ne salarie ni ne subventionne aucun culte. En conséquence, à partir du 1er janvier qui suivra la promulgation de la présente loi, seront supprimées des budgets de l'État, des départements et des communes, toutes dépenses relatives à l'exercice des cultes.
[...] Les établissements publics du culte sont supprimés, sous réserve des dispositions énoncées à l'article 3.

Décret du 25 juillet 2005 portant reconnaissance d'une fondation comme établissement d'utilité publique, NOR: INTA0500200D[15]

Par décret en date du 25 juillet 2005:
Est reconnue comme établissement d'utilité publique la fondation dite « Fondation des œuvres de l'Islam de France », dont le siège est à Paris.
Sont approuvés les statuts de cette fondation.

Instruction du 11 mars 2015, NOR: INTK1504902J, Organisation de consultations avec les représentants des Français musulmans de vos départements en vue de la constitution d'une instance nationale de dialogue (excerpt)[16]

1. Instance de dialogue de l'Islam de France
a) Objectifs de l'instance nationale et des consultations locales
Cette instance est destinée à renforcer le dialogue entre le Gouvernement et les musulmans de France en apportant des réponses concrètes à leurs attentes sur les sujets cultuels ou qui s'y rattachent. Réunie autour du Premier ministre, elle rassemblera, dès juin prochain, les membres du Conseil Français du Culte Musulman, les représentants des grandes mosquées, de la société civile, des imams et des intellectuels. Cette instance n'est pas destinée à remplacer le CFCM, qui continuera à jouer son rôle auprès des pouvoirs publics et de l'opinion nationale.
Les consultations que vous allez mener d'ici à la première réunion de l'instance doivent permettre d'identifier les sujets prioritaires pour les musulmans de France.
Vous pourrez, à cet égard, sonder vos interlocuteurs sur des sujets tels que la formation des imams, les phénomènes de radicalisation chez certains jeunes,

15 Available at http://legifrance.gouv.fr/eli/decret/2005/7/25/INTA0500200D/jo/texte.
16 Available at http://circulaires.legifrance.gouv.fr/pdf/2015/03/cir_39347.pdf.

la prévention des actes antimusulmans, l'organisation et la protection des lieux de cultes, l'enseignement confessionnel, les aumôneries ... mais veillerez à recueillir leur opinions ou tout autre centre d'intérêt qu'ils indiqueraient. Les thématiques que vous dégagerez auront vocation à alimenter l'ordre du jour et les travaux de l'instance nationale.

b) Organisation de la consultation nationale

C'est dans cet esprit qu'il vous est demandé d'organiser une consultation des représentants des Français musulmans dans votre département, d'ici au 1er mai 2015.

À cet effet, vous animerez vous-même une ou plusieurs réunions, l'essentiel étant que ce débat soit vivant et qu'il intéresse le plus grand nombre.

Pour constituer la liste des personnes conviées à cette consultation, vous vous rapprocherez des CRCM, des dirigeants de mosquées, des associations musulmanes et des personnalités marquantes de confession musulmane, religieuses ou non. Vous veillerez à associer des acteurs indépendants, notamment les nouvelles personnalités issues de la sphère associative, du monde de l'entreprise, de l'université, du secteur caritatif ou culturel, des acteurs de la politique de la ville, désireuses de s'investir dans les dossiers de l'Islam de France dans le cadre des lois de la République.

Vous m'informerez régulièrement des thèmes abordés et des principales prises de position. Ces rencontres pourront, si vous le jugez opportun, être médiatisées a posteriori, avec le souci de l'apaisement et de la promotion du vivre ensemble.

Je vous remercie de bien vouloir m'informer des résultats de cette consultation dans les meilleurs délais.

Sauf proposition contraire de votre part, votre correspondant laïcité sera la cheville ouvrière de ce processus, en lien avec la DLPAJ (bureau-central-cultes@interieur.gouv.fr).

CHAPTER 3

State Support for Islamic Religious Communities

The rules governing state support for Islamic religious communities—and for all religious denominations—are twofold. On the one hand, state support for faith groups is prohibited by Article 2 of the 1905 Act on the separation between church and state. On the other hand, there are several exceptions to this ban, which have been made by the legislator or the courts. It should be noted on this point that case law has played a key role in adapting the relevant 1905 Act provisions to the contemporary context of religious pluralism, despite the high symbolic weight of the ban on public funding, which, to a large extent, embodies the separation between state and religious groups. This symbolic weight is likely to explain why state support for religious groups remains a sensitive issue although it can legally be argued that such support is possible. Indeed, the question has arisen of the exact scope of the legislative ban on public funding with regard to the constitutional principle of *laïcité*, as defined today by the courts and the Constitutional Council. This definition implies, in particular, a delicate balance between state neutrality and the guarantee of religious freedom. Besides exceptions introduced progressively since 1905, it is agreed today that state support for faith groups is compatible with the principle of *laïcité*, provided that it meets the condition of general interest and abides by the principle of non-discrimination.[1]

3.1 The Ban on State Support for Religious Groups

The 1905 Act puts an end to the previous system of legal recognition of four religious denominations in force during the nineteenth century (the Catholic Church, the Reformed Church, the Lutheran Church and the Jewish community). The prohibition of state support for religious groups in Article 2 should be read as a consequence of this change in the relations between the state and those four faith groups towards separation. Moreover, Article 19 of the 1905 Act prohibits subsidies for associations having the specific status of religious associations (*associations cultuelles*, see above *1.1 Religious communities as associations*). Funds allocated for repairs to buildings used for public worship,

1 On this point see *Traité de droit français des religions*, 2013, no. 2243 et seq.

classified as historical monuments, are not considered subsidies, but these provisions hardly apply to Muslim associations.

Financially, the combining of Articles 2 and 19 of the 1905 Act proved to be especially disadvantageous for the 1901 Act associations with only partly religious activities: because of their religious activities, they fall within the scope of Article 2 and cannot receive public subsidies, but their other, non-religious, activities prevent them from benefiting from the advantageous tax situation reserved for religious associations under the 1905 Act. This state of the law had been established by the Council of State in a case of 1992 (see below, case 1). The Council of State departed from this legal analysis of the provisions of 1905 in a decisive case of 19 July 2011 (see below, case 2). Indeed, the Council held that public funding of the non-religious activities of 1901 Act associations having a partly religious object does not violate Article 2 of the 1905 Act. The case involved a Catholic church building but is likely to be extended to other faith groups, as indicated by the administrative circular of 29 July 2011 on the legal regime covering places of worship as it results from the renewed case law of the Council of State.

Loi du 9 décembre 1905 concernant la séparation des Églises et de l'État

Article 2, § 1. La République ne reconnaît, ne salarie ni ne subventionne aucun culte. En conséquence, à partir du 1er janvier qui suivra la promulgation de la présente loi, seront supprimées des budgets de l'État, des départements et des communes, toutes dépenses relatives à l'exercice des cultes.

Article 19. Ces associations devront avoir exclusivement pour objet l'exercice d'un culte [...]. Elles ne pourront, sous quelque forme que ce soit, recevoir des subventions de l'État, des départements et des communes. Ne sont pas considérées comme subventions les sommes allouées pour réparations aux édifices affectés au culte public, qu'ils soient ou non classés monuments historiques.

Circulaire du 29 juillet 2011: Édifices du culte: propriété, construction, reparation, entretien, règles d'urbanisme, fiscalité, NOR/IOC/D/11/21246C (excerpt)[2]

Par circulaire du 25 mai 2009, des informations vous ont été apportées sur le droit applicable dans le domaine de l'immobilier cultuel aux fins de répondre aux questions sur l'entretien et la réparation de bâtiments cultuels construits avant ou après 1905, sur la construction de lieu de culte, la mise à disposition de locaux communaux à des fins cultuelles, l'utilisation d'édifice cultuel à des fins non cultuel [sic], etc.
L'évolution de la jurisprudence administrative, notamment les décisions du Conseil d'État du 19 juillet 2011, rend nécessaire d'apporter quelques modifications ou compléments à certaines parties de cette circulaire.
La circulaire NOR/IOC/D/09/10906/C du 25 mai 2009 est donc abrogée.

Case Law

Case 1: The town council of Saint-Louis de la Réunion had granted some subsidies to a Hindu association called 'Société Siva Soupramanien de Saint-Louis'. In a judgment of 26 December 1986, the administrative court of Saint-Denis de La Réunion annulled the town council's decision by which those subsidies had been granted. The Council of State upheld the administrative court's judgment. Its reasoning mainly relied on Article 2 of the Act of 9 December 1905, which provides that 'the Republic neither recognises nor salaries or subsidises any religion'. Indeed, it concludes that no subsidies can be granted to associations carrying out religious activities. In the case at hand, the Council of State noted that the 'Société Siva Soupramanien de Saint-Louis' association was aimed at gathering together its members in order to practise and to study the Hindu religion and to purchase or rent buildings in which to host religious practices. This association was, however, also dedicated to social and cultural activities, which prevented it from benefiting from the rules only applicable to associations having an exclusively religious purpose (*associations cultuelles*). Furthermore, because the 'Société Siva Soupramanien de Saint-Louis' association nevertheless did conduct religious activities, Article 2 of the 1905 Act was enforceable. Accordingly, the Council of State dismissed the City of Saint-Louis

2 The full text of the circular (34 pages) is available at http://circulaire.legifrance.gouv.fr/pdf/2011/08/cir_33668.pdf.

de La Réunion's claim (*Council of State, 09-10-1992, Association Siva Soupramanien de St-Louis, no. 94455*).

Case 2: The applicant was the Federation of the Free Thinking and of Social Action of the Rhône *département*. It applied for judicial review of the Lyon city council's decision to grant a subsidy to contribute to the financing of a lift to make access to the basilica of Fourvière easier for disabled people. The Court took the view that the provisions of the 1905 Act allowed the financing by a city of the maintenance and preservation works under the condition that the equipment at stake corresponded to a local public interest based on the cultural importance of the place of worship and the touristic and economic development of the city and was not of religious use on the one hand, and, on the other hand, that the public subsidy was not granted to a religious association (*association cultuelle*) and was used for financing the equipment only. If those conditions were met, the fact that this equipment might also be used by worshipers did not affect the legality of the City of Lyon's decision (*Council of State, 19-07-2011, Fédération de la libre pensée et de l'action sociale du Rhône, Picquier, no. 308817*).

3.2 Exceptions to the Ban on State Support for Religious Communities

As a matter of fact, state support is almost exclusively indirect, in that it does not mainly consist of direct subsidy but, rather, of providing the means to make worship or religious practice possible or easier. The first noticeable exception appears in the 1905 Act itself in Article 2, which pertains to chaplaincy in various public services such as schools, prisons, hospitals and so on. In the name of freedom of religion, the provisions of Article 2 aim at making access to religious services possible for people unable to leave the buildings of certain public services (see below *9. Islamic chaplaincy in public institutions*). At the time the 1905 Act was passed, it was made clear that these provisions should resolve the latent opposition between Article 1 proclaiming freedom of worship and the ban contained in Article 2.

From 1905, exceptions to Article 2 were made regarding places of worship in particular (see below *5.3 Specific legislation on places of worship*). Islam is undoubtedly concerned but these financial schemes benefit all religious groups. Legislation was passed in 1961 (Act of 29 July 1961) and 2006 (Article L. 1311-2 of the General Code of Local Government).

Finally, among legal exceptions made to the ban on state support for religious groups, one should mention the opportunity offered to make airtime available. Thus, pursuant to Article 56 of Act of 30 September 1986 on freedom of communication, the public TV channel *France Télévisions* is responsible for scheduling weekly programmes run by the main religious groups represented in France. The costs of production are borne by the public channel.

Loi du 9 décembre 1905 concernant la séparation des Églises et de l'État

Article 2, § 2. Pourront toutefois être inscrites auxdits budgets les dépenses relatives à des services d'aumônerie et destinées à assurer le libre exercice des cultes dans les établissements publics tels que lycées, collèges, écoles, hospices, asiles et prisons.

Loi de finances no. 61-825 du 29 juillet 1961

Article 11. Les emprunts pour financer la construction dans les agglomérations en voie de développement d'édifices répondant à des besoins collectifs de caractère religieux par des groupements locaux ou par des associations cultuelles peuvent être garantis par les départements et les communes.
Le ministre des finances et des affaires économiques est également autorisé à donner la garantie de l'État aux emprunts qui seraient émis en France pour le même objet par des groupements ou par des associations à caractère national.

Code rural et de la pêche maritime

Article L. 451-1. Le bail emphytéotique de biens immeubles confère au preneur un droit réel susceptible d'hypothèque; ce droit peut être cédé et saisi dans les formes prescrites pour la saisie immobilière.
Ce bail doit être consenti pour plus de dix-huit années et ne peut dépasser quatre-vingt-dix-neuf ans; il ne peut se prolonger par tacite reconduction.

Code général de la propriété des personnes publiques

Article L. 1311-2. Un bien immobilier appartenant à une collectivité territoriale peut faire l'objet d'un bail emphytéotique prévu à l'article L. 451-1 du code rural et de la pêche maritime, en vue de l'accomplissement, pour le compte de la collectivité territoriale, d'une mission de service public ou en vue de la réalisation d'une opération d'intérêt général relevant de sa compétence ou en vue de l'affectation à une association cultuelle d'un édifice du culte ouvert au public ou en vue de la réalisation d'enceintes sportives et des équipements connexes nécessaires à leur implantation ou, à l'exception des opérations réalisées en vue de l'affectation à une association cultuelle d'un édifice du culte ouvert au public, de leur restauration, de la réparation, de l'entretien-maintenance ou de la mise en valeur de ce bien ou, jusqu'au 31 décembre 2017, liée aux besoins de la justice, de la police ou de la gendarmerie nationales ou, jusqu'au 31 décembre 2017, liée aux besoins d'un service départemental d'incendie et de secours. Ce bail emphytéotique est dénommé bail emphytéotique administratif.

Un tel bail peut être conclu même si le bien sur lequel il porte, en raison notamment de l'affectation du bien résultant soit du bail ou d'une convention non détachable de ce bail, soit des conditions de la gestion du bien ou du contrôle par la personne publique de cette gestion, constitue une dépendance du domaine public, sous réserve que cette dépendance demeure hors du champ d'application de la contravention de voirie.

Tout projet de bail emphytéotique administratif présenté pour la réalisation d'une opération d'intérêt général liée aux besoins de la justice, de la police ou de la gendarmerie nationales dont le loyer est supérieur à un montant fixé par décret en Conseil d'État est soumis à la réalisation d'une évaluation préalable dans les conditions fixées à l'article L. 1414-2.

Les conclusions de baux mentionnées aux alinéas précédents sont précédées, le cas échéant, d'une mise en concurrence et de mesures de publicité, selon des modalités fixées par décret en Conseil d'État.

Loi n. 86-1067 du 30 septembre 1986 relative à la liberté de communication (Loi Léotard)

Article 56: France Télévisions programme le dimanche matin des émissions à caractère religieux consacrées aux principaux cultes pratiqués en France. Ces émissions sont réalisées sous la responsabilité des représentants de ces cultes et se présentent sous la forme de retransmissions de cérémonies cultuelles ou de commentaires religieux. Les frais de réalisation sont pris en charge par la société dans la limite d'un plafond fixé par les dispositions annuelles du cahier des charges.

Case Law

Case 1: The Montreuil-sous-Bois town council had entered into an administrative emphyteutic 99-year lease with a Muslim local association with a view to the building of a mosque. The city council granted a communal parcel of land for an annual rent amounting to one euro. A member of the city council lodged an appeal with the Council of State to request the annulment of the

City Council's resolution approving this contract. She argued that the parcel was at the disposal of the association for free, in breach of Article 2 of the 1905 Act.

In the case at hand, the Council took a stand on two points. On the one hand, the judge deemed that the low annual rent had two counterparts: the religious association involved had a non-profit-making purpose and at the end of the emphyteutic lease the building would be incorporated into the town's assets. On the other hand, the Council specified that the legislator (in 2006) intended to depart from the provisions of Article 2 of the 1905 Act, which forbids public funding of religious denominations. Accordingly, the appeal was dismissed (*Council of State, 19-07-2011, Madame V., no. 320796*).

3.3 Tax Exemptions

Tax exemptions constitute another form of indirect support for religious groups. Religious groups benefit from tax exemptions for their places of worship and have a specific beneficial fiscal regime through the status of religious association.[3]

As regards the latter, Article 200, for individual donors, and Article 238 *bis* of the General Tax Code, for companies, provide for tax reductions on gifts to religious associations and religious institutions of recognised denominations in Alsace-Moselle (*établissements publics des cultes reconnus*). Moreover, gifts and legacies to religious associations are exempt from estate and wealth transfer taxes (Article 757 and 795 of the General Tax Code).

Several tax exemptions are applicable to places of worship owned by religious associations or associations under the 1901 Act formed by a religious group. First, the exemption from property tax (Article 1382, 4° of the General Tax Code) benefits buildings owned by a public entity or a denominational association and used only for worship. Secondly, council tax (Article 1407 of the General Tax Code) does not apply to premises used exclusively for public worship, provided that there is no private use, irrespective of the status of the owner, whether a denominational association or not. Finally, planning tax (Article R. 331-4, 4° of the Town Planning Code), which is payable at the time of the construction of a building, is not applicable to places of worship.

3 The administrative circular NOR/IOC/D/10/16585/C of 23 June 2010 on religious associations provides details on, among others, their tax regime. The circular is available at http://www.legirel.cnrs.fr/spip.php?article96; see also above *1. Status of religious communities.*

Although most of the case law relating to these provisions involves Jehovah's Witnesses—and very often evangelical groups—some cases pertain to Islamic groups.

Loi du 9 décembre 1905 concernant la séparation des Églises et de l'État

Article 24: Les édifices affectés à l'exercice du culte appartenant à l'État, aux départements ou aux communes continueront à être exemptés de l'impôt foncier et de l'impôt des portes et fenêtres.
Les édifices servant au logement des ministres des cultes, les séminaires, les facultés de théologie protestante qui appartiennent à l'État, aux départements ou aux communes, les biens qui sont la propriété des associations et unions sont soumis aux mêmes impôts que ceux des particuliers.
Toutefois, les édifices affectés à l'exercice du culte qui ont été attribués aux associations ou unions en vertu des dispositions de l'article 4 de la présente loi sont, au même titre que ceux qui, appartiennent à l'État, aux départements et aux communes, exonérés de l'impôt foncier et de l'impôt des portes et fenêtres.

Code général des impôts

Article 200: 1. Ouvrent droit à une réduction d'impôt sur le revenu égale à 66 % de leur montant les sommes prises dans la limite de 20 % du revenu imposable qui correspondent à des dons et versements, y compris l'abandon exprès de revenus ou produits, effectués par les contribuables domiciliés en France au sens de l'article 4 B, au profit: [...]
e. D'associations cultuelles et de bienfaisance, ainsi que des établissements publics des cultes reconnus d'Alsace-Moselle;

Article 238 bis: 1. Ouvrent droit à une réduction d'impôt égale à 60% de leur montant les versements, pris dans la limite de 5 pour mille du chiffre d'affaires, effectués par les entreprises assujetties à l'impôt sur le revenu ou à l'impôt sur les sociétés au profit: [...]
b) De fondations ou associations reconnues d'utilité publique ou des musées de France et répondant aux conditions fixées au a, ainsi que d'associations cultuelles ou de bienfaisance et des établissements publics des cultes reconnus d'Alsace-Moselle. La condition relative à la reconnaissance d'utilité publique est réputée remplie par les associations régies par la loi locale maintenue en vigueur dans les départements de la Moselle, du Bas-Rhin et du Haut-Rhin lorsque la mission de ces associations est reconnue d'utilité publique.

Article 757: Les actes renfermant soit la déclaration par le donataire ou ses représentants, soit la reconnaissance judiciaire d'un don manuel, sont sujets aux droits de mutation à titre gratuit. Ces droits sont calculés sur la valeur du don manuel au jour de sa déclaration ou de son enregistrement, ou sur sa valeur au jour de la donation si celle-ci est supérieure. Le tarif et les abattements applicables sont ceux en vigueur au jour de la déclaration ou de l'enregistrement du don manuel.
La même règle s'applique lorsque le donataire révèle un don manuel à l'administration fiscale.
Ces dispositions ne s'appliquent pas aux dons manuels consentis aux organismes d'intérêt général mentionnés à l'article 200.

Article 795: Sont exonérés des droits de mutation à titre gratuit: [...]
10° Les dons et legs faits aux associations cultuelles, aux unions d'associations cultuelles et aux congrégations autorisées;

Code général des impôts

Article 1382, 4°: Sont exonérés de la taxe foncière sur les propriétés bâties: [...]
4° Les édifices affectés à l'exercice du culte appartenant à l'État, aux départements ou aux communes, ou attribués, en vertu des dispositions de l'article 4 de la loi du 9 décembre 1905, aux associations ou unions prévues par le titre IV de la même loi ainsi que ceux attribués en vertu des dispositions de l'article 112 de la loi du 29 avril 1926 aux associations visées par cet article et ceux acquis ou édifiés par lesdites associations ou unions; les édifices affectés à l'exercice du culte qui, dans les départements du Bas-Rhin, du Haut-Rhin et de la Moselle, appartiennent à des associations ayant pour objet exclusif l'exercice d'un culte non reconnu;

Article 1407: I. La taxe d'habitation est due:
1° Pour tous les locaux meublés affectés à l'habitation;
2° Pour les locaux meublés conformément à leur destination et occupés à titre privatif par les sociétés, associations et organismes privés et qui ne sont pas retenus pour l'établissement de la cotisation foncière des entreprises;

Code de l'urbanisme

Article R*331-4: Pour l'application du 1° de l'article L. 331-7, sont exonérées de la part communale ou intercommunale de la taxe d'aménagement les constructions définies ci-après:

1° Les constructions édifiées par l'État, les collectivités territoriales et leurs groupements et exemptées de la taxe foncière sur les propriétés bâties en application du 1° de l'article 1382 du code général des impôts;
2° Les constructions édifiées pour le compte de l'État, des collectivités territoriales ou de leurs groupements, en vertu d'un contrat de partenariat, d'un bail emphytéotique administratif prévu à l'article L. 1311-2 du code général des collectivités territoriales, à l'article L. 6148-2 du code de la santé publique ou à l'article L. 2341-1 du code général de la propriété des personnes publiques, d'un bail prévu à l'article L. 2122-15 du code général de la propriété des personnes publiques, d'un contrat mentionné à l'article 2 de la loi n° 87-432 du 22 juin 1987 relative au service public pénitentiaire ou à l'article 3 de la loi n° 2002-1094 du 29 août 2002 d'orientation et de programmation pour la sécurité intérieure, ou d'une autorisation d'occupation du domaine public assortie de droits réels, qui sont incorporées au domaine de la personne publique conformément aux clauses du contrat, au plus tard à l'expiration de ce contrat, et exemptées de la taxe foncière sur les propriétés bâties en application du 1° de l'article 1382 du code général des impôts;
[...]
4° Les constructions édifiées par les associations cultuelles ou unions d'associations cultuelles et, en Guyane et à Mayotte, par les missions religieuses ou, dans le cadre d'un des contrats mentionnés au 2°, pour le compte de ces associations, unions ou missions;
5° Les constructions édifiées par des groupements autres que des associations cultuelles et des missions religieuses mentionnées au 4° ou, dans le cadre d'un des contrats mentionnés au 2°, pour leur compte, destinées à être exclusivement affectées à l'exercice public d'un culte;
6° Les constructions édifiées dans les départements du Bas-Rhin, du Haut-Rhin ou de la Moselle par les établissements publics du culte et par les associations ayant pour objet exclusif l'exercice d'un culte non reconnu ou, dans le cadre d'un des contrats mentionnés au 2°, pour le compte de ces établissements et associations;
[...]
Le bénéfice des exonérations prévues par le présent article est subordonné à la condition que l'organisme constructeur s'engage, pour lui et ses ayants cause, à conserver à la construction la même affectation pendant une durée minimale de cinq ans à compter de l'achèvement de cette construction.
Toutefois, pour qu'ils puissent bénéficier des dispositions du présent article, les organismes constructeurs doivent avoir une activité strictement conforme à leur objet légal ou statutaire.

Case Law

Case 1: The Islamic association of Lot-et-Garonne asked to be exempted from property tax (Article 1382, 4° of the General Tax Code) on certain premises. The Court decided, however, that the premises in dispute were distinct from the mosque—which was already exempt from property tax—and were not immediate and necessary dependencies of the place of worship (*Administrative court of appeal of Bordeaux, 14-10-2004, no. 01BX00145, 01BX00146, Association Islamique de Lot-et-Garonne*).

Case 2: The Islamic Turkish Association of Franche-Comté sought exemption from council tax (Article 1407 of the General Tax Code) for premises used for the reception of members of the Turkish community to help them perform various administrative formalities. Although the premises concerned were open to any person in need of such help, it was clear that access was not completely free. The premises should accordingly be considered to be occupied as private premises (*Administrative Court of appeal of Nancy, 14-12-1994, no. 93NC00385, Association Islamique Turque de Franche-Comté*).

CHAPTER 4

Muslims in Integration Law

Integration law implies a distinction between the law pertaining to the acquisition of French nationality and the law on aliens. Indeed, relevant texts pursue different aims and apply at different stages of life in French society, in that the acquisition of French nationality requires evidence of assimilation into French society and is considered to be the outcome of the integration process. However, whether regarding the acquisition of French nationality or the obtaining of a residence permit, nationality law and the law on aliens tend to rely on a common view of integration and assimilation, although the assessment of the conditions of republican integration within the meaning of provisions entrenched in the Code for the Entry and Stay of Aliens and Asylum Law (*Code de l'Entrée et du Séjour des Étrangers et du Droit d'Asile*, hereinafter CESEDA) is more flexible than the measures of assimilation.

As regards the application to Islam of both sets of rules, this section stands a little apart, in that in the French context immigrants likely to apply for a residence permit or for the acquisition of French nationality have in common that they often come from 'Muslim' countries. Consequently a regular confusion occurs between religious affiliation and national origin. Islam then characterises these people beyond the question of religion, creating a link between debates on nationality and immigration and those pertaining to values like *laïcité*. As a result, Islam has been and is still considered as an integration-related issue, if not as an obstacle to the integration process. For example, requirements to abide by the principle of equality between men and women and the ban on polygamy—both found in nationality law and the law applicable to foreigners—reflect this ambiguous confusion.

4.1 Islam and French Nationality Law[1]

Nationality law rules generally reflect the political concerns of the time when they were adopted.[2] Texts enforceable in this field are still marked by the

1 See Anne Fornerod, 'Religion et acquisition de la nationalité française', *Revue du droit public et de la science politique en France et à l'étranger*, no. 3/2009, pp. 715–741.

2 Marceau Long (ed.), *Etre français aujourd'hui et demain. Rapport remis au Premier ministre* (Paris: La documentation française, 1988), vol. 2, p. 18.

debates on nationality and integration which took place during the 1980s, thus regularly leading to some confusion between religious Muslim practices and alien customs in administrative circulars. Most of them were adopted before 2012 by the then governing right wing party.

There are three ways of acquiring French nationality: automatically or 'as of right' (by parentage or birth in France)—which will not be addressed here—by declaration (after marriage with a French national, Article 21-2 et seq. of the Civil Code) or by decision of the public authority (naturalisation and reintegration, Article 21-24 et seq.).

4.1.1 *Acquisition of French Nationality by Reason of Marriage*

Pursuant to Article 21-2 of the Civil Code, an alien may, after a period of four years from marriage with a French national, acquire French nationality by way of declaration provided that, at the time of the declaration, an effective and physical community of living can be proved. The foreign spouse must also prove a sufficient knowledge of the French language. These provisions do not call for extended comment, except for the notion of community of living when considered together with the question of bigamy, raised in a couple of cases (see below case 1).

The Government may oppose the acquisition of French nationality by the foreign spouse on grounds of *indignity* or *lack of assimilation* other than linguistic (Article 21-4 of the Civil Code). An effective situation of polygamy or a conviction under Article 222-9 of the Penal Code on mutilation or permanent disability[3]—and implicitly directed at the practice of excision (also called female circumcision)—[4]can justify opposition to the acquisition of French nationality. Both impediments were added by the Act of 24 July 2006, leading to a dubious confusion between the two practices, knowing that polygamy is very often connected with Islam, through personal statute enforceable abroad.

The circular of 24 August 2011 on control of the condition of assimilation in the procedures for acquiring French nationality makes an indirect link between *indignity* and religious practices by referring to 'proselytising behaviour contrary to republican values, like activism in movements or associations considered as extremist or radical, as they encourage the spread of theses contrary or opposed to the essential values of the French community'.

3 Article 222-9 of the Penal Code pertains to 'Acts of violence causing mutilation or permanent disability [which] are punished by ten years' imprisonment and a fine of €150,000.'

4 Rapport Sénat, no. 371, 31 mai 2006, pp. 198–199. Available at http://www.senat.fr/rap/l05-371-1/l05-371-11.pdf.

Religious practices and *assimilation* are addressed together in the administrative circular of 29 December 2009 on the procedure of acquisition of French nationality by reason of marriage, in which one can easily read a reference to the Islamic faith. Annex VIII to this text relates to the Prefectural or consular authorities conducting an investigation to verify the assimilation into the French community of the applicant, his behaviour and his loyalty as well as the emotional and material community of living of the spouses. The text defines assimilation—into the French community—as a 'full commitment to the standards and the values of tolerance, *laïcité*, freedom and equality of the host society'. The Annex further provides that the public official responsible for conducting the investigation should highlight evidence of an intolerant or discriminatory attitude based on gender, race, religion, politics or nationality. The elements on which such an investigation should be based, as provided by the Annex, all pertain to religion and are worth quoting: 'denigration of members of other religious and national communities, belonging to movements advocating a radical practice of religion or violent action and, for the woman, home confinement, wearing, under constraint or not, of conspicuous religious signs, restriction or even prohibition of communication with male people'. The circular of 24 August 2011 stresses the principle of equality between men and women as an essential value, stating that 'everyday discriminatory attitudes vis-à-vis women, such as the refusal to shake hands, reveals a lack of assimilation; such a way of life, be it based on religious precepts, is inconsistent with the values of the Republic.'

These circulars, considered together with case law, call for two remarks. Firstly, case law shows that when applicant's religious affiliation is taken into account during the procedure it overwhelmingly involves individuals of the Muslim faith. Secondly, and as stated in the circular of 24 August 2011, religious practices do not of themselves constitute a lack of assimilation. French nationality can be denied only if these religious practices contradict the essential values of the French community, including *laïcité*. For example, the Council of State annulled a refusal to grant French nationality by marriage to a Tunisian national who claimed to practise his Muslim faith and whose French spouse wore the Islamic headscarf (*Council of State, 19-11-1997, M. Ben Halima, no. 286798*). In another case, the applicant was a member of the Association of Islamic Students in France and had taken part in radio and television programmes as well as seminars in order to raise awareness of Islam. All these factors did not amount to a lack of assimilation (*Council of State, 24-11-1997, Monsieur X., no. 158917*).

As regards lack of assimilation in relation to religious practices, a case concerned an Algerian who was denied the acquisition of French nationality pursuant to Article 21-4 of the Civil Code due to his active membership of an extremist movement and his speeches, particularly in the mosque of Angers, thus demonstrating a rejection of the essential values of French society (*Council of State, 14-10-1998, no. 175186*). However, as illustrated by another case, the circumstance that the applicant's wife wears the Islamic headscarf does not amount to an absence of assimilation of the applicant (*Council of State, 23-03-1994, no. 116144*). The widely publicised case *Madame M.* of 2008 (reported below, see case 2) was a first, in that the religious practice in question consisted of wearing a full veil.

Code civil

Article 21-2: L'étranger ou apatride qui contracte mariage avec un conjoint de nationalité française peut, après un délai de quatre ans à compter du mariage, acquérir la nationalité française par déclaration à condition qu'à la date de cette déclaration la communauté de vie tant affective que matérielle n'ait pas cessé entre les époux depuis le mariage et que le conjoint français ait conservé sa nationalité.
Le délai de communauté de vie est porté à cinq ans lorsque l'étranger, au moment de la déclaration, soit ne justifie pas avoir résidé de manière ininterrompue et régulière pendant au moins trois ans en France à compter du mariage, soit n'est pas en mesure d'apporter la preuve que son conjoint français a été inscrit pendant la durée de leur communauté de vie à l'étranger au registre des Français établis hors de France. En outre, le mariage célébré à l'étranger doit avoir fait l'objet d'une transcription préalable sur les registres de l'état civil français.
Le conjoint étranger doit également justifier d'une connaissance suffisante, selon sa condition, de la langue française, dont le niveau et les modalités d'évaluation sont fixés par décret en Conseil d'État.

Article 21-4: Le Gouvernement peut s'opposer par décret en Conseil d'État, pour indignité ou défaut d'assimilation, autre que linguistique, à l'acquisition de la nationalité française par le conjoint étranger dans un délai de deux ans à compter de la date du récépissé prévu au deuxième alinéa de l'article 26 ou, si l'enregistrement a été refusé, à compter du jour où la décision judiciaire admettant la régularité de la déclaration est passée en force de chose jugée.
La situation effective de polygamie du conjoint étranger ou la condamnation prononcée à son encontre au titre de l'infraction définie à l'article 222-9 du code pénal, lorsque celle-ci a été commise sur un mineur de quinze ans, sont constitutives du défaut d'assimilation.

En cas d'opposition du Gouvernement, l'intéressé est réputé n'avoir jamais acquis la nationalité française.

Circulaire NOR IMIC0900097C du 29 décembre 2009 relative à la procédure d'acquisition de la nationalité française en raison du mariage (excerpt)[5]

Annexe VIII: Rapport d'enquête sur une demande d'acquisition de la nationalité française par déclaration
Conformément à l'article 15 du décret n° 93-1362 du 30 décembre 1993 modifié relatif notamment aux déclarations de nationalité, les services préfectoraux ou consulaires procèdent à une enquête permettant de vérifier l'assimilation du déclarant à la communauté française, sa conduite et son loyalisme ainsi que la communauté de vie affective et matérielle du couple.
Cette rubrique doit comporter des éléments permettant, le cas échéant, de déclarer que l'intéressé n'est pas assimilé à la communauté française
L'assimilation peut se définir:
– par une pleine adhésion aux règles de fonctionnement et aux valeurs de tolérance, de laïcité, de liberté et d'égalité de la société d'accueil;
– par une participation aux activités de la société et pas seulement à son économie.
L'enquête, qui peut éventuellement se dérouler en présence du conjoint, consiste à mesurer le degré d'assimilation du déclarant au travers:
– de son comportement et des propos tenus lors de son audition;
– de ses relations sociales;
– de son comportement familial;
– de ses activités de loisirs.
Le cas échéant, l'agent qui conduira l'enquête devra mettre en évidence les éléments révélateurs mêmes modestes d'une attitude intolérante ou discriminatoire fondée sur des critères de sexe, de race, de religion, de politique ou de nationalité (dénigrement de membres d'autres communautés religieuses ou nationales, appartenance à des mouvements prônant une pratique radicale de la religion ou l'action violente et, pour la femme, confinement au foyer, port sous la contrainte ou non de signes religieux ostentatoires, limitation voire même interdiction de toute communication avec des personnes du sexe masculin, etc.). […]

5 Available at http://circulaire.legifrance.gouv.fr/pdf/2012/01/cir_34452.pdf.

Circulaire NOR IOCN1114306C du 24 août 2011 relative au contrôle de la condition d'assimilation dans les procédures d'acquisition de la nationalité française[6]

L'article 21-4 du code civil précise que «le Gouvernement peut s'opposer par décret en Conseil d'État, pour indignité ou défaut d'assimilation, autre que linguistique, à l'acquisition de la nationalité par le conjoint étranger.»
Deux notions distinctes permettent de fonder une opposition: l'indignité et le défaut d'assimilation. N'est pas comprise dans le champ de cette dernière l'assimilation linguistique qui demeure un motif de refus d'enregistrement.
1.1 L'indignité
La notion d'indignité s'apprécie de plusieurs façons. Elle peut être constatée par la commission de faits répréhensibles avérés, commis en France ou dans un pays étranger, examinés en fonction de leur ancienneté, de leur répétition et de leur gravité. Elle peut tenir compte du loyalisme du déclarant à l'égard des institutions publiques, de l'administration fiscale ou encore des organismes sociaux. [...]
Entrent également dans ce champ les comportements prosélytes contraires aux valeurs républicaines, par exemple le militantisme actif au sein de mouvements ou d'associations considérées comme extrémistes ou radicaux, dès lors qu'ils encouragent la propagation de thèses contraires ou hostiles aux valeurs essentielles de la communauté française.
1.2 Le défaut d'assimilation autre que linguistique
L'assimilation à la communauté française suppose une adhésion aux règles de fonctionnement et aux valeurs de tolérance, de laïcité, de liberté et d'égalité de la société française.
Parmi les faits constitutifs du défaut d'assimilation (autre que linguistique), sont ainsi expressément visées par l'article 21-4 du code civil: «la situation effective de polygamie du conjoint étranger», la condamnation au titre de violences ayant entraîné une mutilation ou une infirmité permanente sur un mineur de quinze ans (l'excision, par exemple). Le défaut d'assimilation est ainsi constaté lorsque le déclarant se trouve formellement dans les liens de plusieurs unions matrimoniales ou dans une situation de fait assimilable à la polygamie déterminée par la présence, dans le même espace de proximité, de l'épouse et de la concubine.
Au rang des valeurs essentielles de la République française figure le principe de l'égalité entre les hommes et les femmes. Par conséquent, l'adoption au

6 Available at http://circulaire.legifrance.gouv.fr/pdf/2011/08/cir_33673.pdf.

quotidien d'attitudes discriminatoires vis-à-vis des femmes, telles que le refus de leur serrer la main, révèle un défaut d'assimilation; un tel mode de vie, fût-il fondé sur des préceptes religieux, est incompatible avec les valeurs de la République. Il en va de même de l'autorité abusive du déclarant à l'égard de son épouse, de ses filles ou de ses sœurs, marquée par exemple par une interdiction de participer à toute vie sociale, le confinement au domicile, le mariage forcé, l'interdiction de poursuivre des études ou de suivre une formation ou encore l'interdiction de signer un contrat d'accueil et d'intégration.
L'effectivité du port du voile ne doit être prise en compte que dans le cadre d'un examen de l'ensemble des éléments du dossier. La stricte observance d'une religion et la manifestation d'un attachement aux principes de cette religion par le port d'un insigne ou d'un vêtement traditionnel ne sont pas suffisantes pour constituer le défaut d'assimilation. Une opposition peut être, cependant, envisagée si le dossier fait apparaître que cet aspect du comportement s'inscrit dans un mode de vie, nettement et objectivement, incompatible avec les valeurs essentielles de la République française. [...]

Case Law

Case 1: The community of living required by Article 21-2 of the Civil Code must be understood as an element of the French conception of monogamous marriage and excludes the contracting of a second marriage before the dissolution of the first. As a consequence, an alien, of Muslim personal statute, who married a foreign woman after he married a French national, cannot apply for French nationality on the ground of his first marriage. In the case in hand, he repudiated his second wife after he had applied for acquiring French nationality (*Court of appeal of Paris, 24-03-1998*).

Case 2: The applicant, a Moroccan woman married to a French man, was seeking the annulment of the decree preventing her from acquiring French nationality (Articles 21-2 and 21-4 of the Civil Code). However, the Council of State considered that the applicant, by wearing the full veil, had "adopted a radical practice of her religion, incompatible with the key values of the French community, notably with the principle of gender equality and, therefore, she did not satisfy the condition of assimilation" (*Council of State, 27-06-2008, Madame M., no. 286798*).

4.1.2 *Acquisition of French Nationality by a Decision of the Government (Naturalisation)*

Unlike the acquisition of French nationality by declaration—most generally because of marriage—which is legally binding when the conditions are met, naturalisation by decree (Article 21-15 of the Civil Code) depends on a discretionary decision of the public authority. This latter mode of acquisition of French nationality also entails an assessment of the assimilation of the applicant to the national community (Article 21-24 of the Civil Code). Still pursuant to Article 21-24, such an assessment is based on knowledge of French language—which proves to be a key criterion in practice—of history, culture and society, of the rights and duties conferred by French nationality. Moreover, the applicants should prove their commitment to essential values and principles of the Republic. Just as for acquisition of French nationality by declaration, it turns out that assimilation is evaluated through religious belonging. In this regard, the administrative circular of 24 August 2011 on control of the conditions of assimilation in the procedures for acquiring French nationality refers to polygamy as a proof of lack of integration or respect by the applicant for the principle of equality. Moreover, it expressly recommends paying attention to the dress code of female applicants. Public officials responsible for carrying out the inquiry should indicate whether the applicants wear "traditional headscarves in use in Northern Africa or Turkey" or "hijab that completely covers the head and neck and, like the chador, is a sign of belonging to a fundamentalist Islam [sic]." Finally, the circular of 24 August 2011 echoes the circular of 29 December 2009 pertaining to acquisition of French nationality by reason of marriage on several points like "intolerant or discriminatory attitude" or "belonging to movements advocating a radical practice of religion or violent action" and, for the woman, "home confinement, wearing, whether under constraint or not, of conspicuous religious signs, restriction or even prohibition of communication with males".

These administrative texts should, however, be put in perspective with case law which shows an overwhelming number of litigations relating to the lack of knowledge of the French language.

Code civil

Art. 21-15: Hors le cas prévu à l'article 21-14-1, l'acquisition de la nationalité française par décision de l'autorité publique résulte d'une naturalisation accordée par décret à la demande de l'étranger.

Article 21-24: Nul ne peut être naturalisé s'il ne justifie de son assimilation à la communauté française, notamment par une connaissance suffisante, selon sa condition, de la langue, de l'histoire, de la culture et de la société françaises, dont le niveau et les modalités d'évaluation sont fixés par décret en Conseil d'État, et des droits et devoirs conférés par la nationalité française ainsi que par l'adhésion aux principes et aux valeurs essentiels de la République.
À l'issue du contrôle de son assimilation, l'intéressé signe la charte des droits et devoirs du citoyen français. Cette charte, approuvée par décret en Conseil d'État, rappelle les principes, valeurs et symboles essentiels de la République française.

Circulaire NOR IOCN1114306C du 24 août 2011 relative au contrôle de la condition d'assimilation dans les procédures d'acquisition de la nationalité française (excerpt)[7]

2. Le contrôle de l'assimilation dans le cadre de la procédure de naturalisation
La naturalisation de l'étranger qui sollicite la nationalité française constitue une prérogative particulière de la puissance publique. L'autorité administrative dispose d'un large pouvoir pour apprécier l'opportunité d'accorder ou non la nationalité française à un candidat à la naturalisation. Le code civil précise que «nul ne peut être naturalisé s'il ne justifie de son assimilation à la communauté française» (article 21-24).
Ainsi, seront considérés comme constitutifs d'un défaut d'assimilation, les éléments révélateurs d'une attitude intolérante ou discriminatoire fondée notamment sur des critères de sexe, de race, de religion ou de nationalité tels que le dénigrement de certaines communautés ou l'appartenance à des mouvements radicaux prônant l'action violente.
De même, une pratique radicale de la religion ou un mode de vie non conforme aux us et coutumes tel que le confinement au foyer, la limitation des relations sociales avec des personnes de l'autre sexe et a fortiori des comportements contraires à l'ordre public (polygamie, pratique de mutilations sexuelles) pourront fonder une décision d'irrecevabilité sur le fondement de l'article 21-24 du code civil.

7 Available at http://circulaires.legifrance.gouv.fr/pdf/2011/08/cir_33673.pdf.

Case Law

Case 1: The applicant was denied French nationality due to his support for an imam belonging to a salafist oriented movement and since deported. Moreover, the applicant had become the treasurer of an association aimed at supporting and helping that imam. By his behaviour, the applicant did not meet the legal requirements for acquiring French nationality (*Council of State, 14-02-2007, no. 279704*).

4.2 Islam and Integration of Aliens

The integration of aliens is regulated by the Code for the Entry and Stay of Foreigners and Asylum Law (CESEDA). As a rule, any alien over the age of eighteen who wishes to stay in France should, within three months of arrival in France, obtain a residence permit (Article L. 311-1 CESEDA).[8] Since the Act of 24 July 2006, the residence of aliens in France has been linked to the requirement of integration in two ways. First, the alien who wishes to settle permanently in France must 'prepare [...] his republican integration into French society' (Article L. 311-9 CESEDA). In this respect, he must conclude with the state a 'welcome and integration contract' for one year, by which he commits himself to attend language training if need be and civic education courses. Civic education includes 'the presentation of French institutions and the values of the Republic, particularly with regard to equality between men and women, *laïcité*, the rule of law, fundamental freedoms ...' (Articles L. 311-9 and R. 311-22 CESEDA). Secondly, when renewing the residence permit, the administrative authority must take into account clear non-compliance with stipulations of the welcome and integration contract with regard to the fundamental values of the Republic and the committedmess of the immigrant's participation in civic and linguistic training (Article L. 311-9 CESEDA). Finally, the issuing of a first ten-year residence permit depends on the integration of the applicant, assessed in particular with regard to his personal commitment to the principles governing the French Republic, the effective protection of these principles and adequate knowledge of the French language (Article L. 314-2 CESEDA).

8 The category of residence permit is traditionally divided between the temporary residence permit and the ten-year residence permit. However, the temporary residence permit covers several sub-categories, making law in this field difficult to understand.

Outside the requirements relating to integration, legal rules likely to conflict with Muslim affiliation are to be found in general provisions of the Code for the Entry and Stay of Foreigners and Asylum Law. Such a conflict between law and faith appears in case law or arises from the reference to polygamy.

Thus, a temporary residence permit can be refused to any person whose stay in France constitutes a threat to public order (Article L. 313-3 CESEDA) (see below, case 2). In addition, polygamy constitutes an obstacle to the issuing of a temporary residence permit (Article L. 313-14 CESEDA) and a ten-year residence permit (Article L. 314-5 CESEDA). As regards the latter and in order to obtain that residence permit, the applicant, if he is married and is a national of a state whose law allows polygamy, should provide a sworn statement that he is not living in France in a polygamous relationship (Article R. 314-1 CESEDA).

Code de l'entrée et du séjour des étrangers et du droit d'asile

Article L. 311-1: Sous réserve des dispositions de l'article L. 121-1 ou des stipulations d'un accord international, tout étranger âgé de plus de dix-huit ans qui souhaite séjourner en France doit, après l'expiration d'un délai de trois mois depuis son entrée en France, être muni d'une carte de séjour.
Ce délai de trois mois peut être modifié par décret en Conseil d'État.

Article L. 311-9: L'étranger admis pour la première fois au séjour en France ou qui entre régulièrement en France entre l'âge de seize ans et l'âge de dix-huit ans, et qui souhaite s'y maintenir durablement, prépare son intégration républicaine dans la société française.
À cette fin, il conclut avec l'État un contrat d'accueil et d'intégration, traduit dans une langue qu'il comprend, par lequel il s'oblige à suivre une formation civique et, lorsque le besoin en est établi, linguistique. L'étranger pour lequel l'évaluation du niveau de connaissance de la langue prévue à l'article L. 411-8 et au deuxième alinéa de l'article L. 211-2-1 n'a pas établi le besoin d'une formation est réputé ne pas avoir besoin d'une formation linguistique. La formation civique comporte une présentation des institutions françaises et des valeurs de la République, notamment l'égalité entre les hommes et les femmes et la laïcité, ainsi que la place de la France en Europe. La formation linguistique est sanctionnée par un titre ou un diplôme reconnus par l'État. L'étranger bénéficie d'une session d'information sur la vie en France et d'un bilan de compétences professionnelles. Toutes ces formations et prestations sont dispensées gratuitement et financées par l'Office français de l'immigration et de l'intégration. Lorsque l'étranger est âgé de seize à dix-huit

ans, le contrat d'accueil et d'intégration doit être cosigné par son représentant légal régulièrement admis au séjour en France.
Lors du renouvellement de la carte de séjour intervenant au cours de l'exécution du contrat d'accueil et d'intégration ou lors du premier renouvellement consécutif à cette exécution, l'autorité administrative tient compte du non-respect, manifesté par une volonté caractérisée, par l'étranger des stipulations du contrat d'accueil et d'intégration s'agissant des valeurs fondamentales de la République, de l'assiduité de l'étranger et du sérieux de sa participation aux formations civiques et linguistiques, à la réalisation de son bilan de compétences professionnelles et, le cas échéant, à la session d'information sur la vie en France. [...]

Article L. 313-3: La carte de séjour temporaire peut être refusée à tout étranger dont la présence en France constitue une menace pour l'ordre public.

Article L. 313-14: La carte de séjour temporaire mentionnée à l'article L. 313-11 ou la carte de séjour temporaire mentionnée au 1° de l'article L. 313-10 peut être délivrée, sauf si sa présence constitue une menace pour l'ordre public, à l'étranger ne vivant pas en état de polygamie dont l'admission au séjour répond à des considérations humanitaires ou se justifie au regard des motifs exceptionnels qu'il fait valoir, sans que soit opposable la condition prévue à l'article L. 311-7.
L'autorité administrative est tenue de soumettre pour avis à la commission mentionnée à l'article L. 312-1 la demande d'admission exceptionnelle au séjour formée par l'étranger qui justifie par tout moyen résider en France habituellement depuis plus de dix ans.

Article L. 314-1: La carte de résident est valable dix ans. Sous réserve des dispositions des articles L. 314-5 et L. 314-7, elle est renouvelable de plein droit.

Article L. 314-2: Lorsque des dispositions législatives du présent code le prévoient, la délivrance d'une première carte de résident est subordonnée à l'intégration républicaine de l'étranger dans la société française, appréciée en particulier au regard de son engagement personnel à respecter les principes qui régissent la République française, du respect effectif de ces principes et de sa connaissance suffisante de la langue française dans des conditions définies par décret en Conseil d'État.
Pour l'appréciation de la condition d'intégration, l'autorité administrative tient compte, lorsqu'il a été souscrit, du respect, par l'étranger, de l'engagement défini à l'article L. 311-9 et saisit pour avis le maire de la commune dans

laquelle il réside. Cet avis est réputé favorable à l'expiration d'un délai de deux mois à compter de la saisine du maire par l'autorité administrative.
Les étrangers âgés de plus de soixante-cinq ans ne sont pas soumis à la condition relative à la connaissance de la langue française.

Article L. 314-5: Par dérogation aux dispositions des articles L. 314-8 à L. 314-12 la carte de résident ne peut être délivrée à un ressortissant étranger qui vit en état de polygamie ni aux conjoints d'un tel ressortissant ni à un ressortissant étranger condamné pour avoir commis sur un mineur de quinze ans l'infraction définie à l'article 222-9 du code pénal ou s'être rendu complice de celle-ci. Une carte de résident délivrée en méconnaissance de ces dispositions doit être retirée.

Article R. 311-22: La formation civique mentionnée à l'article L. 311-9 comporte la présentation des institutions françaises et des valeurs de la République, notamment en ce qui concerne l'égalité entre les hommes et les femmes, la laïcité, l'état de droit, les libertés fondamentales, la sûreté des personnes et des biens ainsi que l'exercice de la citoyenneté que permet notamment l'accès obligatoire et gratuit à l'éducation. Un arrêté du ministre chargé de l'intégration fixe la durée maximale et minimale nécessaire à cette formation. La participation de l'étranger à cette formation est sanctionnée par une attestation nominative établie par l'Agence nationale de l'accueil des étrangers et des migrations et remise à l'étranger par l'organisme ayant assuré la formation.

Article R. 314-1: Pour l'application des dispositions des articles L. 314-8 et L. 314-9, l'étranger présente à l'appui de sa demande de carte de résident ou de carte de résident portant la mention "résident de longue durée-UE":
1° Les indications relatives à son état civil et, le cas échéant, à celui de son conjoint et de ses enfants à charge;
2° S'il est marié et ressortissant d'un État dont la loi autorise la polygamie, une déclaration sur l'honneur selon laquelle il ne vit pas en France en état de polygamie;
3° Trois photographies de face, tête nue, de format 3,5 × 4,5 cm, récentes et parfaitement ressemblantes;
4° Les pièces justifiant:
a) Qu'il entre dans l'un des cas prévus à l'article L. 314-9;
b) Ou, s'il ne relève pas de ces dispositions, des raisons pour lesquelles il entend s'établir durablement en France ainsi que les éléments attestant du caractère suffisant et de la stabilité de ses moyens d'existence et, le cas échéant, les conditions de son activité professionnelle s'il en a une;

5° Pour l'appréciation de la condition d'intégration prévue à l'article L. 314-2:
a) Une déclaration sur l'honneur par laquelle il s'engage à respecter les principes qui régissent la République française;
b) Le cas échéant, le contrat d'accueil et d'intégration conclu en application de l'article L. 311-9 ainsi que l'attestation nominative remise par l'Office français de l'immigration et de l'intégration précisant si les actions prévues au contrat ont été suivies ainsi que les conditions de leur validation;
c) Tout document de nature à attester sa connaissance suffisante de la langue française, notamment le diplôme initial de langue française.
Lorsque les moyens d'existence de l'intéressé sont tirés de l'exercice d'une activité professionnelle soumise à l'autorisation d'une autorité de l'État, cette autorisation peut être accordée ou renouvelée par le préfet.
La demande de carte de résident au titre de l'article L. 314-8, lorsqu'elle est présentée après cinq années de résidence régulière ininterrompue, vaut aussi demande de renouvellement du titre de séjour précédemment détenu. Il en va de même en cas de demande de carte de résident au titre du 1° de l'article L. 314-9, lorsqu'elle est présentée après trois années de résidence régulière ininterrompue, et au titre du 2° du même article lorsqu'elle est présentée par un étranger qui est titulaire depuis au moins trois années de la carte de séjour temporaire mentionnée au 6° de l'article L. 313-11.

Case Law

Case 1: A Moroccan citizen had been denied a residence permit on the basis of Articles L. 314-2 and following of the CESEDA because she wore a full Islamic veil. Indeed, before the first issuing of a residence permit, these provisions require that a foreign individual has integrated into French society, particularly in relation to his/her personal commitment to respect for the principles governing the Republic, to observation of these principles, and to having an adequate command of the French language (*Administrative Court of Châlons-en-Champagne, 23-09-2010, no. 1000648*).

Case 2: The refusal to renew a temporary resident permit on the ground that the applicant is a threat to public order is justified (Article L. 313-3 CESEDA). Indeed, the applicant was a Muslim religious leader who encouraged the faithful to support the fundamentalist Islamic movements and made discriminatory remarks against the faithful of other religions (*Council of State, 22-01-1997, no. 163690*).

Case 3: The National Agency for the Reception of Foreigners and Migration (*Agence Nationale de l'Accueil des Étrangers et des Migrations*, ANAEM)[9] had applied to the equality body HALDE (*Haute Autorité de Lutte contre les Discriminations et pour l'Égalité*) for review of the compatibility of the prohibition of the veil with the principle of non-discrimination in the context of language training. According to HALDE, the obligation to remove a full veil during training did not amount to violations of Articles 9, 14 and 2 of Protocol 1 to the European Convention on Human Rights (*HALDE, 25-09-2008, no. 2008-193*).

9 In 2009, the ANAEM was replaced by the French Office for Immigration and Integration.

CHAPTER 5

Mosques and Prayer Houses

The legal framework applicable to mosques and prayer houses is still determined by the 1905 Act. In addition, besides some general rules contained in urban planning legislation, specific legislation was passed in 1961 and 2006 the purpose of which was precisely to facilitate the building of new places of worship, first and foremost mosques and Muslim prayer houses. In addition, case law plays a critical role in this matter as it has facilitated the updating of the 1905 Act rules on the funding of new places of worship.

In 2012, there were approximately 2,450 mosques and Muslim places of worship 2,450 in Metropolitan France,[1] with a noticeable increase in the past few years. It was stressed that Muslims still make limited use of the opportunity to create 1905 Act religious associations, although this status is advantageous for tax planning.[2] This is due to the preference for 1901 Act associations which arose in the 1980s when the ability to create such associations was opened to foreigners.[3] Moreover, the status of the 1905 Act religious associations requires an exclusively religious purpose, which can prove difficult to achieve for Muslim attitudes to places of worship.[4]

5.1 The Legal Framework Based on the 1905 Act

It is accepted that effective freedom of religion depends on having places of worship. In French law, Article 1 of the Act of 9 December 1905 can be read in this light, in that it provides that public authorities should guarantee the free exercise of religious practices.

However, other provisions (Articles 12 and 13 mainly) pertaining to places of worship entrenched in the 1905 Act are aimed at buildings already in exis-

1 Data from the Senate report on *Local public authorities and the funding of places of worship*, 17 March 2015, p. 25, available at http://www.senat.fr/rap/r14-345/r14-345.html.

2 Senate report on *Local public authorities and the funding of places of worship*, 17 March 2015, p. 27, available at http://www.senat.fr/rap/r14-345/r14-345.html.

3 See above *1.1. Religious communities as associations, and* Janine Ponty, 'Les étrangers et le droit d'association au xxe siècle', *Matériaux pour l'histoire de notre temps*. 2003, no. 69, pp. 24–25.

4 Bernard Godard, Sylvie Taussig (2007).

tence at that time. As a result, mosques and other places of worship built after 1905 do not fall within the scope of these provisions, meaning that they do not benefit from the legal protection of pre-1905 buildings designated for worship. The 34-page-long administrative circular of 29 July 2011, which otherwise recalls the overall applicable law in this field, specifies that post-1905 buildings benefit from the protection of private property entrenched in Article 545 of the Civil Code. However, the scheme put in place in 1905 remains applicable in that it entrusts, as said above, the 1905 Act and 1901 Act associations with the management of religious assets (see above *1.1 Religious Communities as Associations*). Finally, the relevant applicable law is also impacted by Article 2 of the same Act of 1905, which prohibits public funding for religious groups.[5] Accordingly, the main challenge lies in the chance to build new places of worship with this latent contradiction between the two articles of the Act of 1905 (see more precisely *3. State support for Islamic religious communities*).

Loi du 9 décembre 1905 concernant la séparation des Églises et de l'État

Article 1: La République assure la liberté de conscience. Elle garantit le libre exercice des cultes sous les seules restrictions édictées ci-après dans l'intérêt de l'ordre public.

Article 2: La République ne reconnaît, ne salarie ni ne subventionne aucun culte. En conséquence, à partir du 1er janvier qui suivra la promulgation de la présente loi, seront supprimées des budgets de l'État, des départements et des communes, toutes dépenses relatives à l'exercice des cultes.

Code civil

Article 545: Nul ne peut être contraint de céder sa propriété, si ce n'est pour cause d'utilité publique, et moyennant une juste et préalable indemnité.

5 This explains why the issue of places of worship is very often dealt with and analysed in the light of Article 2 of the Act of 1905. Accordingly, see also 3. *State support for Islamic religious communities*.

Circulaire du 29 juillet 2011, NOR/IOC/D/11/21246C, Édifices du culte: propriété, construction, réparation et entretien, règles d'urbanisme, fiscalité (excerpt)[6]

La question de l'immobilier cultuel tient une place importante dans le droit des cultes. Il ne peut y avoir de liberté de culte s'il n'y a pas libre disposition de locaux adaptés aux célébrations publiques d'un culte. Le régime juridique français des biens cultuels est un produit de l'Histoire qui garantit l'affectation cultuelle des biens attribués aux associations cultuelles par la loi du 9 décembre 1905 concernant la séparation des Églises et de l'État et des biens qui étaient avant 1905 ou sont devenus, par application de l'article 1er de la loi du 13 avril 1908, la propriété d'une personne publique (État, communes).
Les difficultés rencontrées dans le domaine immobilier peuvent concerner tant les édifices du culte qui on fait l'objet d'une affectation légale par la loi du 9 décembre 1905 que ceux qui ont été édifiés postérieurement à cette loi.
Les cultes qui étaient peu présents, voire absents, en 1905 se trouvent confrontés à des difficultés importantes, notamment pour l'acquisition de terrain en vue de la construction d'un édifice du culte ou pour la location de locaux pouvant être utilisés comme lieu de culte.
L'affectation cultuelle des édifices du culte construits avant 1905, réglée par les dispositions de l'article 13 de la loi du 9 décembre 1905 et de l'article 5 de la loi du 2 janvier 1907, donne des prérogatives importantes aux affectataires qui sont, pour les cultes protestants et israélite, les présidents des associations cultuelles qui peuvent être, le cas échéant, ministres du culte et, pour le culte catholique, le curé desservant [...].
Les édifices du culte qui ne bénéficient pas de cette affectation légale sont protégés par le droit de la propriété privée qui constitue une sérieuse garantie puisque, en principe, nul ne peut être contraint de céder sa propriété, sauf pour cause d'utilité publique (article 545 du code civil).

5.2 Urban Planning Legislation

Besides the 1905 Act provisions, the scope of which transcends places of worship, there are no legal provisions in urban planning legislation specifically applicable to the building of mosques or Muslim prayer houses. Any building

6 Available at http://circulaires.legifrance.gouv.fr/pdf/2011/08/cir_33668.pdf.

project should abide by general urban planning legislation. For example, pursuant to Article L. 421-1 of the urban planning Code, a building permit should be issued in the case of a mosque or prayer house project. Such a project should be assessed in the light of urban planning law alone. An old ruling explicitly regarding a chaplaincy stated that the 1905 Act and the principle of *laïcité* are not among the legal provisions applicable to a building permit (*Council of State, 07-03-1969, no. 70735*).[7]

In addition, places of worship are subject to local town planning (Article L. 123-1 of the urban planning Code), which includes, among other things, rules on buildings' height or parking areas (Article L. 123-1-2 of the urban planning Code). The latter topic is often at the heart of litigation on mosque building.

Moreover, places of worship are included in the category of buildings open to the public (*Établissements recevant du public*, ERP) and should accordingly abide by safety rules regarding fire risk (administrative order of 25 June 1980).

It should be mentioned that, as with other categories of building—like historical monuments or farm buildings—the Code on construction and housing (Article R. 111-22) provides an exception to rules on energy requirements for places of worship. Indeed, Article R. 111-22-1 states that 'prior to the filing of the application for a building permit, the developer will conduct a study of technical and economic feasibility of various energy supply solutions for heating, ventilation, cooling, domestic hot water and lighting of the premises.'

Beyond law enforcement, the issue of Islamic places of worship is characterised by how it is perceived in the local context either by the neighbourhood or by public authorities.

Code de l'urbanisme

Article L. 123-1: Le plan local d'urbanisme [...] comprend un rapport de présentation, un projet d'aménagement et de développement durables, des orientations d'aménagement et de programmation, un règlement et des annexes. Lorsque le plan local d'urbanisme tient lieu de programme local de l'habitat ou de plan de déplacements urbains, il comprend également un programme d'orientations et d'actions. Chacun de ces éléments peut comprendre un ou plusieurs documents graphiques.
[...]

7 Text of the ruling available at http://www.legifrance.gouv.fr/affichJuriAdmin.do?idTexte=CETATEXT000007639890&dateTexte=.

Article L. 123-1-2: Le rapport de présentation explique les choix retenus pour établir le projet d'aménagement et de développement durables, les orientations d'aménagement et de programmation et le règlement.
Il s'appuie sur un diagnostic établi au regard des prévisions économiques et démographiques et des besoins répertoriés en matière de développement économique, de surfaces et de développement agricoles, de développement forestier, d'aménagement de l'espace, d'environnement, notamment en matière de biodiversité, d'équilibre social de l'habitat, de transports, de commerce, d'équipements et de services.
Il analyse la capacité de densification et de mutation de l'ensemble des espaces bâtis, en tenant compte des formes urbaines et architecturales. Il expose les dispositions qui favorisent la densification de ces espaces ainsi que la limitation de la consommation des espaces naturels, agricoles ou forestiers.
Il établit un inventaire des capacités de stationnement de véhicules motorisés, de véhicules hybrides et électriques et de vélos des parcs ouverts au public et des possibilités de mutualisation de ces capacités.
Il présente une analyse de la consommation d'espaces naturels, agricoles et forestiers au cours des dix années précédant l'approbation du plan ou depuis la dernière révision du document d'urbanisme.
Il justifie les objectifs compris dans le projet d'aménagement et de développement durables au regard des objectifs de consommation de l'espace fixés, le cas échéant, par le schéma de cohérence territoriale et au regard des dynamiques économiques et démographiques.

Article L. 421-1: Les constructions, même ne comportant pas de fondations, doivent être précédées de la délivrance d'un permis de construire.
Un décret en Conseil d'État arrête la liste des travaux exécutés sur des constructions existantes ainsi que des changements de destination qui, en raison de leur nature ou de leur localisation, doivent également être précédés de la délivrance d'un tel permis.

Code de la construction et de l'habitat

Article R. 111-22:[8] La présente sous-section s'applique à la construction de tout bâtiment nouveau, à l'exception des catégories suivantes:
a) Les constructions provisoires prévues pour une durée d'utilisation égale ou inférieure à deux ans;

8 In the same logic, see also, in the same code, Articles R. 131-25 on thermal characteristics and energy performance and R. 134-1 on the diagnosis of energy performance.

b) Les bâtiments à usage agricole, artisanal ou industriel, autres que les locaux servant à l'habitation, qui ne demandent qu'une faible quantité d'énergie pour le chauffage, la production d'eau chaude sanitaire ou le refroidissement;
c) Les bâtiments servant de lieux de culte;
d) Les extensions des monuments historiques classés ou inscrits à l'inventaire en application du code du patrimoine;
e) Les bâtiments indépendants dont la surface de plancher totale nouvelle est inférieure à 50 m^2;
f) Les bâtiments auxquels la réglementation thermique définie à l'article R. 111-20 impose le recours à une source d'énergie renouvelable.
Article R. 111-22-1: Préalablement au dépôt de la demande de permis de construire, le maître d'ouvrage réalise une étude de faisabilité technique et économique des diverses solutions d'approvisionnement en énergie pour le chauffage, la ventilation, le refroidissement, la production d'eau chaude sanitaire et l'éclairage des locaux.

Arrêté du 25 juin 1980 portant approbation des dispositions générales du règlement de sécurité contre les risques d'incendie et de panique dans les établissements recevant du public (ERP)

Article 1: Sont approuvées les dispositions générales ci-jointes du règlement de sécurité contre les risques d'incendie et de panique dans les établissements recevant du public.
[…]

Article GN 1: Classement des établissements
§ 1. Les établissements sont classés en types, selon la nature de leur exploitation:
a) Établissements installés dans un bâtiment:
J Structures d'accueil pour personnes âgées et personnes handicapées;
L Salles d'auditions, de conférences, de réunions, de spectacles ou à usage multiple;
M Magasins de vente, centres commerciaux;
N Restaurants et débits de boissons;
O Hôtels et pensions de famille;
P Salles de danse et salles de jeux;
R Établissements d'éveil, d'enseignement, de formation, centres de vacances, centres de loisirs sans hébergement;
S Bibliothèques, centres de documentation;

T Salles d'expositions;
U Établissements sanitaires;
V *Établissements de culte*;

Case Law[9]

Case 1: An Islamo-French cultural association had obtained a building permit for a mosque. Several inhabitants of the surrounding area lodged an appeal against the municipal bye-law granting the permit. The Council of State held that the building permit met the requirements of zoning regulations by dismissing several claims of the applicants:

1. The planned building was not such as to affect the residential nature of the zone.
2. The zoning regulations demanded that the parking area correspond to the purpose of the building. By providing for 102 parking spaces the planned building abided by those regulations.
3. The mosque will be 24.35 metres high, which is within the local 25 metre height limit (*Council of State, 03-02-1992, Madame Raymonde E., no. 118855*).

5.3 Specific Legislation on Places of Worship

In principle, religious groups are responsible for building places of worship using their own funds. For historical reasons,[10] Catholic church buildings dating from before 1905 are maintained out of public funds. Moreover, the Catholic Church's estate is larger than that of any other faith group, due to its historical role. This leads to a discriminatory situation with regard to other religious groups in need of places of worship. In order to reduce this gap, two legal mechanisms have been set up: the loan guarantee and the emphyteutic lease. The former was created by the Act of 29 July 1961 (now Articles L. 2252-4 and L. 3231-5 of the General Code of Local Government) and allows cities (*communes*) and counties (*départements*) to guarantee loans contracted by religious groups for the funding of the building of places of worship in new urban areas. This bill

9 Although there is no leading judicial case here, it is worth showing how general legislation applies to mosques.

10 See Anne Fornerod, 'The places of worship in France and the public/private divide', S. Ferrari, S. Pastorelli (eds), *Religion in public spaces* (Farnham: Ashgate, 2012), pp. 323–336.

was aimed at making up for the shortage of places of worship affecting religious groups at a time of urban growth, when new urban areas were deprived of religious buildings.

The second mechanism consists in resorting to emphyteutic leases that is for a local authority to 'mak[e] land available to an association using a long-term lease (18 to 99 years) to erect a building of worship' on its private domain (Article L. 451-1 of the Rural Code). This opportunity was extended to the public domain of local authorities by the Order of 21 April 2006 relating to the legislative part of the General Code of Ownership by Public Entities that allows for resorting to administrative emphyteutic leases 'with the view to assign a building of worship open to public to a religious association' (Article L. 1311-2 of the General Code of Local Government). This means that these provisions cannot benefit associations other than religious ones (*associations cultuelles*).

In the case *Mrs. v.*, of 19 July 2011, the Council of State clarified the hitherto unclear legal situation concerning emphyteutic leases entered into for the building of places of worship, in the main for mosques. Indeed, administrative courts had repeatedly avoided leases agreed between cities and Muslim associations to provide land to facilitate the construction of mosques on the ground that the rent being charged at a nominal amount was akin to a public subsidy, which is forbidden by Article 2 of the 1905 Act. In this decision, the Council of State specified that the legislator intended in 2006 to depart from the provisions of the 1905 Act. Also, in respect of low rents, which was at the heart of the disputes (see below), the Council of State gave the impression that it was making a specific feature of this type of emphyteutic lease by doubly justifying it: by the 'fact that its titleholder engages in non-profit activities' and by including in the estate of the local authorities concerned 'the building, whose design, construction, maintenance and conservation costs they will not have borne'.

Code général des collectivités territoriales

Article L. 2252-4: Une commune peut garantir les emprunts contractés pour financer, dans les agglomérations en voie de développement, la construction, par des groupements locaux ou par des associations cultuelles, d'édifices répondant à des besoins collectifs de caractère religieux.

Article L. 3231-5: Les départements peuvent garantir les emprunts contractés pour financer, dans les agglomérations en voie de développement, la construction, par des groupements locaux ou par des associations cultuelles, d'édifices répondant à des besoins collectifs de caractère religieux.

Article L. 1311-2: Un bien immobilier appartenant à une collectivité territoriale peut faire l'objet d'un bail emphytéotique prévu à l'article L. 451-1 du code rural et de la pêche maritime, en vue de l'accomplissement, pour le compte de la collectivité territoriale, d'une mission de service public ou en vue de la réalisation d'une opération d'intérêt général relevant de sa compétence ou en vue de l'affectation à une association cultuelle d'un édifice du culte ouvert au public ou en vue de la réalisation d'enceintes sportives et des équipements connexes nécessaires à leur implantation ou, à l'exception des opérations réalisées en vue de l'affectation à une association cultuelle d'un édifice du culte ouvert au public, de leur restauration, de la réparation, de l'entretien-maintenance ou de la mise en valeur de ce bien ou, jusqu'au 31 décembre 2017, liée aux besoins de la justice, de la police ou de la gendarmerie nationales ou, jusqu'au 31 décembre 2017, liée aux besoins d'un service départemental d'incendie et de secours. Ce bail emphytéotique est dénommé bail emphytéotique administratif.
Un tel bail peut être conclu même si le bien sur lequel il porte, en raison notamment de l'affectation du bien résultant soit du bail ou d'une convention non détachable de ce bail, soit des conditions de la gestion du bien ou du contrôle par la personne publique de cette gestion, constitue une dépendance du domaine public, sous réserve que cette dépendance demeure hors du champ d'application de la contravention de voirie.
[...]
Les conclusions de baux mentionnées aux alinéas précédents sont précédées, le cas échéant, d'une mise en concurrence et de mesures de publicité, selon des modalités fixées par décret en Conseil d'État.

Code rural et de la pêche maritime

Article L. 451-1: Le bail emphytéotique de biens immeubles confère au preneur un droit réel susceptible d'hypothèque; ce droit peut être cédé et saisi dans les formes prescrites pour la saisie immobilière.
Ce bail doit être consenti pour plus de dix-huit années et ne peut dépasser quatre-vingt-dix-neuf ans; il ne peut se prolonger par tacite reconduction.

Case Law

Case 1: The Montreuil-sous-Bois town council had agreed an administrative emphyteutic lease of 99 years with the *Fédération cultuelle des associations musulmanes de Montreuil* (Religious federation of the Muslim associations of Montreuil) with a view to the building of a mosque. The town council granted a communal parcel of land for an annual rent amounting to one euro. An appeal was lodged with the Council of State to request the annulment of the town council's resolution implementing this contract on the ground that the parcel was at the disposal of the association for free, in breach of Article 2 of the 1905 Act, which prohibits public funding for religious denominations.

In the case at hand, the council took a position on two points. On the one hand, the judge deemed the low annual rent to have two counterparts: the religious association involved had a non-profit-making purpose and at the end of the emphyteutic lease the building would be reincorporated into the town's estate. On the other hand, the Council specified that in 2006 the lawmaker (creating Article L. 1311-2 of the General Code of Local Government) intended to depart from the provisions of Article 2 of the 1905 Act. Accordingly, the appeal was dismissed (*Council of State, 19-07-2011, Mrs V., no. 320796*).

CHAPTER 6

Burial and Cemeteries

Managing cemeteries and burials is a public service, run by each municipality and subject to specific supervisory powers of the mayor (Article L. 2213-8 of the General Code of Local Government). Although the courts have recognised the ability to maintain existing denominational cemeteries, no new religious, privately run cemetery can be created.

Beyond safety and health reasons, which for example forbid burials in places of worship and hospitals (Article L. 2223-10 of the General code for local government), the applicable law is characterised by the principle of neutrality of public cemeteries and the religious freedom of funeral rites. The regulation of burial and cemeteries is mainly based on old legislative texts inherited from the 'golden age' of *laïcité* at the end of the 19th century, while more contemporary administrative circulars endeavour to meet the requirements of religious pluralism by addressing the issue of denominational burial places.

Code général des collectivités territoriales

Article L. 2213-8: Le maire assure la police des funérailles et des cimetières.

Article L. 2223-10: Aucune inhumation ne peut avoir lieu dans les églises, temples, synagogues, hôpitaux, chapelles publiques, et généralement dans aucun des édifices clos et fermés où les citoyens se réunissent pour la célébration de leurs cultes, ni dans l'enceinte des villes et bourgs.
Toutefois, le maire peut, à titre d'hommage public, autoriser, dans l'enceinte de l'hôpital, et après avis de son conseil d'administration, la construction de monuments pour les fondateurs et bienfaiteurs de l'établissement, lorsqu'ils en ont exprimé le désir dans leurs actes de donation, de fondation ou de dernière volonté.

6.1 Religious Neutrality of Cemeteries

The principle of the neutrality of public cemeteries derives from the Act of 14 November 1881. This Act repeals the Decree of 23 prairial year XII,[1] which provided that public cemeteries should include denominational sections for the four religious groups recognised during this period (see above *1.1 Religious communities as associations*) or that each recognised religious group could have its own cemetery.

In this logic of the neutrality of cemeteries, it should be noted that Article 28 of the 9 December 1905 Act prohibits the display of religious symbols or emblems on public monuments or in public spaces—such as cemeteries—except on individual graves.

Loi du 14 novembre 1881, dite loi sur la neutralité des cimetières

Article unique: L'article 15 du décret du 23 prairial an XII est expressément abrogé.[2]

Loi du 9 décembre 1905 concernant la séparation des Églises et de l'État

Article 28: Il est interdit, à l'avenir, d'élever ou d'apposer aucun signe ou emblème religieux sur les monuments publics ou en quelque emplacement public que ce soit, à l'exception des édifices servant au culte, des terrains de sépulture dans les cimetières, des monuments funéraires, ainsi que des musées ou expositions.

6.2 Freedom of Funerals

The freedom of funerals is laid down in the Act of 15 November 1887, whose Article 3 notably protects the right to have religious funerals or not. This might lead one to consider the wish not to be cremated. These provisions are still applied and regularly give rise to litigation (see below *Case law*).

1 This refers to the revolutionary calendar created in 1792 and applied until 1806. The date of 23 prairial an XII corresponds to 12 June 1804.

2 See below 6.4 *Cemeteries in Alsace-Moselle*.

In addition, the law pertaining to funerals is marked by the principle of non-discrimination on grounds of religion. Thus, according to Articles L. 2213-7, L. 2213-9 and L. 2213-13 of the General Code for Local Government, the mayor, who is in charge of ensuring funerals, cannot make any distinction or recommendation based on the belief or religion of the deceased.

Loi du 15 novembre 1887 sur la liberté des funérailles

Article 3: Tout majeur ou mineur émancipé, en état de tester, peut régler les conditions de ses funérailles, notamment en ce qui concerne le caractère civil ou religieux à leur donner et le mode de sa sépulture.
Il peut charger une ou plusieurs personnes de veiller à l'exécution de ses dispositions. [...]

Code général des collectivités territoriales

Article L. 2213-7: Le maire ou, à défaut, le représentant de l'État dans le département pourvoit d'urgence à ce que toute personne décédée soit ensevelie et inhumée décemment sans distinction de culte ni de croyance.

Article L. 2213-9: Sont soumis au pouvoir de police du maire le mode de transport des personnes décédées, le maintien de l'ordre et de la décence dans les cimetières, les inhumations et les exhumations, sans qu'il soit permis d'établir des distinctions ou des prescriptions particulières à raison des croyances ou du culte du défunt ou des circonstances qui ont accompagné sa mort.

Article L. 2213-13: Il ne peut être établi, même par voie d'arrêté, de prescriptions particulières applicables aux funérailles, selon qu'elles présentent un caractère civil ou religieux.

Case Law

Case 1: A widow and her children were litigating over the burial circumstances of the deceased who was Muslim. The widow had chosen cremation, which is known as contrary to Islamic tradition. According to the Court, where the deceased's will is unclear and gives rise to differences between the members of the family, the solution should tend to be compatible with their religious beliefs. In this regard, by ordering the family to choose cremation instead of burial, the decision of the court of appeal was in breach of the Act of 15 November 1887. However, the Court of Cassation inscribed its decision in well-established case law which consists in entrusting the best qualified relative of the deceased with deciding the arrangements for the burial where the deceased's last wish is unknown. The Court eventually held that in the case at hand the widow was best placed to decide (*Court of Cassation, 02-02-2010, no. 10-11.295*).

Case 2: A widow wanted her husband to be buried in a denominational area of the cemetery, while the deceased's children wanted him to be cremated. When a disagreement arises among a family on the exact wish of the decease regarding his/her funeral, the judge has first to find out the deceased's intentions and then to designate the best qualified person to decide the manner of the funeral. In the case at hand, the Court took into account the fact that, although he did not practise regularly, the deceased was of the Muslim tradition and had not abandoned this religious tradition. Moreover, he had expressed the will to be buried and not cremated (*Court of cassation, 15-06-2005, no. 05-15.839*).

6.3 Denominational Burial Places

The regulation of denominational burial places is marked by uncertainty from a legal point of view. Indeed, allocating spaces reserved to deceased according to their religious beliefs within cemeteries is theoretically in breach of the 1881 Act and the principle of neutrality of cemeteries. However, public authorities face increasing claims on this point, especially from Muslim families, and try to meet such requests. Accordingly, the Ministry of Home Affairs (in charge of matters pertaining to religious groups and activities) adopted three administrative circulars in 1975, 1991 and 2008, all encouraging mayors to deal positively with such requests, within the limits allowed by their powers in this matter. The texts of 1975 and 1991 explicitly refer to the 'burial of French people of Islamic faith'. Above all this first circular was intended to regulate the specific situation of Muslim immigrant workers who died in France at that time.

The regulation of 19 February 2008 aims at encouraging mayors to use their supervisory powers in order to deal positively with the requests of families. More specifically, the regulation refers to an old court case (*Valès*, see below) which states that the mayor is entitled to decide on the location of graves within the town cemetery and hence to *de facto* group them according to the religious beliefs of the deceased. It falls within the authority of the mayor whether or not to give a positive answer and to find a balance between the neutrality of common spaces in a town cemetery and the principle of individual freedom of religion.

Although there are approximately 300 denominational burial spaces, supporters of 'strong' *laïcité* still argue that they are unlawful.[3]

Circulaire du ministère de l'Intérieur du 19 février 2008, NOR/INT/A/08/00038/C. Police des lieux de sépulture: Aménagement des cimetières—Regroupements confessionnels des sépultures (excerpt)

Mon attention est régulièrement appelée par les maires, les représentants des cultes, voire les particuliers, sur les difficultés rencontrées à l'occasion du décès d'une personne dont la famille, ou un proche, souhaite qu'elle soit inhumée selon les règles ou les usages définis par sa religion, ceux-ci n'étant pas toujours compatibles avec les dispositions législatives et réglementaires, ou lorsque des conflits s'élèvent entre les membres d'une famille sur les modalités des funérailles, le lieu et les modes de sépulture. Aussi, me semble-t-il nécessaire de rappeler aux maires les éléments essentiels du droit concernant la police des funérailles et des cimetières en développant plus particulièrement les questions liées aux demandes de regroupement confessionnels des sépultures.

Tel est l'objet de la présente circulaire qui annule et remplace les circulaires des 28 novembre 1975 et 14 février 1991. [...]

Il convient de signaler que les associations cultuelles sont de plus en plus nombreuses à faire part du dilemme auquel sont confrontées les familles, qui ont à choisir entre le renvoi du corps dans le pays d'origine, considéré comme trop onéreux par certaines d'entre elles, et l'inhumation du défunt en France, sachant que les règles propres à son culte (orientation des tombes, durée illimitée des sépultures, etc.) peuvent ne pas être satisfaites. Si le principe de laïcité des lieux publics, en particulier des cimetières, doit être clairement affirmé, il apparaît souhaitable, par souci d'intégration des familles issues de l'immigration, de favoriser l'inhumation de leurs proches sur le territoire français.

Le maire a en effet la possibilité de déterminer l'emplacement affecté à chaque tombe (CE, 21 janvier 1925, *Valès*)[4] et donc de rassembler les sépultures de personnes de même confession, sous réserve que les principes de neutralité des parties publiques du cimetière et de liberté de choix de sépulture de la famille soient respectés.

3 See the report issued by the *Défenseur des droits* (a Protection of Rights Body created in March 2011) in October 2012, available at http://defenseurdesdroits.fr/sites/default/files/atoms/files/ddd_r_20121029_legislation_funeraire.pdf.

4 The right date is 28 January 1925.

Tel est le sens des deux circulaires qui vous ont été préalablement adressées en 1975 et 1991 et sur lesquelles je souhaite à nouveau appeler votre attention, car le développement d'espaces confessionnels me paraît être la solution à privilégier pour résoudre les difficultés qui me sont le plus souvent signalées. Pour répondre favorablement aux familles souhaitant que leurs défunts reposent auprès de coreligionnaires, je vous demande d'encourager les maires à favoriser, en fonction des demandes, l'existence d'espaces regroupant les défunts de même confession, en prenant soin de respecter le principe de neutralité des parties communes du cimetière ainsi que le principe de liberté de croyance individuelle.

Case Law

Case 1: The applicant was denied the space for a grave for which he had applied to the town cemeteries service. According to the Council of State, the mayor did not deny the applicant's right to obtain such a space, but was entitled within his supervisory powers in this field to refuse to grant the grave in the spot wanted by the applicant. The mayor's power to decide the location of a grave in a town cemetery is still based on this case, as is indicated in the 2008 administrative circular (*Council of State, 28-01-1925, Valès, no. 82.046*).

6.4 Cemeteries in Alsace-Moselle

The provisions of local law are particularly worthy of note on this matter with regard to Islam. Indeed, the above mentioned decree of 23 prairial year XII is still in force in the three *départements* of Bas-Rhin, Haut-Rhin and Moselle. These provisions made the creation of a public Muslim cemetery possible in Strasbourg in 2012.

Décret du 23 prairial an XII (12 juin 1804)

Article 15: Dans les communes où on professe plusieurs cultes, chaque culte a un lieu d'inhumation particulier. Lorsqu'il n'y a qu'un seul cimetière, on le partage par des murs, haies ou fossés, en autant de parties qu'il y a de cultes différents, avec une entrée particulière pour chacune, et en proportionnant cet espace au nombre d'habitants de chaque culte.

CHAPTER 7

Education and Schools

Historically, schooling played a key role in the opposition between the state and the Catholic Church, which culminated in the 1880s. At that time, the struggle of the governing republicans against the moral and intellectual influence of the Catholic Church found its most significant expression in school institutions and is reflected in several Acts which are still in force. The French school system is thus 'characterized by a strong State presence in the organisation and funding of education.'[1] This explains the clear prominence of public schools, that is schools run by the state. Moreover, public schools are governed by the principle of *laïcité*, inherited from the 'school Acts' adopted during the Third Republic (1870–1940). Compulsory, free and *laïque* education was set up by the Ferry Act (after the name of the Minister Jules Ferry) of 28 March 1882 (*see 7.1. Compulsory education*). Thus, under the Act of 30 October 1886, education is entrusted to *laïque* teachers only in public primary schools (today Article L. 141-5 of the Education Code). The importance of *laïcité* in the state-run school system does not leave much room for religious education (see below *7.2*).

Religious groups are nevertheless not excluded from the school system. Their involvement in education relies on the principle of freedom of education, and most private schools are denominational (see below *7.3 Private schools*). The public and private sectors include three types of schools: primary (*école élémentaire*), and lower (*collège*) and upper (*lycée*) secondary schools.[2]

7.1 Compulsory Education

The right to education is entrenched in paragraph 13 of the Preamble to the 1946 Constitution, which is still in force and which also provides that 'free, public and *laïque* education at all levels is a duty of the State'. These provisions are reiterated by Article L. 141-1 of the Education Code.

---

1 For a general view of the French education system see https://webgate.ec.europa.eu/fpfis/mwikis/eurydice/index.php/France:Overview.

2 A large majority of children—if not all—however, start school earlier by attending nursery school, even though it is optional (*Ecole maternelle*). Unless otherwise indicated, secondary schools cover *collège* (for pupils from the ages of 12 to 16) and *lycée* (for pupils from the ages of 16 to 18).

Education—not necessarily conducted in school—is compulsory for all children from the ages of 6 to 16 (Article L. 131-1 of the Education Code). Compulsory education should be combined with the fundamental freedom of education.[3] This explains why homeschooling is permitted (Article L. 131-2) and that compulsory education should be distinguished from school attendance. Homeschooling remains tightly regulated and is subject to control by the public authorities responsible for education (Article L. 131-10 et seq. of the Education Code). Avoiding the requirement to educate a child without legitimate reason is punishable with a fine (Article R. 624-7 of the Penal Code). Moreover, it is particularly dealt with in the context of the fight against abuse by cults.

School attendance is imposed on pupils only when they are enrolled at an educational establishment. Article L. 511-1 states that the obligations of pupils involve the performance of tasks inherent in their studies, including school attendance. More precisely, Article R. 511-11 sets out various obligations for pupils arising from school attendance, such as submission to teaching hours defined by the school curriculum or modes of knowledge assessment. Article L. 131-8 of the Education Code expressly lists several reasons justifying school absence, such as the child's illness or a 'solemn family meeting', but does not include religious reasons. Any other reason is assessed by the state authority responsible for educational matters. The Council of State addressed the issue of absence for religious holidays in a case of 14 April 1995, *Consistoire central des israëlites de France* (see below), in which the administrative judge sought to combine freedom of religion and the obligation to go to school. This analysis was applied to Muslim pupils who refused to attend sports lessons: the wearing of the Islamic headscarf for religious reasons and preventing them from attending sports courses did not amount to a legitimate reason for avoiding the school attendance requirement (*Council of State, 27-11-1996, no. 170209, Époux Wissaadane et Époux Chedouane*).

Constitution de la République française du 27 octobre 1946. Préambule

La nation garantit l'égal accès de l'enfant et de l'adulte à l'instruction, à la formation professionnelle et à la culture. L'organisation de l'enseignement public gratuit et laïque à tous les degrés est un devoir de l'État.

3 It was recognized as a constitutional freedom by the Constitutional Council in its decision of 23 November 1977, no. 77-87 DC, *Liberté d'enseignement et de conscience.*

Code de l'éducation

Article L. 111-1: L'éducation est la première priorité nationale. Le service public de l'éducation est conçu et organisé en fonction des élèves et des étudiants. Il contribue à l'égalité des chances et à lutter contre les inégalités sociales et territoriales en matière de réussite scolaire et éducative. Il reconnaît que tous les enfants partagent la capacité d'apprendre et de progresser. Il veille à l'inclusion scolaire de tous les enfants, sans aucune distinction. Il veille également à la mixité sociale des publics scolarisés au sein des établissements d'enseignement. Pour garantir la réussite de tous, l'école se construit avec la participation des parents, quelle que soit leur origine sociale. Elle s'enrichit et se conforte par le dialogue et la coopération entre tous les acteurs de la communauté éducative.
Outre la transmission des connaissances, la Nation fixe comme mission première à l'école de faire partager aux élèves les valeurs de la République. Le service public de l'éducation fait acquérir à tous les élèves le respect de l'égale dignité des êtres humains, de la liberté de conscience et de la laïcité. Par son organisation et ses méthodes, comme par la formation des maîtres qui y enseignent, il favorise la coopération entre les élèves. [...]

Article L. 131-1: L'instruction est obligatoire pour les enfants des deux sexes, français et étrangers, entre six ans et seize ans.
La présente disposition ne fait pas obstacle à l'application des prescriptions particulières imposant une scolarité plus longue.

Article L. 131-2: L'instruction obligatoire peut être donnée soit dans les établissements ou écoles publics ou privés, soit dans les familles par les parents, ou l'un d'entre eux, ou toute personne de leur choix. [...]

Article L. 131-8: Lorsqu'un enfant manque momentanément la classe, les personnes responsables doivent, sans délai, faire connaître au directeur ou à la directrice de l'établissement d'enseignement les motifs de cette absence. Les seuls motifs réputés légitimes sont les suivants: maladie de l'enfant, maladie transmissible ou contagieuse d'un membre de la famille, réunion solennelle de famille, empêchement résultant de la difficulté accidentelle des communications, absence temporaire des personnes responsables lorsque les enfants les suivent. Les autres motifs sont appréciés par l'autorité de l'État compétente en matière d'éducation. Celle-ci peut consulter les assistantes sociales agréées par elle, et les charger de conduire une enquête, en ce qui concerne les enfants en cause.

Article L. 131-10: Les enfants soumis à l'obligation scolaire qui reçoivent l'instruction dans leur famille, y compris dans le cadre d'une inscription dans un établissement d'enseignement à distance, sont dès la première année, et tous les deux ans, l'objet d'une enquête de la mairie compétente, uniquement aux fins d'établir quelles sont les raisons alléguées par les personnes responsables, et s'il leur est donné une instruction dans la mesure compatible avec leur état de santé et les conditions de vie de la famille. Le résultat de cette enquête est communiqué à l'autorité de l'État compétente en matière d'éducation.
Lorsque l'enquête n'a pas été effectuée, elle est diligentée par le représentant de l'État dans le département.
L'autorité de l'État compétente en matière d'éducation doit au moins une fois par an, à partir du troisième mois suivant la déclaration d'instruction par la famille, faire vérifier que l'enseignement assuré est conforme au droit de l'enfant à l'instruction tel que défini à l'article L. 131-1-1.
Ce contrôle prescrit par l'autorité de l'État compétente en matière d'éducation a lieu notamment au domicile des parents de l'enfant. Il vérifie notamment que l'instruction dispensée au même domicile l'est pour les enfants d'une seule famille.
Ce contrôle est effectué sans délai en cas de défaut de déclaration d'instruction par la famille, sans préjudice de l'application des sanctions pénales.
Le contenu des connaissances requis des élèves est fixé par décret.
Les résultats de ce contrôle sont notifiés aux personnes responsables avec l'indication du délai dans lequel elles devront fournir leurs explications ou améliorer la situation et des sanctions dont elles seraient l'objet dans le cas contraire.
Si, au terme d'un nouveau délai fixé par l'autorité de l'État compétente en matière d'éducation, les résultats du contrôle sont jugés insuffisants, les parents sont mis en demeure, dans les quinze jours suivant la notification, d'inscrire leur enfant dans un établissement d'enseignement public ou privé et de faire connaître au maire, qui en informe l'autorité de l'État compétente en matière d'éducation, l'école ou l'établissement qu'ils auront choisi.

Article L. 131-12: Les modalités du contrôle de l'obligation, de la fréquentation et de l'assiduité scolaires sont déterminées par décret en Conseil d'État.

Article L. 141-1: Comme il est dit au treizième alinéa du Préambule de la Constitution du 27 octobre 1946 confirmé par celui de la Constitution du 4 octobre 1958, "la Nation garantit l'égal accès de l'enfant et de l'adulte à l'instruction, à la formation et à la culture; l'organisation de l'enseignement public gratuit et laïque à tous les degrés est un devoir de l'État".

Article L. 141-5: Dans les établissements du premier degré publics, l'enseignement est exclusivement confié à un personnel laïque.

Article L. 511-1: Les obligations des élèves consistent dans l'accomplissement des tâches inhérentes à leurs études; elles incluent l'assiduité et le respect des règles de fonctionnement et de la vie collective des établissements.

Article R. 511-11: L'obligation d'assiduité mentionnée à l'article L. 511-1 consiste, pour les élèves, à se soumettre aux horaires d'enseignement définis par l'emploi du temps de l'établissement. Elle s'impose pour les enseignements obligatoires et pour les enseignements facultatifs dès lors que les élèves se sont inscrits à ces derniers.
Les élèves doivent accomplir les travaux écrits et oraux qui leur sont demandés par les enseignants, respecter le contenu des programmes et se soumettre aux modalités de contrôle des connaissances qui leur sont imposées.
Les élèves ne peuvent se soustraire aux contrôles et examens de santé organisés à leur intention.

Code pénal

Article R. 624-7: Le fait, pour l'un ou l'autre parent d'un enfant soumis à l'obligation scolaire ou pour toute personne exerçant à son égard l'autorité parentale ou une autorité de fait de façon continue, après avertissement donné par le directeur académique des services de l'éducation nationale agissant sur délégation du recteur d'académie et mise en œuvre des procédures définies à l'article R. 131-7 du code de l'éducation, de ne pas imposer à l'enfant l'obligation d'assiduité scolaire sans faire connaître de motif légitime ou d'excuse valable ou en donnant des motifs d'absence inexacts est puni de l'amende prévue pour les contraventions de la 4e classe.
Le fait de faciliter, par aide ou assistance, la commission de la contravention prévue au présent article est puni des mêmes peines.

Case Law

Case 1: The National Jewish Board of France had applied for judicial review of Article 3-5 of the decree of 30 August 1985 on compulsory school attendance, claiming violation of freedom of religion. According to the Council of State, these provisions do not prohibit students who request it to benefit from individual leave of absence for religious practice or festivals, provided that it is compatible with the fulfillment of their educational obligations (*Council of State, 14-04-1995, no. 125148, Consistoire central des israëlites de France*).

7.2 Religious Education

Since the nineteenth century, school has been considered as the most appropriate place for the transmission of republican values like *laïcité*, thus excluding religious references or the teaching of religion.[4] By substituting moral and civic education for religious courses in public primary schools, the Act of 28 March 1882 laid down the principle of *laïcité* of the curriculum. Since then religious education has been provided outside public school curricula (Article L. 141-4 of the Education Code). Furthermore, the state is committed to taking all necessary measures to ensure that at all levels of education pupils' freedom to practise religion and to obtain religious education is assured (Article L. 141-2). Hence, a day off is aimed at allowing pupils of primary schools to attend religious education taught by religious leaders (Article L. 141-3, § 1), but in secondary schools, this mainly takes the form of spiritual assistance through chaplaincies (see below *9.4 Islamic chaplaincy at school*).

Religious instruction is optional in private schools (Article L. 141-3, § 2). The administrative circular no. 85-105 of 13 March 1985 on the standard status of contracts agreed between the state and private schools (Article 5) states that when religious courses and practices take place in the school, they should be included in the timetable in such a way that pupils unwilling to attend them are not obliged to do so.[5]

According to Article L. 111-1, the first mission of school is to share with students the values of the Republic, beyond the transmission of knowledge. It is worth emphasising that the Guidance and Programming Act of 8 July 2013 for Restructuring Schools added to these provisions that within the public educational service pupils should acquire knowledge of the equal dignity of human beings, freedom of conscience and *laïcité*. Moreover, this 2013 Act introduces moral and civic courses (Articles L. 311-4 and L. 312-15 of the Education Code) planned to begin with the school year starting in 2015.

In addition, unlike in many other countries, there is no specific separate teaching about religions in French public schools. There is, however, an ongoing debate about this. Although the school curriculum includes the history of religions in history and geography classes, the growing lack of awareness of pupils in this field has become problematic in a society increasingly characterised by cultural and religious diversity. Along with the social debate on *laïcité*, this has given rise to broader and lasting thinking about this issue since

4 For private schools see below section 7.3.

5 Text of the circular available at http://circulaires.legifrance.gouv.fr/pdf/2009/04/cir_834.pdf.

the late 1980s. The European Institute of Religious Science[6] was created in 2002 after a recommendation in the philosopher Régis Debray's report on *Teaching about religions in laïque school.* In collaboration with the Ministry of National Education this institute provides teaching personnel and school institutions with 'expertise and advice on current and historical issues involving secularity and religious questions'.[7] A certain reluctance, however, remains among teaching personnel to having classes specifically dedicated to the study of religions and religiosity or a body of teachers trained expressly in the field.[8] A bill on teaching about religions was brought before the National Assembly on 21 January 2015[9] by several MPs aiming at adding to Article L. 312-15 of the Education Code that 'civic and moral courses also cover teaching about monotheist religions such as Christianity, Islam and Judaism'.

Code de l'éducation

Article L. 141-2: Suivant les principes définis dans la Constitution, l'État assure aux enfants et adolescents dans les établissements publics d'enseignement la possibilité de recevoir un enseignement conforme à leurs aptitudes dans un égal respect de toutes les croyances.
L'État prend toutes dispositions utiles pour assurer aux élèves de l'enseignement public la liberté des cultes et de l'instruction religieuse.

Article L. 141-3: Les écoles élémentaires publiques vaquent un jour par semaine en outre du dimanche, afin de permettre aux parents de faire donner, s'ils le désirent, à leurs enfants l'instruction religieuse, en dehors des édifices scolaires.
L'enseignement religieux est facultatif dans les écoles privées.

Article L. 141-4: L'enseignement religieux ne peut être donné aux enfants inscrits dans les écoles publiques qu'en dehors des heures de classe.

Article L. 311-4: Les programmes scolaires comportent, à tous les stades de la scolarité, des enseignements destinés à faire connaître la diversité et la richesse des cultures représentées en France. L'école, notamment grâce à un enseignement moral et civique, fait acquérir aux élèves le respect de la

6 This institute had its statutes revised in 2006: see below.
7 See the Institute's website at http://www.iesr.ephe.sorbonne.fr/index5539.html.
8 *Traité de droit français des religions*, op. cit., no. 3067.
9 Text available at http://www.assemblee-nationale.fr/14/propositions/pion2515.asp.

personne, de ses origines et de ses différences, de l'égalité entre les femmes et les hommes ainsi que de la laïcité.

Article L. 312-15: Outre les enseignements concourant aux objectifs définis à l'article L. 131-1-1, l'enseignement moral et civique vise notamment à amener les élèves à devenir des citoyens responsables et libres, à se forger un sens critique et à adopter un comportement réfléchi. Cet enseignement comporte, à tous les stades de la scolarité, une formation aux valeurs de la République, à la connaissance et au respect des droits de l'enfant consacrés par la loi ou par un engagement international et à la compréhension des situations concrètes qui y portent atteinte. Dans ce cadre est donnée une information sur le rôle des organisations non gouvernementales œuvrant pour la protection de l'enfant.

Circulaire n. 85-105 du 13 mars 1985 (Éducation nationale): Participation des collectivités territoriales aux dépenses de fonctionnement (matériel) des établissements d'enseignement privés sous contrat

Art. 5.—L'établissement contractant s'engage selon les dispositions de l'article 3 du décret n. 60-389 à respecter les règles et les programmes de l'enseignement public et à se conformer à l'horaire de cet enseignement.
(Éventuellement). Dans les cas visés au décret n. 75-658 du 16 juillet 1975, une dérogation est accordée en considération de l'intérêt des méthodes pédagogiques propres à l'établissement dans les limites ci-après.
Cette dérogation ne saurait avoir pour effet d'entraver le passage normal d'un élève d'une classe souscontrat à la classe suivante d'un établissement d'enseignement public.
Si des cours et exercices religieux ont lieu dans l'établissement, ils seront placés à des heures telles que les élèves dont la famille ne souhaite pas qu'ils y participent ne soient ni contraints de les suivre ni laissés sans surveillance ou dans l'oisiveté. À cet effet, l'avis des familles ou des élèves majeurs sera recueilli.

Arrêté du 6 mars 2006 portant création à l'École pratique des hautes études de l'Institut européen en sciences des religions, NOR: MENS0600741A (excerpt)[10]

Article 1: Il est créé à l'École pratique des hautes études un institut dénommé Institut européen en sciences des religions (IESR).

Article 2: L'IESR a pour mission de participer à la formation initiale et continue des enseignants et des formateurs des établissements d'enseignement et de formation, pour la connaissance des faits religieux, notamment par des cours et séminaires, en favorisant la publication d'ouvrages pédagogiques et par la constitution d'une documentation directement accessible, en particulier par internet.
Il organise, à la demande d'autres partenaires institutionnels, des actions de formation visant à diffuser dans la société la connaissance du fait religieux.
L'IESR a comme interlocuteurs privilégiés les recteurs, les responsables des instituts universitaires de formation des maîtres, les inspecteurs des disciplines concernées par l'enseignement du fait religieux ainsi que les instances européennes compétentes et les institutions internationales, pour permettre une meilleure connaissance des modalités d'enseignement des religions et pour favoriser une réflexion commune sur le contenu des enseignements.
L'IESR a une activité de recherche concernant l'enseignement des faits religieux en France et en Europe. Il organise, seul et avec des partenaires français ou étrangers, des séminaires, colloques et programmes de recherche concernant son objet de recherche. Il peut être habilité à constituer une bibliothèque rassemblant les ouvrages pédagogiques et didactiques spécialisés dans l'enseignement des religions.
Pour l'exercice de ses missions, l'IESR s'appuie sur les compétences scientifiques de l'École pratique des hautes études. Il est habilité à développer un réseau régional qui contribue à ses travaux au plan local en liaison avec, notamment, les recteurs d'académie, les responsables des instituts universitaires de formation des maîtres et des inspections d'académie.

10 Text available at http://legifrance.gouv.fr/eli/arrete/2006/3/6/MENS0600741A/jo/texte.

7.3 Private Schools

The ability to open and run private schools derives from the principle of freedom of education, which has its roots in several Acts adopted during the nineteenth century. The Guizot Act of 28 June 1833 applies to primary schools, while the Falloux Act of 15 March 1850 affirms the freedom of education for secondary schools and notably provides that public authorities can grant premises and subsidies to private schools. The main currently applicable provisions come from the Act of 31 December 1959 on the relationship between the state and private schools (also known as the Debré Act) and are today entrenched in the Education Code. Thus, Article L. 151-1 proclaims the freedom of education and guarantees its exercise to properly opened private schools.

The opening of a private school is subject to prior declaration to the mayor of the locality where the school premises will be located. The mayor can oppose the opening where the premises are not suitable on grounds of morals or hygiene (Article L. 441-1 of the Education Code). Article L. 441-2 of the Education Code sets a similar procedure for the educational authorities in the *département* and the state authorities competent in educational matters. In the absence of objections, within one month after the application the school can open without further formalities.

Private schools can operate under a contract (*sous contrat*) with the state which reflects their willingness to be part of the public educational service, or off contract (*hors contrat*). In the first case, they receive public funding and must abide by state regulations regarding their curricula and some professional requirements of the teaching personnel. In the second case, schools are not publicly funded and are free to set their own curricula (Article L. 442-3). Moreover, state control is limited to the verification of compliance with the provisions concerning compulsory education, public order and morals (Article L. 442-2). Pupils attending off contract private schools are subject to the principle of compulsory education. They are assumed to have acquired the 'common core of knowledge' (Article D. 131-11 of the Education Code) defined in the Article Annexe to Article D. 122-1 of the Education Code. The process of acquisition of this common knowledge should be compatible with various criteria such as the age and health of the pupils (Article D. 131-12 of the Education code).

Schools of the first category may be further divided into schools under a simple contract (*contrat simple*) and schools under an association contract (*contrat d'association*). The simple contract (Article L. 442-12 of the Education Code) is open to fully private primary schools. Teaching personnel are paid by the state but work under private law, and these schools are subject to government requirements as to curriculum and testing (Article L. 442-1). Municipalities may contribute to the costs of private schools with a simple contract.

Schools operating under an association contract are subject, in addition, to inspection by government school inspectors over pedagogy and the selection of teachers, in exchange for receiving operating costs as well as salaries. The status of teaching personnel is equivalent to that of of public schools. Primary and secondary private schools can apply for an association contract for public education with the state provided that they meet a recognised educational need (*besoin scolaire reconnu*) (Article L. 442-5). This notion of 'educational need' is not legally defined. The Constitutional Council held that this need assessment relies on a quantitative appreciation of training needs but it can also be based on qualitative elements like the *caractère propre* (that is the—religious—orientation of the private school) and the request of families (Constitutional Council, 18-01-1985, no. 84-185 DC). In addition to the salaries of the teaching personnel, the operational costs of schools operating under an association contract are publicly funded (Article L. 442-9).

In 2014, around 14% of children attended a private primary school (of one kind or another) and 21% a private secondary school (lower and upper secondary schools). Catholic schools amounted to 97% of private primary schools and 90% of private secondary schools. 99% of Catholic primary and 98% of Catholic secondary schools operate under contract.[11]

Private schools in France are overwhelmingly denominational, and more precisely Catholic (about 90%). There are only four Protestant private schools operating under contract while approximately thirty recently created Evangelical schools operate off contract. The limited number of pupils attending these schools can be explained by the traditional commitment of the Protestant faith to republican institutions and especially the *laïque* public school. Finally, about 30,000 Jewish pupils are enrolled in 250 private schools under contract.[12]

Muslim private schools number over thirty today, at all levels of education, but only two are operating under contract.[13] Most of them were created after the passing of the Act of 15 March 2004 prohibiting the conspicuous wear-

---

11 Figures established from the data provided by the Ministry of national education, available at http://cache.media.education.gouv.fr/file/2014/30/5/DEPP_grands_chiffres_2014_355305.pdf.

12 Figures from Arnaud Haquet, 'L'enseignement privé musulman dans une République laïque', *Revue Française de Droit Administratif*, 2009, p. 515.

13 These schools are: the *La Medersa Taalim oul-Islam* primary school (Saint-Denis de la Réunion) operating under contract and the Averroès secondaryHigh School (Lille) operating under contract.

ing of religious symbols in public school (see below *12.2.2 Prohibition of religious dress for pupils*). The expected increase in the creation of such schools related to that did not occur immediately. Several legal and non-legal reasons may explain the initially limited number of Muslim private schools given the large number of pupils possibly belonging to the Muslim faith. First, parents willing to make space for religious values in the education of their children can rely on other denominational private schools. Indeed, the provisions of Article L. 442-1 of the Education Code establish a balance between the—religious—orientation of the private school (its '*caractère propre*') and the respect of freedom of conscience. Hence, despite this orientation, all pupils have access to private schools under contract regardless of their religion, opinion or origin. This makes it possible for Muslim pupils to attend Catholic private schools. In this regard, it is worth stressing that religious education is optional in private schools (Article L. 141-3). Secondly, the negative and even hostile reactions towards such projects to create Muslim private schools may be discouraging (see below, cases 1 and 2 regarding the secondary High schools *Averroès* in Lille and *Al Kindi* in Decines). Financial considerations weigh heavily on such projects. Indeed, the opportunity to make a simple contract (Article R. 442-49) or an association contract (Article R. 442-33)—and the related public support—arises only after five years of operation. This condition is aimed at testing the seriousness of the initiative, but it also means that the necessary resources have to be found for this period. One observes, however, an increase in the opening of off-contract private schools, including Muslim schools.

Code de l'éducation

Article L. 131-2: L'instruction obligatoire peut être donnée soit dans les établissements ou écoles publics ou privés, soit dans les familles par les parents, ou l'un d'entre eux, ou toute personne de leur choix.

Article L. 151-1: L'État proclame et respecte la liberté de l'enseignement et en garantit l'exercice aux établissements privés régulièrement ouverts.

Article L. 151-2: Les collectivités territoriales de la République concourent à la liberté de l'enseignement dans les conditions prévues par les articles L. 442-6 et L. 442-7.

Article L. 151-3: Les établissements d'enseignement du premier et du second degré peuvent être publics ou privés.

Les établissements publics sont fondés et entretenus par l'État, les régions, les départements ou les communes.
Les établissements privés sont fondés et entretenus par des particuliers ou des associations.

Article L. 151-4: Les établissements d'enseignement général du second degré privés peuvent obtenir des communes, des départements, des régions ou de l'État des locaux et une subvention, sans que cette subvention puisse excéder le dixième des dépenses annuelles de l'établissement. Le conseil académique de l'éducation nationale donne son avis préalable sur l'opportunité de ces subventions.

Article L. 441-1: Toute personne qui veut ouvrir une école privée doit préalablement déclarer son intention au maire de la commune où il veut s'établir, et lui désigner les locaux de l'école.
Le maire remet immédiatement au demandeur un récépissé de sa déclaration et fait afficher celle-ci à la porte de la mairie, pendant un mois.
Si le maire juge que les locaux ne sont pas convenables, pour des raisons tirées de l'intérêt des bonnes mœurs ou de l'hygiène, il forme, dans les huit jours, opposition à l'ouverture de l'école, et en informe le demandeur.
La même déclaration doit être faite en cas de changement des locaux de l'école, ou en cas d'admission d'élèves internes.

Article L. 441-2: Le demandeur adresse la déclaration mentionnée à l'article L. 441-1 au représentant de l'État dans le département, à l'autorité de l'État compétente en matière d'éducation et au procureur de la République; il y joint en outre, pour l'autorité de l'État compétente en matière d'éducation, son acte de naissance, ses diplômes, l'extrait de son casier judiciaire, l'indication des lieux où il a résidé et des professions qu'il a exercées pendant les dix années précédentes, le plan des locaux affectés à l'établissement et, s'il appartient à une association, une copie des statuts de cette association.
L'autorité de l'État compétente en matière d'éducation, soit d'office, soit sur la requête du procureur de la République, peut former opposition à l'ouverture d'une école privée, dans l'intérêt des bonnes mœurs ou de l'hygiène.
Si le demandeur est un instituteur public révoqué désireux de s'installer dans la commune où il exerçait, l'opposition peut être faite dans l'intérêt de l'ordre public.
À défaut d'opposition, l'école est ouverte à l'expiration d'un délai d'un mois à compter du dépôt de la déclaration d'ouverture, sans aucune formalité.

Article L. 441-7: Pendant le mois qui suit le dépôt des pièces requises par l'article L. 441-5, le recteur, le représentant de l'État dans le département et le procureur de la République peuvent se pourvoir devant le conseil académique de l'éducation nationale et s'opposer à l'ouverture de l'établissement, dans l'intérêt des bonnes mœurs ou de l'hygiène. Après ce délai, s'il n'est intervenu aucune opposition, l'établissement peut être immédiatement ouvert.
En cas d'opposition, le conseil académique se prononce contradictoirement dans le délai d'un mois.
Appel de la décision rendue peut être interjeté dans les dix jours à compter de la notification de cette décision. L'appel est reçu par l'autorité de l'État compétente en matière d'éducation; il est soumis au Conseil supérieur de l'éducation et jugé contradictoirement dans le délai d'un mois.
Le demandeur peut se faire assister ou se faire représenter par un conseil devant le conseil académique et devant le Conseil supérieur.
En aucun cas, l'ouverture ne peut avoir lieu avant la décision d'appel.

Article L. 442-1: Dans les établissements privés qui ont passé un des contrats prévus aux articles L. 442-5 et L. 442-12, l'enseignement placé sous le régime du contrat est soumis au contrôle de l'État. L'établissement, tout en conservant son caractère propre, doit donner cet enseignement dans le respect total de la liberté de conscience. Tous les enfants sans distinction d'origine, d'opinion ou de croyances, y ont accès.

Article L. 442-2: Le contrôle de l'État sur les établissements d'enseignement privés qui ne sont pas liés à l'État par contrat se limite aux titres exigés des directeurs et des maîtres, à l'obligation scolaire, à l'instruction obligatoire, au respect de l'ordre public et des bonnes mœurs, à la prévention sanitaire et sociale.
L'autorité de l'État compétente en matière d'éducation peut prescrire chaque année un contrôle des classes hors contrat afin de s'assurer que l'enseignement qui y est dispensé respecte les normes minimales de connaissances requises par l'article L. 131-1-1 et que les élèves de ces classes ont accès au droit à l'éducation tel que celui-ci est défini par l'article L. 111-1.

Article L. 442-3: Les directeurs d'écoles élémentaires privées qui ne sont pas liées à l'État par contrat sont entièrement libres dans le choix des méthodes, des programmes et des livres, sous réserve de respecter l'objet de l'instruction obligatoire tel que celui-ci est défini par les articles L. 131-1-1 et L. 131-10.

Article L. 442-5: Les établissements d'enseignement privés du premier et du second degré peuvent demander à passer avec l'État un contrat d'association

à l'enseignement public, s'ils répondent à un besoin scolaire reconnu qui doit être apprécié en fonction des principes énoncés aux articles L. 141-2, L. 151-1 et L. 442-1.
Le contrat d'association peut porter sur une partie ou sur la totalité des classes de l'établissement. Dans les classes faisant l'objet du contrat, l'enseignement est dispensé selon les règles et programmes de l'enseignement public. Il est confié, en accord avec la direction de l'établissement, soit à des maîtres de l'enseignement public, soit à des maîtres liés à l'État par contrat. Ces derniers, en leur qualité d'agent public, ne sont pas, au titre des fonctions pour lesquelles ils sont employés et rémunérés par l'État, liés par un contrat de travail à l'établissement au sein duquel l'enseignement leur est confié, dans le cadre de l'organisation arrêtée par le chef d'établissement, dans le respect du caractère propre de l'établissement et de la liberté de conscience des maîtres.
[...]
Les dépenses de fonctionnement des classes sous contrat sont prises en charge dans les mêmes conditions que celles des classes correspondantes de l'enseignement public.
Les établissements organisent librement toutes les activités extérieures au secteur sous contrat.

Article L. 442-9: Les dépenses de fonctionnement des classes sous contrat d'association des établissements d'enseignement privés du second degré sont prises en charge sous la forme de contributions forfaitaires versées par élève et par an et calculées selon les mêmes critères que pour les classes correspondantes de l'enseignement public.

Article L. 442-12: Les établissements d'enseignement privés du premier degré peuvent passer avec l'État un contrat simple suivant lequel les maîtres agréés reçoivent de l'État leur rémunération qui est déterminée compte tenu notamment de leurs diplômes et des rémunérations en vigueur dans l'enseignement public.
Le contrat simple porte sur une partie ou sur la totalité des classes des établissements. Il entraîne le contrôle pédagogique et le contrôle financier de l'État.
Peuvent bénéficier d'un contrat simple les établissements justifiant des seules conditions suivantes: durée de fonctionnement, qualification des maîtres, nombre d'élèves, salubrité des locaux scolaires. Ces conditions sont précisées par décret.
Les communes peuvent participer dans les conditions qui sont déterminées par décret aux dépenses des établissements privés qui bénéficient d'un contrat simple.

Il n'est pas porté atteinte aux droits que les départements et les autres personnes publiques tiennent de la législation en vigueur.

Article R. 442-33: Peuvent demander à passer avec l'État un contrat d'association à l'enseignement public les établissements d'enseignement privés du premier degré et du second degré ouverts depuis cinq ans au moins à la date d'entrée en vigueur du contrat. Toutefois, ce délai peut être ramené, par décision du préfet du département, à un an dans les quartiers nouveaux des zones urbaines lorsque ces quartiers comprennent au moins 300 logements neufs.
Les classes des établissements faisant l'objet de la demande de contrat doivent répondre à un besoin scolaire reconnu, apprécié conformément aux dispositions de l'article L. 442-5, et en ce qui concerne les classes des établissements du second degré, en fonction des schémas prévisionnels, des plans régionaux et de la carte des formations supérieures prévus aux articles L. 214-1 et L. 214-2. Le contrat ne peut être conclu que dans les conditions fixées par l'article L. 442-14.
Les conditions fixées par l'article L. 442-13 à la conclusion des contrats s'apprécient, notamment en ce qui concerne les effectifs, dans le cadre du département pour le premier degré et le premier cycle du second degré et dans le cadre de la région pour les lycées.
Les établissements présentent leurs demandes suivant les conditions fixées par les articles R. 442-59 à R. 442-61. Pour les classes faisant l'objet de la demande de contrat, ils disposent de locaux et d'installations appropriés.

Article R. 442-49: Peuvent demander à passer avec l'État, dans les conditions prévues aux articles R. 442-59 à R. 442-61, un contrat simple d'une durée de trois ans au moins, les établissements d'enseignement privés du premier degré ouverts depuis cinq ans au moins à la date d'entrée en vigueur du contrat.
Toutefois, ce délai peut être ramené par décision du préfet du département à un an dans les quartiers nouveaux des zones urbaines lorsque ces quartiers comprennent au moins 300 logements neufs.
Le contrat ne peut être conclu que dans les conditions fixées par l'article L. 442-14.
Les établissements disposent, pour les classes faisant l'objet de la demande de contrat, de locaux et d'installations appropriés aux exigences de la salubrité et de l'hygiène conformément aux dispositions du chapitre Ier du titre III du livre III de la partie I du code de la santé publique et de celles du livre Ier du code de la construction et de l'habitation.

Les effectifs d'élèves des classes faisant l'objet de la demande de contrat sont ceux des classes correspondantes de l'enseignement public, toutes conditions de fonctionnement étant égales.

Article D. 131-11: Le contenu des connaissances requis des enfants relevant de l'obligation scolaire qui reçoivent une instruction dans leur famille ou dans les classes des établissements d'enseignement privés hors contrat est défini par l'annexe mentionnée à l'article D. 122-1.

Article D. 131-12: La progression retenue pour l'acquisition de ces connaissances et compétences doit être compatible avec l'âge de l'enfant et son état de santé, tout en tenant compte des aménagements justifiés par les choix éducatifs effectués. Elle doit avoir pour objet d'amener l'enfant, à l'issue de la période de l'instruction obligatoire, à la maîtrise de l'ensemble des exigences du socle commun.

Article D. 122-1: Le socle commun prévu à l'article L. 122-1-1 est défini à l'annexe à la présente section.

Article Annexe: L'établissement d'un socle commun des savoirs indispensables répond à une nécessité ressentie depuis plusieurs décennies en raison de la diversification des connaissances. L'article 9 de la loi du 23 avril 2005 d'orientation et de programme pour l'avenir de l'école en arrête le principe en précisant que la scolarité obligatoire doit au moins garantir à chaque élève les moyens nécessaires à l'acquisition d'un socle commun constitué d'un ensemble de connaissances et de compétences qu'il est indispensable de maîtriser pour accomplir avec succès sa scolarité, poursuivre sa formation, construire son avenir personnel et professionnel et réussir sa vie en société. De plus, par l'article 2 de la même loi, "la nation fixe comme mission première à l'école de faire partager aux élèves les valeurs de la République".
Pour toutes ces raisons, le socle commun est le ciment de la nation: il s'agit d'un ensemble de valeurs, de savoirs, de langages et de pratiques dont l'acquisition repose sur la mobilisation de l'école et qui suppose, de la part des élèves, des efforts et de la persévérance.
La définition du socle commun prend également appui sur la proposition de recommandation du Parlement européen et du Conseil de l'Union européenne en matière de "compétences clés pour l'éducation et l'apprentissage tout au long de la vie".
Elle se réfère enfin aux évaluations internationales, notamment au Programme international pour le suivi des acquis des élèves (PISA), qui propose

une mesure comparée des connaissances et des compétences nécessaires tout au long de la vie.

Cinq générations après les lois scolaires fondatrices de la IIIe République, une génération après l'instauration du collège unique, le socle constitue une référence commune, pour tous ceux qui confient leurs enfants à l'école, mais aussi pour tous les enseignants.

L'enseignement obligatoire ne se réduit pas au socle commun. Bien que désormais il en constitue le fondement, le socle ne se substitue pas aux programmes de l'école primaire et du collège; il n'en est pas non plus le condensé. Sa spécificité réside dans la volonté de donner du sens à la culture scolaire fondamentale, en se plaçant du point de vue de l'élève et en construisant les ponts indispensables entre les disciplines et les programmes. Il détermine ce que nul n'est censé ignorer en fin de scolarité obligatoire sous peine de se trouver marginalisé. L'école doit offrir par ailleurs à chacun les moyens de développer toutes ses facultés.

Maîtriser le socle commun c'est être capable de mobiliser ses acquis dans des tâches et des situations complexes, à l'école puis dans sa vie; c'est posséder un outil indispensable pour continuer à se former tout au long de la vie afin de prendre part aux évolutions de la société; c'est être en mesure de comprendre les grands défis de l'humanité, la diversité des cultures et l'universalité des droits de l'homme, la nécessité du développement et les exigences de la protection de la planète.

Le socle commun s'organise en sept compétences. Cinq d'entre elles font l'objet, à un titre ou à un autre, des actuels programmes d'enseignement: la maîtrise de la langue française, la pratique d'une langue vivante étrangère, les compétences de base en mathématiques et la culture scientifique et technologique, la maîtrise des techniques usuelles de l'information et de la communication, la culture humaniste. Deux autres domaines ne font pas encore l'objet d'une attention suffisante au sein de l'institution scolaire: il s'agit, d'une part, des compétences sociales et civiques et, d'autre part, de l'autonomie et de l'initiative des élèves.

Case Law

Case 1: The applicant had applied to open a Muslim private secondary high school (*Lycée*), called 'Averroès', whose premises were located in the Islamic Religious Centre in Lille. In 2002, the city security commission had issued an unfavourable opinion regarding the school's establishment in that Centre. The Public Prosecutor then appealed to the academic council for national education of Lille (local education authority in its litigation role), which decided to oppose the opening of the high school for security reasons. This decision was appealed to the High Council of Education.

On the basis of Article L. 441-7 of the Education Code, the High Council eventually held that there was no longer an impediment to the opening of the Averroès school for two reasons:

- the unfavourable opinion of the security commission had been withdrawn;
- the application by the Public prosecutor had been too late (after one month);

Accordingly, the ruling of the academic council for national education of Lille was annulled (*Decision of the High Council of Education—litigation role, 23-05-2003, no. 2132*).

Case 2: The applicant had applied to the chief education officer (*recteur d'académie*) of the school district of Lyon to declare that he intended to open a secondary high school called *Al Kindi*. The Chief education officer issued a decision opposing the opening of the school on the ground that the head of the school, already holding a position as teacher in another school, could not effectively ensure the management of the private school. The academic council for national education of Lyon upheld the Chief education officer's decision. The applicant appealed to the High Council of Education.

According to the High Council, pursuant to Article L. 441-7 of the Education Code, the academic council for national education was competent to adjudicate on an objection to a secondary high school opening only on grounds of morals or hygiene. An administrative decision opposing such an opening based on another ground did not fall within the competence of that council. Considering that the objection in the case at hand relied on the fact that the school head occupied a position in another high school, preventing him from ensuring the actual management of the *Al Kindi* school, the court concluded that such a ground was not within the competence of the academic council. Accordingly, the Lyon academic council for national education was not competent to adjudicate on this application and its ruling had to be annulled (*Decision of the High Council of Education—litigation role, 08-11-2006, no. 2135*).

CHAPTER 8

Further and Higher (Tertiary) Education

Higher education differs from secondary in its relation to knowledge and religion. Article L. 151-6 of the Education Code, stating that higher education is free, derives from the Act of 12 July 1875 on freedom of university education. Moreover, the higher education public service is *laïque* and independent of any political, economic, religious or ideological influence (Article L. 141-6 of the Education Code). However, the purpose of these provisions differs from that in primary and secondary education in the sense that they are meant to foster the objectivity of research and knowledge. Teaching personnel and students have freedom of speech and thought (based on Article 11 of the Declaration of the Rights of Man and of Citizens for the former[1] and on Article L. 811-1 of the Education Code for the latter[2]).

Although they are much more limited in number and purpose than primary and secondary schools, private universities can be created. For faith groups, the challenge is not so much to disseminate religion as it is to set up structures likely to favour an in-depth knowledge of religious tradition and to provide training for religious leaders.

Déclaration des droits de l'homme et du citoyen, 26 août 1789

Article 11: La libre communication des pensées et des opinions est un des droits les plus précieux de l'Homme: tout Citoyen peut donc parler, écrire, imprimer librement, sauf à répondre de l'abus de cette liberté dans les cas déterminés par la Loi.

Code de l'éducation

Article L. 141-6: Le service public de l'enseignement supérieur est laïque et indépendant de toute emprise politique, économique, religieuse ou idéologique; il tend à l'objectivité du savoir; il respecte la diversité des opinions.

1 The right, for teaching-research personnel, to the free communication of ideas and of opinions was confirmed by the Constitutional Council in decision no. 83-165 DC of 20 January 1984, relating to the Act on higher education.

2 On these issues see *Traité de droit français des religions*, no. 3262 ff.

> Il doit garantir à l'enseignement et à la recherche leurs possibilités de libre développement scientifique, créateur et critique.
>
> Article L. 151-6: L'enseignement supérieur est libre.

8.1 Training of Teachers for Islamic Religious Education

The training of teachers for Islamic religious education is not an issue since there is no religious education in primary and secondary schools, regardless of which religion. This is the case also in Alsace-Moselle, where religious education is provided, but where Islam does not belong to the category of 'recognised faith groups' benefiting from this ability (see above *1. Status of religious communities*). Nor is there Islamic religious education training for teachers at universities.

8.2 Imam Training in Public Tertiary Education

Imam training actually encompasses two issues: the chance to set up structures for theological studies organised on the lines of other religious theological traditions (see below *8.3. Law on private universities*) and the training of religious leaders exercising responsibilities in religious associations or likely to serve as chaplains, for example. In a system of separation between Church and state, both would logically fall within the responsibility of religious institutions. This training for religious leaders remains an issue for public authorities mainly on grounds of public policy, causing and revealing their involvement in the organisation of Islam in France.[3] It also explains why imam training has a limited legal basis and does not rely on relevant texts but, rather, is indirectly broached through other questions. It reflects that accommodating Islam within the French system of the state-Religion relationship and French law in general is work in progress and is still partly connected with the issue of social integration. For example, according to recent data, a significant majority of imams

3 Already on religious policy under the Old Regime, that is before the 1789 Revolution, the historian Gabriel Le Bras asserted that 'the states fear their preachers' ... Le Bras (Gabriel), *La police religieuse dans l'ancienne France*, Cours d'histoire du droit public de 1940–1941, handout, p. 11.

working in France come from abroad.[4] This raises concerns in particular about imams preaching in foreign languages and expressing radical religious views. Although it would amount to an unlawful requirement to demand that imams preach in French, the monitoring of radical speechs in mosques, to a limited extent, leads to the expulsion of imams, who are subject to the legislation on foreigners.[5]

Although imam training in public tertiary education is not regulated as such, several public universities offer degrees intended to provide knowledge of law and republican values and institutions, relying on the framework provided by Article L. 613-2 of the Education Code which allows each—private or public—university to set up its own one-year degree with the curriculum of its choice. These degrees officially do not address imams alone but all individuals interested in this kind of training. Such degrees number ten today, and others are set to open in the next few years.[6]

Code de l'éducation

Article L. 613-2: Les établissements peuvent aussi organiser, sous leur responsabilité, des formations conduisant à des diplômes qui leur sont propres ou préparant à des examens ou des concours.
Les présidents et directeurs d'établissements publics d'enseignement supérieur rendent publique sur leur site internet la liste des diplômes qui leur sont propres et des enseignants intervenant dans ces formations.

4 Parliamentary question no. 74929 of 3 March 2015, available at http://questions.assemblee-nationale.fr/q14/14-74929QE.htm; the exact data, however, vary according to the sources, all claiming to be based on information from public authorities.

5 On this question see the parliamentary question of 20 November 2007 and the ministerial response of 20 May 2008, available at http://questions.assemblee-nationale.fr/q13/13-11070QE.htm.

6 The first university degree started in 2008 with the 'inter-culturality, *laïcité*, religions' decree in the private Catholic Institute of Paris, in coordination with the Ministry of Home Affairs. The nine other degrees are hosted by public universities (Strasbourg, Lyon, Lille, Toulouse, Paris-Sud, Paris-Sorbonne, Montpellier, Aix and Bordeaux).

8.3 Law on Private Universities

The ability to create a denominational private university relies on the now codified Act of 12 July 1875 (Article L. 731-1 et seq. of the Education Code). Opening a private university is conditional on the making of a declaration to the local education authority (*rectorat*) which includes, among others, the names of the teachers, the location of the premises, and the object of the lessons that will be taught. Premises should satisfy the health and safety rules applicable to teaching institutions. Non-EU citizens wanting to create a private university are subject to the Decree of 5 December 1850 and should obtain an express authorisation from the local education authority. In the context of tension between the state and the Catholic Church was adopted the Act of 18 March 1880, which denies private universities the right to give out high school graduations (*collation des grades*, see Article L. 613-1 of the Education Code), and forbids them from being called universities (Article L. 731-14 of the Education Code). Degrees awarded by private universities are not recognised by the state, except for those of the Catholic and Protestant faculties in Strasbourg which, for historical reasons, are included in the public university system. Accordingly, private institutions that want to prepare students for a public degree must conclude an agreement with a public university over the sitting of exams (Article L. 613-7 of the Education Code). In practice, only Catholic private institutions provide general academic studies curricula comparable to those delivered in public universities, while other denominational private universities focus on theological studies. There are three faculties of Protestant theology and one rabbinical school. These faculties, together with the seven Catholic faculties, also provide training for religious leaders.

Compared to the academic level and history of other denominational traditions, Islamic private higher education is rather limited. To our knowledge, there is no declared Muslims private higher education institution. Moreover, due to very rapid changes in the creation, organisation and closing of private—non-declared—Muslim institutions providing courses on Islam and/or training for religious leaders, it is particularly difficult to provide a clear and reliable view of this field.

Décret du 5 décembre 1850 sur les conditions auxquelles les étrangers peuvent être admis à enseigner en France

Article premier (modifié par le décret n° 86-642 du 19 mars 1986): Pour ouvrir et diriger une école *primaire* ou secondaire libre, tout étranger admis à jouir des droits civils en France est soumis aux mêmes obligations que les natio-

naux. Il devra, en outre, avoir préalablement obtenu et produire une autorisation spéciale du recteur accordée après avis du conseil de l'Éducation nationale institué dans chaque académie.
Cette dernière condition est imposée à tout étranger appelé à remplir dans un établissement d'instruction primaire ou secondaire libre une fonction de surveillance ou d'enseignement.
L'autorisation accordée par le recteur, après avis du conseil de l'Éducation nationale institué dans chaque académie, pourra toujours être retirée dans les mêmes formes.

Code de l'éducation

Article L. 613-1: L'État a le monopole de la collation des grades et des titres universitaires [...].

Article L. 731-1: Tout Français ou tout ressortissant d'un autre État membre de la Communauté européenne ou d'un autre État partie à l'accord sur l'espace économique européen, âgé de vingt-cinq ans, n'ayant encouru aucune des incapacités prévues par l'article L. 731-7, ainsi que les associations formées légalement dans un dessein d'enseignement supérieur, peuvent ouvrir librement des cours et des établissements d'enseignement supérieur, aux seules conditions prescrites par le présent titre.

Article L. 731-14: Les établissements d'enseignement supérieur privés ne peuvent en aucun cas prendre le titre d'universités. Les certificats d'études qu'on y juge à propos de décerner aux élèves ne peuvent porter les titres de baccalauréat, de licence ou de doctorat.
Le fait, pour le responsable d'un établissement de donner à celui-ci le titre d'université ou de faire décerner des certificats portant le titre de baccalauréat, de licence ou de doctorat, est puni de 30,000 euros d'amende.
Est puni de la même peine le responsable d'un établissement qui décerne des diplômes portant le nom de master, ou qui décerne des diplômes en référence au grade de master sans avoir été accrédité ou autorisé par l'État, dans l'un ou l'autre cas.

CHAPTER 9

Islamic Chaplaincy in Public Institutions

Islamic chaplaincy in public institutions is regulated by Article 2 of the 1905 Act which provides the legal basis for chaplaincy in 'closed' public institutions in general. Chaplaincies are intended for users incarcerated movement in certain public institutions and therefore unable to attend worship. At the time the 1905 Bill was being discussed a member of parliament argued that it would be contradictory to sanction freedom of worship in Article 1 and then to forbid public funding for faith groups in Article 2, that is to deprive individuals of concrete access to worship. Provisions were added subsequently stating that the costs of chaplaincies may be included in the state's and local authorities' budgets in order to ensure the free exercise of religion in public institutions.

Beyond the religious freedom requirements, the issue of chaplaincy is nowadays often analysed in the light of the struggle against discrimination on grounds of religion.[1] The implementation of these provisions relating to Islamic chaplaincies has for long been significantly delayed due to the lack of a Muslim representative body able to appoint chaplains. The creation of the French Council for Muslim Faith in April 2003 (*Conseil Français du Culte Musulman*)[2] critically contributed to improving this situation for all chaplaincies. The relevant texts reflect slight variations according to the public service concerned, leading to a separate analysis.

Loi du 9 décembre 1905 concernant la séparation des Églises et de l'État

Article 2: La République ne reconnaît, ne salarie ni ne subventionne aucun culte. En conséquence, à partir du 1er janvier qui suivra la promulgation de la présente loi, seront supprimées des budgets de l'État, des départements et des communes, toutes dépenses relatives à l'exercice des cultes.
Pourront toutefois être inscrites auxdits budgets les dépenses relatives à des services d'aumônerie et destinées à assurer le libre exercice des cultes dans

1 See, among others, Conseil d'État (2004), *Rapport public 2004. Un siècle de laïcité* (Paris: La documentation française), p. 392 and Bernard Stasi (2003), *Commission de réflexion sur l'application du principe de laïcité dans la République: rapport au Président de la République* (Paris: La documentation française), pp. 39–40, 63 and 67.

2 See above, *2.1. The French Council for the Muslim Faith.*

> les établissements publics tels que lycées, collèges, écoles, hospices, asiles et prisons.

9.1 Islamic Chaplaincy in Hospital

Pursuant to Article R. 1112-46 of the Code of Public Health, hospital managing authorities must make it possible for people who are hospitalised to worship by giving them access to a religious leader. The obligation for hospitals can be fulfilled by enabling patients to meet a religious leader of their faith and does not require access to a specifically dedicated room (see *Council of State, 28-01-1955, Sieurs Aubrun et Villechenoux*). The administrative circular of 2 March 2006 on the rights of hospital patients recalls the principle entrenched in the Code of Public Health and adds that religious practice should be compatible with the proper functioning of the institution and that any proselytism is forbidden.

Chaplains are hired temporarily or permanently, through an employment contract or on a voluntary basis. They are officially hired by a hospital upon suggestion by the Muslim national or local representative authorities (*Conseil régional du culte musulman*). The administrative circular of 20 December 2006 pertaining to chaplaincy in hospitals expressly states that chaplains are hired upon the suggestion of religious authorities and that in the absence of a clearly identified religious authority chaplaincy cannot be provided (*Circulaire DHOS/P1/2006/538, II.1—Le choix des aumôniers*).

Like all chaplains in hospital, Muslim chaplains operate within a framework provided by the administrative circular of 5 September 2011 relating to the Charter of chaplaincies in hospitals and completing the administrative circular of 20 December 2006 on chaplains in hospital. The 2011 circular primarily aims at facilitating the daily dialogue between chaplains and hospital management. Further, the circular provides that a civil servant is responsible for religious issues in each hospital. It is worth noting that the Charter contained in this circular was drafted with the help of religious representatives including a Muslim.

Finally, a National Council for Islamic Chaplaincy in Hospital was created in April 2013, and this takes the form of an association. Its purpose is to provide for the training of chaplains, help and support for chaplains, and to establish links between chaplains.[3]

---

3 See the announcement of its creation on the website of the *Journal Officiel*: http://

Article R. 1112-46 of the Code of Public Health[4]

Les hospitalisés doivent être mis en mesure de participer à l'exercice de leur culte. Ils reçoivent, sur demande de leur part adressée à l'administration de l'établissement, la visite du ministre du culte de leur choix.

Circulaire DHOS/E1/DGS/SD1B/SD1C/SD4A/2006/90 du 2 mars 2006 relative aux droits des personnes hospitalisées et comportant une charte de la personne hospitalisée (excerpt)[5]

L'établissement de santé doit respecter les croyances et convictions des personnes accueillies. Dans les établissements de santé publics, toute personne doit pouvoir être mise en mesure de participer à l'exercice de son culte (recueillement, présence d'un ministre du culte de sa religion, nourriture, liberté d'action et d'expression, rites funéraires ...). Toutefois, l'expression des convictions religieuses ne doit porter atteinte ni au fonctionnement du service, ni à la qualité des soins, ni aux règles d'hygiène, ni à la tranquillité des autres personnes hospitalisées et de leurs proches. Tout prosélytisme est interdit, qu'il soit le fait d'une personne hospitalisée, d'un visiteur, d'un membre du personnel ou d'un bénévole.

Circulaire DHOS/P1/2006/538 du 20 décembre 2006 relative aux aumôniers des établissements mentionnés à l'article 2 de la loi n° 86-33 du 9 janvier 1986 portant dispositions statutaires relatives à la fonction publique hospitalière[6]

I—Le service du culte dans les établissements mentionnés à l'article 2 de la loi du 9 janvier 1986
I.1—Une obligation à caractère législatif

www.journal-officiel.gouv.fr/association/index.php?ACTION=Rechercher&HI_PAGE=1&HI_COMPTEUR=0&original_method=get&WHAT=conseil+national+&JTH_ID=&JAN_BD_CP=&JRE_ID=&JAN_LIEU_DECL=Prefecture%2Fpuyd%F4me&JTY_ID=&JTY_WALDEC=&JTY_SIREN=&JPA_D_D=&JPA_D_F=&rechercher.x=23&rechercher.y=2.

4 Available at http://www.legifrance.gouv.fr/affichCodeArticle.do?idArticle=LEGIARTI000006908220&cidTexte=LEGITEXT000006072665.

5 Available at http://circulaires.legifrance.gouv.fr/pdf/2009/04/cir_10571.pdf.

6 Available at http://circulaires.legifrance.gouv.fr/pdf/2009/04/cir_4364.pdf.

[...] Ce sont les aumôniers qui ont la charge d'assurer, dans ces établissements, le service du culte auquel ils appartiennent et d'assister les patients qui en font la demande par eux-mêmes ou par l'intermédiaire de leur famille, ou ceux qui, lors de leur admission, ont souhaité déclarer appartenir à tel ou tel culte. Ainsi, bien que la loi du 9 décembre 1905 susmentionnée ait posé le principe selon lequel « La République ne reconnaît, ne salarie ni ne subventionne aucun culte », l'article 2 de cette même loi a prévu que « Pourront toutefois être inscrites aux budgets les dépenses relatives à des services d'aumônerie et destinées à assurer le libre exercice des cultes dans les établissements publics tels que lycées, collèges, écoles, hospices, asiles et prisons. »
C'est à ce titre qu'il appartient aux établissements relevant du titre IV du statut général des fonctionnaires d'assurer le fonctionnement d'un service d'aumônerie destiné à répondre aux besoins spirituels des patients ou résidents qu'ils accueillent. [...]
I.2—L'organisation de ce service
Les conseils d'administration fixent les effectifs des aumôniers, en tenant compte de l'importance des établissements, de leur rayon d'attractivité et des données démographiques relatives au bassin de vie qu'ils desservent. Il en découle que cette fonction peut être assurée, de façon permanente ou temporaire, soit par des aumôniers rémunérés recrutés en qualité de contractuels, soit par des aumôniers bénévoles qui devront cependant, pour être autorisés à exercer leur mission, remplir les mêmes conditions que ceux qui sont rémunérés.
Lorsque les besoins le justifient, les aumôniers peuvent être employés à plein temps. Ils peuvent alors éventuellement être logés dans l'établissement par nécessité absolue du service. Ils doivent en tout état de cause pouvoir disposer d'un local de permanence pour recevoir à proximité du lieu réservé à la prière. Les cultes sont célébrés au sein des établissements soit dans une chapelle, lorsqu'il s'en trouve une dans l'enceinte de l'établissement, et pour les seuls cultes qui peuvent s'y pratiquer, soit dans une salle de prière rendue disponible à cet effet. Il est possible de prévoir une salle polyvalente, partagée entre différentes aumôneries, dès lors qu'il y a accord entre les aumôniers de différents cultes. Ces obligations doivent cependant être conciliées tant avec les exigences du service hospitalier qu'avec les possibilités de l'établissement (Conseil d'État, 28 janvier 1955, *Sieurs Aubrun et Villechenoux*). Les directions veilleront particulièrement à la bonne signalisation de ces locaux et à ce que les personnes hospitalisées ou les résidents disposent d'une information claire sur les différents services d'aumônerie de l'établissement.
Les établissements étant tenus d'assurer la permanence du service, il leur appartient de procéder, pendant leurs périodes de congés (congés annuels,

congés de maladie, congés de formation, …), au remplacement des aumôniers habituellement affectés à ce service, en concertation avec ces derniers.
Il convient enfin de rappeler ici que, dans les départements du Bas-Rhin, du Haut-Rhin et de la Moselle où le régime « concordataire » est en vigueur, la procédure de recrutement des aumôniers par les établissements prévue par la présente circulaire s'applique de plein droit aux différents cultes, que ceux-ci soient ou non reconnus, même si, jusqu'à présent, les établissements disposaient, pour les cultes reconnus, de bénévoles mis à disposition par des associations cultuelles pouvant recevoir à cette fin des subventions publiques.
II.1—Le choix des aumôniers
Des services d'aumônerie, au sens de l'article 2 de la loi de 1905, peuvent être mis en place pour chaque culte qui le demande, en fonction des besoins exprimés ou recensés par l'établissement hospitalier, social ou médico-social concerné. Quel que soit le culte auquel ils appartiennent, les aumôniers sont recrutés ou autorisés par les chefs d'établissement sur proposition des autorités cultuelles dont ils relèvent en fonction de leur organisation interne: évêchés, consistoires israélites central, régionaux ou locaux, aumônier national hospitalier du conseil français du culte musulman ou des conseils régionaux du culte musulman et commissions nationale ou régionale des aumôneries des établissements sanitaires, sociaux et médicosociaux de la Fédération protestante de France ou présidents des Conseils régionaux de l'Église réformée de France, etc … En l'absence d'autorité cultuelle clairement identifiée, il ne peut être donné droit à une demande de mise en place d'un service d'aumônerie.
II.2—Le statut des aumôniers
Les aumôniers sont affectés dans un emploi d'agent contractuel, sur proposition des autorités religieuses qui seront consultées, le cas échéant, sur la résiliation de contrat par l'administration. Ils sont donc des agents publics non titulaires soumis aux dispositions générales applicables aux agents contractuels des établissements mentionnés à l'article 2 de la loi nº 86-33 du 9 janvier 1986 portant dispositions statutaires relatives à la fonction publique hospitalière prévues par le décret du 6 février 1991 cité en référence, et ils doivent à ce titre remplir les conditions générales d'accès à la fonction publique fixées à l'article 3 du dit décret.
Le contrat doit préciser le temps hebdomadaire consacré à l'établissement. Sous réserve des dispositions mentionnées à l'alinéa suivant, le contrat est établi pour une durée minimale de trois ans et peut être renouvelé par reconduction expresse ou tacite dans la mesure où l'intéressé remplit toujours les conditions de l'article 3 du décret du 6 février 1991 et que l'agrément des autorités ecclésiastiques dont il dépend est maintenu.

La cessation des fonctions pourra résulter soit de la résiliation du contrat, sur l'initiative de l'une ou l'autre des parties contractantes, ladite résiliation étant obligatoire si l'aumônier n'est plus agréé par les autorités religieuses dont il relève et qui l'auront présenté à l'administration (Conseil d'État, nº 13567 du 17 octobre 1980, *Sieur Pont*), soit du licenciement pour faute grave.
[...]

Circulaire nº DGOS/RH4/2011/356 du 5 septembre 2011 relative à la charte des aumôneries dans les établissements mentionnés à l'article 2 de la loi 86-33 du 9 janvier 1986 portant dispositions statutaires relatives à la fonction publique hospitalière[7]

Le Ministère de la santé a souhaité promouvoir l'élaboration d'une charte nationale des aumôneries des établissements relevant de la fonction publique hospitalière.
En complément des dispositions fixées par la circulaire NºDHOS/P1/2006/538 du 20 décembre 2006 relative aux aumôniers des établissements mentionnés à l'article 2 de la loi nº 86-33 du 9 janvier 1986 portant dispositions statutaires relatives à la fonction publique hospitalière, le besoin de mieux définir un certain nombre de principes fondamentaux et d'harmoniser la pratique des aumôniers hospitaliers dans le respect de leurs cultes respectifs, des droits des patients hospitalisés et des valeurs de la République, a été exprimé.
Des expériences d'élaboration de chartes menées à l'initiative de certaines autorités religieuse ont révélé la demande existant en ce domaine et l'intérêt qu'il y aurait à les étendre au plan national.
Le rapport sur l'application du principe de laïcité dans les établissements de santé établi en septembre 2009 par Michelle Bressand et Philippe Barbezieux, Conseillers Généraux des établissements de santé, a également mis en évidence que si les dispositions de la circulaire DHOS/G/2005/57 du 2 février 2005 relative à la laïcité dans les établissements de santé ont globalement répondu aux attentes de la communautés hospitalières et des usagers, des progrès sont possibles sur les conditions d'exercice des différents cultes.
La charte nationale des aumôneries relevant de la fonction publique hospitalière aujourd'hui diffusée est le résultat d'un travail qui a réuni autour de la Direction Générale de l'Offre de Soins:
– les aumôniers nationaux des cultes catholique, protestant, juif et musulman
– la Fédération Hospitalière de France
– le Collectif inter-associatif sur la santé

7 Available at http://circulaire.legifrance.gouv.fr/pdf/2011/09/cir_33766.pdf.

– le bureau central des cultes du ministère de l'Intérieur
Son premier objectif est de faciliter le dialogue quotidien entre les aumôniers et les directions d'établissement.
Par ailleurs, la circulaire NOR IOCK1103788C du ministre de l'intérieur du 21 avril 2011 a défini des principes d'action tendant à rappeler l'importance du principe de laïcité et ses conditions d'application. Elle prévoit la désignation d'un référent laïcité dans chaque préfecture, qui sera appelé à être l'interlocuteur naturel des représentants locaux des cultes et des administrateurs et élus en matière de laïcité et de liberté religieuse, en lien avec le bureau central des cultes du ministère de l'intérieur. Il sera également appelé à présider une conférence départementale de la liberté religieuse réunissant au niveau local les référents des différents services publics et les représentants des cultes.
La mise en oeuvre de ces actions suppose qu'un agent soit désigné en qualité de correspondant chargé des questions de laïcité et de pratique religieuse: dans chaque établissement de santé, ce référent sera chargé de chercher avec les différentes obédiences, la meilleure prise en compte des convictions religieuses des usagers en fonction des règles de fonctionnement du service et pourra s'appuyer sur les principes posés par cette charte; dans chaque Agence régionale de santé (ARS), un référent désigné devra assurer, en lien avec les services compétents de la direction générale de l'offre de soins, le suivi de ces questions. Cette prise en compte sera déclinée au sein des délégations territoriales des ARS. Le référent participera à la conférence départementale de la liberté religieuse évoquée par la circulaire NOR IOCK1103788C. À ce titre, il travaillera en liaison avec le correspondant «laïcité» désigné par le préfet.
La charte vise également à ce titre à être un support pour l'action des différents acteurs en région et pour le dialogue régional à établir et développer entre les représentants des différents cultes, les établissements et les référents qui seront désignés dans chaque ARS.
Les participants à l'élaboration de ce texte, et notamment les aumôniers nationaux interlocuteurs directs de la DGOS, s'engagent à en assurer le suivi, l'évaluation et à le faire évoluer au regard des besoins qui s'exprimeront au sein des établissements comme des régions.
Vous voudrez bien faire part, sous le présent timbre, des difficultés qui pourraient se présenter dans l'application de la présente circulaire.
Préambule
La Constitution du 4 octobre 1958 rappelle que «La France est une République … laïque …» qui «assure l'égalité devant la loi de tous les citoyens sans distinction d'origine, de race ou de religion» et qui «respecte toutes les croyances.»

C'est dans ce cadre constitutionnel que s'applique la loi du 9 décembre 1905 qui a posé dans son article 2, les termes d'un équilibre selon lequel, à la fois, «La République ne reconnaît, ne salarie ni ne subventionne aucun culte» et «Pourront toutefois être inscrites aux budgets les dépenses relatives à des services d'aumônerie et destinées à assurer le libre exercice des cultes dans les établissements publics tels que lycées, collèges, écoles, hospices, asiles et prisons.» en raison du caractère particulier de ces lieux.

Ces principes généraux ont été réaffirmés dans la Charte du patient hospitalisé (Circulaire DGS/DH/95 n° 22 du 6 mai 1995 relative aux droits des patients hospitalisés et comportant une Charte du patient hospitalisé) qui précise notamment que «L'établissement de santé doit respecter les croyances et convictions des personnes accueillies. Un patient doit pouvoir, dans la mesure du possible, suivre les préceptes de sa religion (recueillement, présence d'un ministre du culte de sa religion, nourriture, liberté d'action et d'expression, ...). Ces droits s'exercent dans le respect de la liberté des autres».

C'est aux aumôniers des établissements mentionnés à l'article 2 de la loi du 9 janvier 1986 qu'incombe la charge d'assurer, dans ces établissements, le service du culte qu'ils représentent et d'assister les patients qui en font la demande par eux-mêmes ou par l'intermédiaire de leur famille, ou ceux qui, lors de leur admission, ont souhaité déclarer appartenir à tel ou tel culte.

La présente Charte a pour objet de rappeler les principes généraux de fonctionnement des aumôneries des établissements relevant de la Fonction Publique Hospitalière, principes régulateurs tant pour les aumôniers qui, après avoir été désignés par les autorités cultuelles dont ils relèvent, ont été recrutés par les établissements hospitaliers, sociaux et médico-sociaux ou qui y exercent leur ministère à titre bénévole que pour les directions d'établissement. Elle concerne tous les cultes et a vocation à s'appliquer sur tout le territoire de la République.

Les autorités cultuelles peuvent nommer des aumôniers nationaux chargés de gérer et coordonner leurs activités d'aumôneries. Ils sont les interlocuteurs directs de la DGOS. Les aumôniers nationaux des cultes catholique, protestant, juif et musulman ont contribué à l'élaboration de cette charte.

1. Statut des ministres du culte

La désignation des aumôniers

La circulaire du 20 décembre 2006 (Circulaire N°DHOS/P1/2006/538 du 20 décembre 2006 relative aux aumôniers des établissements mentionnés à l'article 2 de la loi n° 86-33 du 9 janvier 1986 portant dispositions statutaires relatives à la fonction publique hospitalière) rappelle les modalités de recrutement des aumôniers au sein des établissements de santé:

– Des services d'aumônerie, au sens de l'article 2 de la loi de 1905, peuvent être mis en place pour chaque culte qui le demande, en fonction des besoins exprimés ou recensés par l'établissement hospitalier, social ou médico-social concerné.
– Quel que soit le culte auquel ils appartiennent, les aumôniers sont recrutés en qualité d'agents contractuels ou autorisés en tant que bénévoles par les chefs d'établissement sur proposition des autorités cultuelles dont ils relèvent en fonction de leur organisation interne.
En l'absence d'autorité cultuelle clairement identifiée, il ne peut être donné droit à une demande de mise en place d'un service d'aumônerie.
En cas d'interrogation, les référents au sein des ARS, le préfet ou le bureau central des cultes du ministère de l'Intérieur peuvent être saisis.
L'aumônier est un agent public
Recruté sur la base d'un contrat de droit public (Décret n° 91-155 du 6 février 1991 relatif aux dispositions générales applicables aux agents contractuels des établissements mentionnés à l'article 2 de la loi n° 86-33 du 9 janvier 1986 modifiée portant dispositions statutaires relatives à la fonction publique hospitalière), l'aumônier est, quels que soient son mode d'exercice et sa quotité de travail dans l'établissement, un agent public. S'il est bénévole, il est considéré comme un collaborateur occasionnel du service public. Dans un cas comme dans l'autre, il est soumis à l'autorité du directeur et au règlement intérieur de l'établissement. Il respecte les règles et la déontologie qui s'imposent à tout intervenant interne ou externe de l'hôpital. Il est tenu à la plus stricte confidentialité en ce qui concerne la vie personnelle et familiale des personnes rencontrées.
Le principe de neutralité
L'aumônier respecte le principe de neutralité. La jurisprudence administrative rappelle que ce principe de neutralité s'impose à tous les agents publics. Comme le précise la Charte du patient hospitalisé, « Tout prosélytisme est interdit, qu'il soit le fait d'une personne accueillie dans l'établissement, d'une personne bénévole, d'un visiteur ou d'un membre du personnel. »
Le planning de présence
Le planning de présence des aumôniers contractuels ou bénévoles est régulièrement porté à la connaissance de la direction de l'établissement. En cas de pluralité d'aumôniers pour un même culte, un aumônier référent, proposé par l'autorité cultuelle, est désigné comme interlocuteur direct de l'administration.
La formation
Outre la connaissance des textes religieux de référence, des cultures et pratiques religieuses et de l'accompagnement spirituel propres au culte qu'il

représente, l'aumônier salarié ou bénévole s'oblige à une formation permanente, dans les disciplines fondamentales pour l'exercice de sa mission dans un établissement hospitalier, social ou médico-social et notamment:
– La connaissance de la culture hospitalière et du fonctionnement du service public
– Les principales règles d'hygiène à l'hôpital
– Les libertés publiques en établissement de santé;
– La psychologie de l'écoute des personnes en souffrance;
– Le questionnement éthique.
Cette formation peut être proposée par l'établissement ou par l'autorité cultuelle.
L'intervention des auxiliaires bénévoles
Aux côtés des aumôniers, rémunérés ou bénévoles, les autorités cultuelles peuvent désigner des auxiliaires bénévoles qui doivent être agréés par l'administration dans les mêmes conditions que les aumôniers.
II. Mission et champ d'intervention des ministres du culte au sein des établissements relevant de la fonction publique hospitalière
Mission et champ d'intervention
Les aumôniers exercent au sein d'une institution dans laquelle s'applique le principe de «laïcité». Recrutés au nom et pour le culte qu'ils représentent, ils y assurent une «fonction» qui, par essence, relève du religieux et du spirituel. À la différence de la mission de soin ou d'hébergement qui s'impose à l'établissement à l'égard de tout patient ou résidant, l'action de l'aumônier est «conditionnelle» dans la mesure où les aumôniers «ont la charge d'assurer, dans ces établissements, le service du culte auquel ils appartiennent et d'assister les patients qui en font la demande par eux-mêmes ou par l'intermédiaire de leur famille, ou ceux qui, lors de leur admission, ont souhaité déclarer appartenir à tel ou tel culte» (Circulaire susmentionnée du 20 décembre 2006).
Les demandes d'accompagnement ou de soutien des personnes hospitalisées, de leur famille et de leurs proches doivent être prises en compte dans le respect de leur communauté d'appartenance. Les personnels soignants sont attentifs à repérer et à transmettre d'éventuelles demandes. Les aumôniers des différents cultes relaient entre eux les demandes de patients ou résidants concernant un autre culte.
Au-delà du rôle de visite au patient qui le demande, ou le cas échéant, d'ordonnateur de rituels mortuaires, l'aumônier apporte son concours à l'équipe soignante; son action ne se fait pas au seul bénéfice du patient qui l'a demandé: sa présence, par la dimension éthique qu'il porte, est enrichissante pour tous. L'aumônier, éclaire le cas échéant l'équipe médicale et soignante

sur les implications que peuvent avoir certaines de leurs décisions au regard des convictions et pratiques religieuses des patients. Sa démarche doit être cohérente avec la démarche de soins.

L'aumônier en raison même de sa spécificité, joue pleinement son rôle d'agent public, à titre permanent ou occasionnel, en contribuant à l'amélioration du service rendu aux usagers des établissements publics qui les accueillent, notamment en oeuvrant à la médiation nécessaire à la bonne compréhension de l'organisation du service public par les usagers. Il peut par ailleurs être sollicité pour des actions de formation interne à l'établissement, en vue de diffuser la connaissance des traditions religieuses.

Inscription de cette mission dans un projet spécifique de chaque culte

Chaque culte élabore un projet qui valide la démarche de l'(des) aumônier(s) et le cas échéant, des auxiliaires bénévoles qui interviennent en son nom. Au regard de l'établissement et des autorités cultuelles concernées, ce projet contribue à préciser les modalités de leur intervention.

À cet égard l'esprit de ce projet doit permettre:

– de se rendre proche de la personne fragilisée par l'expérience de la maladie, en respectant ce qui touche à l'intime de l'être, ce qui est source de souffrances difficiles à maîtriser et à saisir;

– de manifester, avec une considération adaptée à chaque personne, dans son caractère unique, l'attention d'une humanité solidaire;

– de veiller au respect de la dignité de chacun—personne malade, soignant et proche—dans l'expression de ses convictions, de ses options, de ses aspirations.

Dans le cadre de ce projet, les aumôniers référents transmettent chaque année à la direction de l'établissement:

– la liste remise à jour des membres bénévoles en activité ainsi que leurs affectations et les formations suivies dans le cadre de l'aumônerie

– un rapport d'activité ou une évaluation écrite de la mission accomplie

III. Le rôle de l'établissement dans l'accès au culte

Au sein de chaque établissement un référent chargé du service des aumôneries hospitalières est désigné. Il est l'interlocuteur privilégié des représentants des différents cultes et doit faciliter les relations entre les aumôniers, les services et les usagers de l'hôpital.

Le référent est en charge:

– d'organiser l'information des patients et de leur famille dès l'admission et tout au long du séjour sur la possibilité de faire appel à un ministre du culte de leur choix. L'organisation des aumôneries hospitalières doit notamment figurer dans le livret d'accueil.

– de rédiger le projet de service des aumôneries

Ce projet de service, révisable chaque année, doit permettre de rechercher avec les différentes obédiences, la meilleure prise en compte des convictions des uns et des règles de fonctionnement des autres. Il est établi en partenariat avec tous les cultes et sur la base de leurs projets spécifiques.

Ce texte référentiel valide la démarche des aumôniers et des auxiliaires bénévoles des cultes en:
. contribuant à expliciter leur mission au sein de l'établissement en vue d'une juste reconnaissance de leur activité.
. précisant les conditions d'intervention et les précautions requises dans l'exercice de la mission confiée.
. précisant les moyens mis à disposition des aumôneries (nombre d'aumôniers recrutés ou autorisés, locaux, organisation de l'information sur le service des aumôneries, etc.)
. rappelant le principe d'une évaluation annuelle des prestations proposées par chacun des cultes sur la base du rapport d'activité du service

– de rédiger le rapport d'activité du service des aumôneries
Un rapport d'activité annuel est établi sur la base de ceux présentés par les différents cultes, Ce rapport d'activité est présenté et discuté avec les référents des cultes représentés dans l'établissement. Il est également présenté à la CRUQPC (Commission des relations avec les usagers et de la qualité de la prise en charge).
Ont participé à l'élaboration de cette charte nationale:
Monsieur [...]—Aumônier national musulman des hôpitaux
Monsieur [...]—Aumônier national protestant des établissements sanitaires et médico-sociaux
Madame [...]—Aumônier national catholique des hôpitaux
Monsieur [...]—Aumônier général israélite des hôpitaux de France
Monsieur [...]—Responsable du pôle Ressources Humaines hospitalières—Fédération Hospitalière de France
Madame [...]—Attachée au Pôle Ressources Humaines Hospitalières—Fédération Hospitalière de France
Madame [...]—Médiateur santé—Collectif inter-associatif sur la santé
Monsieur [...]—Chef du bureau central des cultes—Ministère de l'Intérieur
Madame [...]—Adjointe au sous-directeur des ressources humaines du système de santé—DGOS—Secrétariat d'État à la santé
Monsieur [...]—Chargé de mission—Sous-direction des ressources humaines du système de santé—DGOS—Secrétariat d'État à la santé

9.2 Islamic Chaplaincy in the Army

The army is not mentioned in the list of public services likely to host chaplaincies in the 1905 Act, for the reason that previous, still applicable, legislation passed in July 1880 specifically addressed this issue. A decree of 1 June 1964 settled the applicable law, which was thoroughly revised in 2005[8] and 2008. Since a decree of 16 March 2005, chaplains have been given the rank of military chaplains, which is equivalent to officer status. Military head-chaplains are appointed by the Minister of Defence from among the candidates proposed by each religious denomination, thus leaving a certain margin of appreciation and decision to the Minister. Other chaplains are appointed by the Minister as well, upon the suggestion of the head-chaplain (Article 5 of the Decree 2008-1524 of 30 December 2008 on military chaplains).

The ordinance of the Minister of Defence of 16 March 2005 created the first position of Muslim head-chaplain in the army, and it was updated in June 2012. In 2011, thirty Muslim chaplains worked in the army.[9] As with chaplains in hospitals, the appointment of chaplains in the army depends on agreement delivered by the competent religious authority. Once this authority decides to put an end to the chaplain's mission, the public authority has no choice but to draw the consequences and dismiss him.

Loi du 8 juillet 1880 relative à l'abrogation de la loi du 20 mai 1874 sur l'aumônerie militaire[10]

Art. 1er.—La loi des 20 mai–3 juin 1874, sur l'aumônerie militaire est abrogée.

Art. 2.—Il sera attaché des ministres des différents cultes aux camps, forts détachés, et aux garnisons placées hors de l'enceinte des villes, contenant un rassemblement de deux mille hommes au moins et éloignés des églises paroissiales et des temples de plus de trois kilomètres, ainsi qu'aux hôpitaux et pénitenciers militaires.

8 Decree no. 2005-247 of 16 March 2005 on the special status of military chaplains amending the decree of 1964.

9 See the minutes of the hearing of chief chaplains in the army at Parliament available at http://www.assemblee-nationale.fr/13/cr-cdef/10-11/c1011031.asp.

10 Text and explanations available at http://www.legirel.cnrs.fr/spip.php?article285.

Décret n. 64-498 du 1 juin 1964 portant règlement d'administration publique relatif aux ministres du culte attachés aux forces armées[11]

Article 1: Des ministres des différents cultes sont attachés:
a) Aux camps, forts détachés, garnisons et hôpitaux mentionnés à l'article 2 de la loi susvisée du 8 Juillet 1880 ainsi qu'aux formations et établissements des armes dans lesquels le libre exercice du culte serait impossible sans l'existence d'un service d'aumônerie;
b) Aux forces mobilisées.
Sont assimilées aux forces mobilisées:
Les unités qui doivent pouvoir être mises en action sans aucun délai de préparation et sans mobilisation préalable;
Les forces stationnées en dehors du territoire métropolitain;
Les forces navales et bâtiments désignés par le ministre des armées.

Article 2: Le chef d'état-major des armées assure la coordination du soutien matériel des cultes incombant aux forces armées. À ce titre, il veille à un traitement égal entre les cultes dont les aumôneries ont été organisées au sein des forces armées par arrêtés du ministre de la défense.
Pour l'organisation du service des cultes, l'aumônier en chef de chaque culte est placé auprès du chef d'état-major des armées. Il peut être assisté au maximum de quatre adjoints placés auprès des chefs d'états-majors de chaque armée et du directeur général de la gendarmerie nationale. Un aumônier de zone de défense de chaque culte peut être placé auprès des officiers généraux de zone de défense.
La direction centrale du service du commissariat des armées assiste le chef d'état-major des armées et les aumôniers en chef pour l'exercice de leurs attributions.

Décret n. 2008-1524 du 30 décembre 2008 relatif aux aumôniers militaires

Chapitre 1er: dispositions générales
Article 1: Les aumôniers militaires sont des militaires servant en vertu d'un contrat.
Ils détiennent le grade unique d'aumônier militaire, sans correspondance avec la hiérarchie militaire générale. Ils sont soumis aux dispositions applicables aux officiers en tant qu'elles ne sont pas contraires aux dispositions du présent décret.

11 Version resulting from the revision by the Decree no. 2005-248 of 16 March 2005.

Ils peuvent en outre recevoir l'appellation d'aumônier militaire en chef, d'aumônier militaire en chef adjoint ou d'aumônier militaire de zone de défense, sur décision du ministre de la défense, en fonction des responsabilités exercées.

Article 2: Les aumôniers militaires assurent, au sein des armées et formations rattachées, le soutien religieux du personnel de la défense et des militaires de la gendarmerie nationale, qui le souhaitent.
Ils peuvent être consultés par le commandement dans leur domaine de compétences.

Article 3: L'aumônier militaire en chef organise et supervise l'activité des aumôniers de son culte et assure la liaison entre les autorités militaires et les autorités religieuses. Il est le conseiller particulier du chef d'état-major des armées.
L'aumônier militaire en chef adjoint est placé auprès d'un des chefs d'état-major d'armée ou du directeur général de la gendarmerie nationale, dont il est le conseiller particulier. Il coordonne l'activité des aumôniers de son culte au sein de cette armée ou de la gendarmerie.
L'aumônier militaire de zone de défense est chargé, dans les limites géographiques de la zone de défense et de sécurité, du suivi des activités des aumôniers de son culte au sein des organismes des armées et formations rattachées.

Article 4: Les aumôniers militaires relèvent conjointement:
1° De l'aumônier militaire en chef de leur culte, pour ce qui concerne les questions relatives à leur culte;
2° De l'autorité militaire, pour ce qui concerne les modalités d'exercice de leurs missions au sein des armées et formations rattachées. Ils ne peuvent recevoir d'ordres que des commandants de formation administrative ou des autorités militaires commandant des bases dont la liste est fixée par arrêté du ministre de la défense. Ils n'ont ni le pouvoir de donner des ordres ni celui de prononcer des sanctions.

Article 5: Les aumôniers militaires en chef sont nommés par le ministre de la défense, parmi les candidats proposés par chaque culte, conformément à ses règles d'organisation. Les autres aumôniers sont nommés par le ministre de la défense sur proposition de l'aumônier militaire en chef de leur culte.

Article 6: L'arrêté ministériel de nomination des aumôniers militaires leur confère le grade d'aumônier militaire et, le cas échéant, l'appellation correspondant aux fonctions exercées.

Chapitre 2: recrutement
Article 7: Les aumôniers militaires souscrivent un engagement au titre du service du commissariat des armées.
Les contrats des aumôniers militaires sont à durée déterminée et renouvelables jusqu'à la limite d'âge du grade d'aumônier militaire.

Article 8: Sans préjudice des conditions fixées à l'article L. 4132-1 du code de la défense, pour souscrire un contrat d'aumônier militaire, il faut:
1° Être en règle au regard des obligations du code du service national;
2° N'avoir aucune mention au bulletin n° 2 du casier judiciaire qui soit incompatible avec l'exercice des fonctions auxquelles il est postulé;
3° Être titulaire du baccalauréat de l'enseignement secondaire ou d'un titre reconnu équivalent.

Article 9: Lorsque les aumôniers militaires étaient déjà engagés au moment de leur nomination au grade d'aumônier militaire, ils résilient cet engagement et signent un nouveau contrat qui prend effet à la date de leur nomination au grade d'aumônier militaire.
[...]

Chapitre 5: fin du contrat
[...]

Article 18: Les contrats sont résiliés par le ministre de la défense:
1° D'office:
[...]
2° Sur demande écrite de l'intéressé, agréée par le ministre de la défense;
3° Sur demande écrite de l'autorité religieuse militaire dont relève l'intéressé formulée, sauf circonstances particulières, avec un préavis de six mois.

Arrêté du 15 juin 2012 portant organisation des aumôneries militaires[12]

Article 1: Il est institué, au sein des forces armées, une aumônerie militaire pour l'exercice de chacun des cultes catholique, israélite, protestant et musulman.

12 Available at http://www.legirel.cnrs.fr/spip.php?article74.

> Article 2: Une aumônerie militaire est dirigée par un aumônier militaire qui prend, parmi les appellations suivantes, celle correspondant à son culte:
> – aumônier militaire en chef du culte catholique;
> – aumônier militaire en chef du culte israélite;
> – aumônier militaire en chef du culte protestant;
> – aumônier militaire en chef du culte musulman.
>
> Article 3: Un aumônier en chef adjoint de chaque culte est placé auprès du chef d'état-major de chaque armée et auprès du directeur général de la gendarmerie nationale. [...]

9.3 Islamic Chaplaincy in Prison[13]

Besides the 1905 Act, the right of prisoners to have access to chaplaincy is confirmed by the Prison Act of 24 November 2009 in that it derives from their right to freedom of religion and the related right to practise (Article 26). Moreover, Article 40 of the same Act makes an exception to control over prisoners' mail when it is exchanged with chaplains. In addition, the 2009 Act reflects the specificity of the prison public service, for it provides that this practice has no limits other than those imposed by security and order in prison facilities (Article 26). The specific combination of freedom of religion and security requirements in prison may explain why the Code of Criminal Procedure, in which the applicable law is set out, provides many details on how religious life in prison should be regulated, including access to chaplaincy.

The Criminal procedure Code states that 'Every detainee must be able to meet the requirements of his religious, moral or spiritual life' (Article R. 57-9-3). This provision directly link these requirements to the visit of a chaplain and attendance at worship. Detainees should be informed upon their arrival in prison of their right to be visited by a chaplain (Article R. 57-9-3).

Approved chaplains are responsible for all that pertains to chaplaincy, which covers celebrations, religious meetings and dialogue with prisoners (Article R. 57-9-4). Premises are chosen and granted by the administrative head of the prison.

13 On this issue see Béraud and Galembert (2014, p. 5) and, more generally, Béraud, Galembert and Rostaing (2013).

Access to chaplains and the chaplaincy is governed by a particularly liberal set of legal rules. Thus, detainees can meet a chaplain of their faith, at their request and as often as necessary. No measure or sanction may interfere with this right (Article R. 57-9-6).

However, chaplaincy regulation is also marked by concern for security. As an example, although detainees are allowed to keep religious ritual items (Article R. 57-9-7), this right has certain limits defined by a note on religious practice in prison of 16 July 2014. Among others, the prison administration should 'fight against all forms of proselytism and against radical and sectarian abuse'. Moreover, it is worth noting that this note of July 2014 prohibits 'the wearing of signs by which detainees conspicuously manifest a religious affiliation'.[14] More precisely, 'veils and prayer clothing are allowed in cells and prayer rooms'. This text thus echoes the Act of 15 March 2004 applicable to public schools, although it might be reasonably understood that this ban procedes from security consideration rather than from ideological reasons aimed at asserting the principle of *laïcité*. Still according to this 14-page note—which includes a picture—authorised Islamic objects are prayer calendars, rosaries, prayer carpets and *siwak*.

According to the administrative circular of 20 September 2012 the appointment of a national head chaplain involves an application by the faith group to the directorate of the prison administration (*Direction de l'administration pénitentiaire*). The first Muslim national chaplain for prisons was designated by the French Council for Muslim Faith in May 2005. The approval of a national chaplain constitutes a step prior to the creation of a prison chaplaincy for the faith group concerned. The application is examined by both the prison administration and the ministry of home affairs.

The procedure for the appointment of chaplains is settled by the Code of Criminal Procedure as well (Article D. 439 of the Code of Criminal Procedure and following). It is worth noting that chaplaincy appears in this part of the Code of Criminal Procedure among 'actions aimed at preparing reintegration of detainees'.

The number of Muslim chaplains and the related funding have increased significantly in recent years. While there were only twenty-three chaplains in 1996—including eight voluntary chaplains[15]—there are now eighty-six sala-

---

14 See also Article R. 57-6-18 of the Code of Criminal Procedure on internal rules of prisons.

15 Information from the response to a parliamentary question (question no. 15281, *Journal Officiel*, Sénat, 25/04/1996, p. 987; ministerial response, *Journal Officiel*, Sénat, 20/06/1996, p. 1533).

ried and seventy-nine voluntary chaplains.[16] However, unlike in the army and in hospitals (with contract position), chaplains in prison do not have the status of public officials. Chaplains are not salaried but, as of 2005, receive a fixed allowance (Article 1 of Decree no. 2005-1546 of 8 December 2005). According to the national chaplain for prison, this lack of real professional status would explain the difficulty in recruiting Muslim chaplains.[17]

The issue of Muslim chaplains in prison should be considered in light of a specific context of Muslims representing approximately half of detainees.[18] Hence, the frame provided by chaplaincy is critical, combining the requirements of freedom of religion and concern related to religious radicalism.[19]

Décret n°2005-1546 du 8 décembre 2005 portant création d'une indemnité allouée aux ministres du culte des aumôneries des établissements pénitentiaires

Article 1: En vue de leur permettre d'assurer les missions qui leur sont confiées, une indemnité forfaitaire est allouée aux ministres du culte des aumôneries des établissements pénitentiaires.

16 Figures from Jean-René Lecerf, *Avis présenté au nom de la commission des lois constitutionnelles, de législation, du suffrage universel, du Règlement et d'administration générale sur le projet de loi de finances pour 2015*, Tome VIII, Administration Pénitentiaire, no. 114, 20 November 2014, Senate, p. 53. Available at http://www.senat.fr/rap/a14-114-8/a14-114-81.pdf.

17 During his hearing for the report: Jean-René Lecerf, *Avis présenté au nom de la commission des lois constitutionnelles, de législation, du suffrage universel, du Règlement et d'administration générale sur le projet de loi de finances pour 2015*, Tome VIII, Administration Pénitentiaire, no. 114, 20 November 2014, Senate, p. 53. Available at http://www.senat.fr/rap/a14-114-8/a14-114-81.pdf.

18 See Farhad Khosrokhavar, *L'Islam dans les prisons*, Paris, Balland, coll. 'Voix et regards', 2004 and 'Radicalization in Prison: The French Case', *Politics, Religion & Ideology*, vol. 14, issue 2, 2013, pp. 284–306.

19 See for example parliamentary question no. 96754 (JO, 21/12/2010 p. 13654) and ministerial response (JO, 08/03/2011, p. 2315). See also Jean-René Lecerf, *Avis présenté au nom de la commission des lois constitutionnelles, de législation, du suffrage universel, du Règlement et d'administration générale sur le projet de loi de finances pour 2015*, tome VIII, Administration Pénitentiaire, no. 114, 20 November 2014, Sénat, p. 53. Available at http://www.senat.fr/rap/a14-114-8/a14-114-81.pdf, pp. 46ff.

Loi n° 2009-1436 du 24 novembre 2009 pénitentiaire[20]

Article 26: Les personnes détenues ont droit à la liberté d'opinion, de conscience et de religion. Elles peuvent exercer le culte de leur choix, selon les conditions adaptées à l'organisation des lieux, sans autres limites que celles imposées par la sécurité et le bon ordre de l'établissement.

Article 40: Les personnes condamnées et, sous réserve que l'autorité judiciaire ne s'y oppose pas, les personnes prévenues peuvent correspondre par écrit avec toute personne de leur choix.
Le courrier adressé ou reçu par les personnes détenues peut être contrôlé et retenu par l'administration pénitentiaire lorsque cette correspondance paraît compromettre gravement leur réinsertion ou le maintien du bon ordre et la sécurité. En outre, le courrier adressé ou reçu par les prévenus est communiqué à l'autorité judiciaire selon les modalités qu'elle détermine.
Ne peuvent être ni contrôlées ni retenues les correspondances échangées entre les personnes détenues et leur défenseur, les autorités administratives et judiciaires françaises et internationales, dont la liste est fixée par décret, et les aumôniers agréés auprès de l'établissement.
Lorsque l'administration pénitentiaire décide de retenir le courrier d'une personne détenue, elle lui notifie sa décision.

Code de procédure pénale

Article D. 439: L'agrément des aumôniers est délivré par le directeur interrégional des services pénitentiaires après avis du préfet du département dans lequel se situe l'établissement visité, sur proposition de l'aumônier national du culte concerné.

Article R. 57-9-3: Chaque personne détenue doit pouvoir satisfaire aux exigences de sa vie religieuse, morale ou spirituelle.
À son arrivée dans l'établissement, elle est avisée de son droit de recevoir la visite d'un ministre du culte et d'assister aux offices religieux et aux réunions cultuelles organisées par les personnes agréées à cet effet.

20 Available at http://www.legifrance.gouv.fr/affichTexte.do?cidTexte=JORFTEXT000021312171&categorieLien=id.

Article R. 57-9-4: Les offices religieux, les réunions cultuelles et l'assistance spirituelle aux personnes détenues sont assurés, pour les différents cultes, par des aumôniers agréés.

Article R. 57-9-5: Les jours et heures des offices sont fixés par les aumôniers en accord avec le chef d'établissement. Ils sont organisés dans un local déterminé par le chef d'établissement.

Article R. 57-9-6: Les personnes détenues peuvent s'entretenir, à leur demande, aussi souvent que nécessaire, avec les aumôniers de leur confession. Aucune mesure ni sanction ne peut entraver cette faculté.
L'entretien a lieu, en dehors de la présence d'un surveillant, soit dans un parloir, soit dans un local prévu à cet effet, soit dans la cellule de la personne détenue et, si elle se trouve au quartier disciplinaire, dans un local déterminé par le chef d'établissement.
Les personnes détenues occupées à une activité collective de travail qui demandent à s'entretenir avec un aumônier bénéficient de cet entretien en dehors des heures de travail, ou, à titre exceptionnel, en interrompant leur activité, si cette interruption n'affecte pas l'activité des autres personnes détenues.

Article R. 57-9-7: Les personnes détenues sont autorisées à recevoir ou à conserver en leur possession les objets de pratique religieuse et les livres nécessaires à leur vie spirituelle.

Article R. 57-6-18: Le règlement intérieur type pour le fonctionnement de chacune des catégories d'établissements pénitentiaires, comprenant des dispositions communes et des dispositions spécifiques à chaque catégorie, est annexé au présent titre.
Le chef d'établissement adapte le règlement intérieur type applicable à la catégorie dont relève l'établissement qu'il dirige en prenant en compte les modalités spécifiques de fonctionnement de ce dernier. Il recueille l'avis des personnels.

Article Annexe à l'article R. 57-6-18: RÈGLEMENT INTÉRIEUR TYPE DES ÉTABLISSEMENTS PÉNITENTIAIRES [*excerpt*]

Article 18
L'assistance spirituelle
Les modalités de l'organisation de l'assistance spirituelle sont prévues aux articles R. 57-9-3 à R. 57-9-7.

Chaque personne détenue peut exercer le culte de son choix, à titre individuel dans sa cellule ou collectivement dans les salles prévues à cet effet, en présence des intervenants d'aumônerie.
Le port des vêtements religieux est interdit dans les lieux à usage collectif, à l'exception de la salle de culte. Les vêtements et objets de culte doivent être transportés dans un sac de la cellule à la salle de culte.
La personne détenue peut correspondre avec les aumôniers agréés de l'établissement sous pli fermé.

Décret n. 2005-1546 du 8 décembre 2005 portant création d'une indemnité allouée aux ministres du culte des aumôneries des établissements pénitentiaires

Article 1: En vue de leur permettre d'assurer les missions qui leur sont confiées, une indemnité forfaitaire est allouée aux ministres du culte des aumôneries des établissements pénitentiaires.

Circulaire du 20 septembre 2012 relative à l'agrément des aumôniers rémunérés ou bénévoles, des auxiliaires bénévoles d'aumônerie des établissements pénitentiaires et des accompagnants occasionnels d'aumônerie, NOR: JUSK1240021C

La nomination d'un aumônier national implique nécessairement une demande du culte concerné, qui sollicite en ce sens la direction de l'administration pénitentiaire.
Lorsqu'un culte adresse à l'administration pénitentiaire une demande pour constituer une aumônerie de prison, il est nécessaire qu'il propose l'agrément d'un aumônier national. Cette demande fait l'objet d'un examen en lien avec le ministère de l'Intérieur (bureau central des cultes). Cet examen s'appuie sur le fondement des principes de la loi de 1905, de la jurisprudence administrative, et sur des considérations d'ordre public. Il permet au directeur de l'administration pénitentiaire de prendre sa décision, en fonction des besoins de la population pénale.

Note NOR/JUSK1440001N du 16 juillet 2014 relative à la pratique du culte en détention[21]

S'il incombe aux aumôniers d'assurer le service du culte et d'offrir aux personnes détenues qui le souhaitent une assistance spirituelle, il s'ensuit des obligations positives pour l'administration pénitentiaire:
– obligation d'organiser l'accès aux cultes pour garantir l'effectivité de la liberté religieuse reconnue aux personnes détenues (I);
– obligation de lutter contre toute forme de prosélytisme et contre les dérives radicales et sectaires (II);
– obligation de neutralité de l'ensemble des personnes qui participent au service public pénitentiaire (III).
Ainsi, sans empiéter sur les prérogatives religieuses dévolues aux aumôniers de prison, l'administration organise et fixe le cadre d'exercice de la vie cultuelle en détention.
La présente circulaire a pour objet de rappeler les principes et modalités de l'exercice du culte en détention.
Elle concerne tous les cultes et s'applique sur l'ensemble du territoire de la République.
[...]
C—Les restrictions apportées aux pratiques cultuelles
1. Les regroupements à caractère cultuel
Les prières collectives et regroupements à caractère religieux ne sont autorisés qu'en salle polycultuelle, en présence des intervenants d'aumônerie.
2—Le port de signes religieux
Le port de signes par lesquels les personnes détenues manifestent ostensiblement une appartenance religieuse est interdit.
Ainsi, certains objets ou vêtements ne sont autorisés que dans des lieux limitativement identifiés. C'est le cas des voiles et des vêtements de prière qui ne sont autorisés qu'en cellule et en salle polycultuelle: lors des trajets de la cellule à la salle de culte, ceux-ci sont transportés dans un sac. Pour des raisons de sécurité, cette règle s'applique également à la djellaba même s'il s'agit d'un vêtement coutumier plutôt que d'un vêtement cultuel: celle-ci ne peut être revêtue qu'en cellule ou en salle de culte; elle est transportée dans un sac lors des trajets de la cellule à la salle de culte.
En revanche, les impératifs de sécurité s'opposent à ce que des tapis de prière soient transportés à l'intérieur de la détention. Ainsi, les personnes détenues

21 Available at http://circulaires.legifrance.gouv.fr/pdf/2014/08/cir_38686.pdf.

sont autorisées à conserver un tapis de prière en cellule et des tapis de prière peuvent être entreposés dans la salle de culte.

9.4 Islamic Chaplaincy at School

Chaplains in school were established in 1802 to provide religious courses in upper secondary schools. In the 1880s, religious education was separated from school curricula but still delivered by chaplains and chaplaincies, which were maintained for boarding schools to allow pupils to have access to worship. This initial ambiguity in the exact basis for chaplaincy in school, between freedom of worship and religious education, has remained until today. This explains why Article R. 141-3 provides that *religious instruction* is provided by chaplains. Although chaplaincies are compulsory for boarding schools pursuant to Article 2 of the 1905 Act (and Article R. 141-2 of the Education Code), they constitute only an option in other cases and are in all cases created upon request of the pupils' parents (Article R. 141-3 ff. of the Education Code). Moreover, chaplaincies are funded by families, except where the 1905 Act is implemented (Article R. 141-7).

Islamic chaplaincy at school is purely theoretical as none has been created so far. An overwhelming majority of chaplaincies are Catholic. This also comes from the relation to public school adopted by other faith groups, which traditionally do not conceive it as the most appropriate place to transmit religious knowledge and awareness.

Code de l'Éducation

Article L. 141-2: Suivant les principes définis dans la Constitution, l'État assure aux enfants et adolescents dans les établissements publics d'enseignement la possibilité de recevoir un enseignement conforme à leurs aptitudes dans un égal respect de toutes les croyances.
L'État prend toutes dispositions utiles pour assurer aux élèves de l'enseignement public la liberté des cultes et de l'instruction religieuse.

Article R. 141-1: Dans les écoles élémentaires publiques, il n'est pas prévu d'aumônerie. L'instruction religieuse est donnée, si les parents le désirent, à l'extérieur des locaux et en dehors des heures de classe, dans le respect des dispositions des articles L. 141-3 et L. 141-4.

Article R. 141-2: Dans les établissements publics d'enseignement comportant un internat, une aumônerie est instituée à la demande de parents d'élèves.

Article R. 141-3: L'instruction religieuse prévue à l'article R. 141-2 est donnée par les aumôniers et ministres des différents cultes dans l'intérieur des établissements.

Article R. 141-4: Les lycées, collèges, et généralement tous établissements publics d'enseignement du niveau du second degré ne recevant pas d'internes et non encore pourvus d'un service d'aumônerie peuvent en être dotés, à la demande de parents d'élèves. La décision est prise par le recteur dans des conditions et selon des procédures déterminées par arrêté du ministre chargé de l'éducation.
Si la sécurité ou la santé des élèves le justifie, le recteur peut, après avis du chef d'établissement, autoriser les aumôniers à donner l'enseignement religieux à l'intérieur des établissements.

Article R. 141-5: Dans les cas prévus aux R. * 141-2, R. 141-3 et R. 141-4, l'instruction religieuse est donnée par les aumôniers aux heures laissées libres par l'horaire des cours et leçons, suivant un emploi du temps dressé par le chef de l'établissement.

Article R. 141-6: Les aumôniers sont proposés à l'agrément du recteur par les autorités des différents cultes.
Le recteur peut autoriser l'aumônier à se faire aider par des adjoints si le nombre ou la répartition des heures d'instruction religieuse le rend nécessaire.

Article R. 141-7: Les frais d'aumônerie sont à la charge des familles, sous réserve de l'application des dispositions de l'article 2 de la loi du 9 décembre 1905 concernant la séparation des Églises et de l'État.

Circulaire du ministre de l'Éducation nationale n° 88-112 du 22 avril 1988 sur l'enseignement religieux et les aumôneries dans l'enseignement public, NOR: MENL8800692C[22]

Texte adressé aux recteurs, aux inspecteurs d'académie, directeurs des services départementaux de l'Éducation, et aux chefs d'établissement.

22 Available at http://circulaires.legifrance.gouv.fr/pdf/2009/04/cir_949.pdf.

Il est apparu nécessaire de préciser les modalités d'application de la réglementation relative à l'enseignement religieux et aux aumôneries dans l'enseignement public fixée par le décret n° 60-391 du 22 avril 1960 et l'arrêté du 8 août 1960. Les nombreuses modifications qui ont marqué le système éducatif au cours des dix dernières années ont une incidence sur le fonctionnement des services d'aumônerie. Ainsi, la décentralisation a modifié le statut des établissements et confié aux conseils d'administration des responsabilités en matière d'organisation du temps scolaire et d'utilisation des locaux qui doivent être prises en compte. De même, les lois relatives à l'amélioration des relations entre l'administration et les usagers ("Motivation des actes administratifs"—"Informatique, fichiers et liberté") modifient les procédures instituées en 1960.

La présente circulaire traite uniquement de l'enseignement religieux dispensé dans les établissements publics d'enseignement par les services d'aumônerie.

Les circulaires du 8 août 1960, du 8 septembre1961, du 27 octobre 1961, du 13 juin 1962, n° IV-67-351, du 27 décembre 1967 et n° 79-452 du 19 décembre 1979 sont abrogées.

I.—Création d'aumôneries

Pour les établissements publics d'enseignement du second degré, la création d'une aumônerie est liée à l'existence d'une demande émanant des familles. Les demandes présentées par les parents, les représentants légaux d'élèves ou par les élèves majeurs doivent être établies individuellement, à l'exclusion de toute formule collective portant seulement la signature des intéressés. Elles sont adressées au chef d'établissement.

Elles peuvent être établies sur formulaire ou sur papier libre dès lors que le culte choisi, le nom de la famille, l'adresse, la signature, portés à la main, manifestent clairement la volonté de la famille intéressée.

I A.—Dans les établissements comportant un internat, l'institution du service d'aumônerie est de droit dès qu'elle a été demandée.

Le chef d'établissement fait alors connaître au recteur:

- l'effectif, par classe et par confession, des élèves désireux de suivre un enseignement religieux;
- l'horaire prévu pour chaque groupe;
- les locaux où l'enseignement doit être donné.

I B.—Les établissements qui ne comportent pas d'internat peuvent être dotés d'un service d'aumônerie sur décision du recteur.

1) Dans le délai prévu à l'article de l'arrêté du 8 août 1960, c'est-à-dire *deux semaines après la rentrée scolaire*, le chef d'établissement doit adresser au

recteur un dossier comprenant la totalité des demandes reçues, la répartition des élèves intéressés entre les différents cultes et les différentes classes, les conditions dans lesquelles cet enseignement peut être donné, soit à l'intérieur, soit à l'extérieur de l'établissement, compte tenu des considérations suivantes:
– organisation de la semaine scolaire, avec indication des activités scolaires ou parascolaires organisées le mercredi;
– proximité ou éloignement des lieux de culte;
– caractéristiques des élèves concernés (âge, répartition entre externes et demi-pensionnaires ...);
– contraintes externes telles que les horaires des services de transport scolaire;
– existence ou non, à l'intérieur de l'établissement, de locaux pouvant être utilisés pour l'enseignement religieux;
– avis du conseil d'administration de l'établissement sur les conditions de fonctionnement du service d'aumônerie. Si le conseil d'administration n'a pu être saisi de cette question dans le délai donné au chef d'établissement pour établir son rapport, cet avis devra parvenir comme complément au recteur avant l'échéance laissée à celui-ci pour décision.
Compte tenu de la brièveté du délai imparti, il est souhaitable que les demandes des familles et l'avis du conseil d'administration soient recueillis avant la fin de l'année scolaire précédant celle de l'envoi du dossier au recteur.
2) II appartient au recteur seul de juger du bien fondé de la demande. Le chef d'établissement doit lui transmettre la totalité des demandes qui lui ont été adressées, accompagnées de toutes observations et suggestions qu'il estimerait devoir formuler personnellement. Le recteur peut demander les éléments d'information complémentaires et s'entourer des avis qu'il juge nécessaires.
L'appréciation du recteur porte sur deux points distincts:
– sur l'opportunité de la création d'une aumônerie. La règle générale doit être d'accorder satisfaction aux voeux des demandeurs, même si ceux-ci ne représentent qu'un très faible pourcentage de l'effectif total de l'établissement. Un refus, en effet, leur porte préjudice alors que la création du service de l'aumônerie ne nuit en rien aux convictions ni à la liberté de conscience des autres membres de la communauté scolaire;
– sur l'opportunité d'organiser l'enseignement à l'intérieur de l'établissement. Le recteur dispose à cet égard de la liberté d'appréciation la plus large.
I C .—Que l'établissement scolaire comporte ou non un internat, l'organisation du service d'aumônerie ne devient définitive qu'après l'agrément par le recteur sur proposition des autorités religieuses concernées, du responsable

de l'aumônerie et, éventuellement, des personnes qui l'aideront en qualité d'adjoint (cf. articles 6 et 7 du décret nº 60-391 du 22 avril 1960).
La désignation d'un adjoint peut être autorisée quand le nombre ou la répartition des heures d'enseignement le rend nécessaire.
Pour tenir compte de situations locales, le recteur peut, à la demande de l'autorité religieuse et après avis des chefs d'établissement, être conduit à autoriser la constitution d'équipes de responsables d'aumônerie nommément désignés en vue d'exercer soit dans un ensemble d'établissements scolaires, soit auprès d'élèves d'un même établissement mais de niveaux différents.
I D .—La décision du recteur sur la création de l'aumônerie doit être notifiée au chef d'établissement *avant le 1er novembre*.
Le recteur peut demander un complément d'information qui doit être fourni dans la quinzaine qui suit, ou prescrire des modifications ou un complément aux dispositions proposées.
Dans toute la mesure du possible, l'ensemble des décisions du recteur nécessaires au fonctionnement d'une aumônerie doit ainsi intervenir dans le courant du premier trimestre pour permettre à l'aumônerie d'entrer en activité lors de la rentrée scolaire du second trimestre.
Lorsqu'un établissement doté d'une aumônerie change de statut ou de locaux, le service d'aumônerie sera maintenu, sauf empêchement qu'il appartiendra au recteur d'apprécier.
Les décisions négatives du recteur devront être motivées au sens de la loi nº 86-76 du 17 janvier 1986 qui élargit le domaine de la loi nº 79-587 du 11 juillet 1979 relative à la motivation des actes administratifs à une nouvelle catégorie de décisions: les refus d'autorisation (cf. ma note de service nº 87.435 du 18 décembre 1987 annexe A.6.—BO nº 2 du 14 janvier 1988).

II.—Fonctionnement de l'aumônerie
Une fois connu l'agrément du recteur, le responsable de l'aumônerie sera reçu par le chef d'établissement qui examinera avec lui les conditions de fonctionnement de l'aumônerie.
II A.—Inscription des élèves
Lors de la création du service d'aumônerie, ou lors de la première inscription d'un élève dans l'établissement, le chef d'établissement doit informer l'élève, s'il est majeur, ou ses parents ou représentants légaux de l'existence d'un service d'aumônerie.
1 .—Pour le premier cycle
S'il s'agit d'une première inscription de l'élève dans l'établissement, les parents ou représentants légaux indiquent, sur la fiche d'inscription qu'ils doi-

vent remplir et qui doit comporter une rubrique à cet effet, ou à défaut, sur un feuillet ad hoc annexé à cette fiche, s'ils désirent que l'élève suive les activités du service d'aumônerie; dans l'affirmative, ils précisent le culte choisi.

2.—Pour le second cycle

Les élèves font eux-mêmes cette demande. Pour les élèves mineurs, les parents en seront informés et pourront s'y opposer.

3.—Dispositions communes

S'agissant des élèves en cours de scolarité, leur inscription aux activités du service de l'aumônerie sera effectuée dans des délais fixés d'un commun accord par le chef d'établissement et le responsable de l'aumônerie, ou à défaut à tout moment de l'année. Les formulaires d'inscription dans l'établissement scolaire ou tout autre document comportant des questions relatives à l'enseignement religieux doivent préciser clairement que les réponses à ces questions sont facultatives. En outre, les chefs d'établissement devront faire savoir aux parents ou à l'élève majeur que l'inscription aux activités du service d'aumônerie peut entraîner la nécessité de conserver l'enregistrement de cette inscription dans un fichier manuel ou informatisé. À cet effet, ils devront impérativement recueillir l'accord exprès des intéressés. Les dispositions de la loi n° 78-17 du 6 janvier 1978, notamment ses articles 27 et 31, les notes de service n° 85-470 du 13 décembre 1985 et n° 87-99 du 31 mars 1987 portant publication de délibérations de la commission nationale de l'informatique et des libertés doivent être respectées. Le choix fait lors de la première inscription vaut tant qu'il n'a pas été modifié par écrit. Les noms et adresses des élèves inscrits seront tenus à la disposition du responsable de l'aumônerie qui devra refuser de recevoir les élèves non inscrits et les renvoyer au chef d'établissement responsable de leur scolarité auprès des familles. Le chef d'établissement, dès le commencement des activités du service d'aumônerie, informera par écrit les personnes concernées des conditions d'organisation de ces activités et de leur horaire. Il peut en autoriser l'affichage.

II B.—Conditions d'organisation de l'aumônerie

1) L'enseignement religieux prend place dans le cadre du temps scolaire normal de l'établissement dont les principes sont fixés par le conseil d'administration en vertu de l'article 2 du décret n° 85-924 du 30 août 1985 relatif aux EPLE.

En règle générale, il est dispensé le mercredi ou, en cas d'empêchement, aux heures laissées libres à l'emploi du temps. À cet égard, une concertation préalable entre le chef d'établissement et le responsable de l'aumônerie est indispensable pour fixer cet horaire en fonction de contraintes multiples (activités socio-éducatives de l'établissement, organisation d'études dirigées et d'activités de soutien, activités organisées par la collectivité territoriale

pendant les heures d'ouverture de l'établissement (art. 26 de la loi du 22 juillet 1983) modification des heures d'entrée et de sortie de l'établissement par le maire (art. 27 de la loi du 22 juillet 1983), transports scolaires, etc). Il sera également tenu compte de la disponibilité des responsables de l'aumônerie.
Lorsqu'une modification de l'organisation du temps scolaire est envisagée par le conseil d'administration de l'établissement, les autorités des différents cultes concernés doivent être consultées, avant décision du conseil d'administration, au même titre que les autres partenaires de l'établissement scolaire.
Si pour une raison particulière (cérémonies, visites médicales, sorties et voyages, activités exceptionnelles de l'établissement, etc.), les élèves ne peuvent se rendre à l'aumônerie, le chef d'établissement en avertit, au moins deux jours à l'avance, te responsable de l'aumônerie. La rencontre ainsi supprimée est récupérée par accord entre eux.
2) En vue de faciliter le libre exercice du service de l'aumônerie lorsqu'il fonctionne à l'intérieur de l'établissement, le chef d'établissement devra réserver à des heures déterminées une salle permettant au responsable de l'aumônerie de recevoir les élèves inscrits. Une délibération du conseil d'administration pourra prévoir d'affecter spécifiquement un local de l'établissement à l'aumônerie.
3) Dans le cas où l'aumônerie a été créée à l'intérieur de l'établissement, un certain nombre d'activités religieuses sont néanmoins susceptibles d'avoir lieu à l'extérieur. Les internes peuvent, après accord écrit de leurs parents, être autorisés à participer à ces sorties organisées sous la surveillance du responsable de l'aumônerie.
Il C.—Modalités administratives de fonctionnement
II convient de distinguer deux situations précises.
1) Les services d'aumônerie fonctionnant à l'intérieur de l'établissement scolaire
Pendant le temps où les élèves sont placés sous la garde du responsable de l'aumônerie, la responsabilité de l'État est substituée à celle du responsable de l'aumônerie dans les conditions de la loi du 5 avril 1937. En cas d'accident, le responsable de l'aumônerie doit donc, comme les enseignants, en rendre compte, verbalement et par écrit, au chef d'établissement.
Le responsable de l'aumônerie n'assiste à aucun conseil de caractère administratif ou pédagogique. À l'intérieur de l'établissement, son activité est uniquement consacrée à l'instruction et à la formation religieuse des élèves qui lui sont confiés.
Les dépenses relatives au culte et à l'enseignement religieux sont à la charge des familles, les collectivités publiques pouvant y contribuer conformément aux dispositions de l'article 2 de la loi du 9 décembre 1905.

2) Les services d'aumônerie fonctionnant en dehors de l'établissement scolaire

Les élèves devant, pour assister aux activités du service d'aumônerie, quitter l'établissement et y revenir, la responsabilité du chef d'établissement est dégagée pendant la durée de leur absence. C'est au responsable de l'aumônerie qu'il appartient de venir les chercher et de les ramener à l'établissement, où leur retour sera contrôlé dans les conditions réglementaires.

Si les activités de l'aumônerie se situent en début ou en fin de période scolaire, le trajet entre le domicile et le local d'aumônerie est assimilé au trajet entre le domicile et l'établissement scolaire et les élèves peuvent l'effectuer sans accompagnement.

Dans les établissements ne comportant pas d'aumônerie, l'enseignement religieux est laissé à la discrétion des familles. Toutefois, dans les collèges, les chefs d'établissement doivent, avant d'établir l'organisation de la semaine scolaire, se mettre en rapport avec les autorités religieuses compétentes afin de s'assurer que les familles qui le désirent soient en mesure de faire donner à leurs enfants l'instruction religieuse de leur choix.

Par ailleurs, les chefs d'établissement sont responsables de l'application du règlement intérieur de l'établissement, qui rappelle notamment le devoir pour chaque membre de la communauté scolaire de veiller au respect des principes de laïcité et de pluralisme ainsi que le devoir de tolérance et de respect d'autrui dans sa personnalité et dans ses convictions (cf. article 3 du décret n° 85-924 d'août 1985).

Quelles que soient les modalités selon lesquelles sera organisé et dispensé l'enseignement religieux, les chefs d'établissement ont un rôle déterminant dans l'application de cette réglementation qui suppose une importante concertation avec les responsables de l'aumônerie. S'il survient des difficultés, ils voudront bien, si la négociation locale n'aboutit pas, en rendre compte par la voie hiérarchique au recteur d'académie, qui étudiera le problème posé en liaison avec l'autorité religieuse compétente.

CHAPTER 10

Employment and Social Law

In employment and social law, one must distinguish between the private and the public sectors. Although the principle of non-discrimination on grounds of religion apply to both sectors (see the preamble to the Constitution of 1946 which is still in force), the principle of *laïcité* does not apply in the private sector (10.1), while it constitutes the main source of the law applicable to civil servants (10.2).

Préambule de la Constitution française du 27 octobre 1946[1]

Alinéa 5: Chacun a le devoir de travailler et le droit d'obtenir un emploi. Nul ne peut être lésé, dans son travail ou son emploi, en raison de ses origines, de ses opinions ou de ses croyances.

10.1 Employment and Social Law in the Private Sector

General labour law regulates religious beliefs and practices in the private workplace. Any general and absolute prohibition on employees to manifest their religion or beliefs, unless justified by the nature of the task to be carried out and proportionate to the aim pursued, is unlawful (Article L. 1121-1 of the Labour Code). For example, the dismissal of a cook is justified considering her refusal to taste non-halal food and its negative impact on the efficient running of the business (*Court of appeal of Pau, 18-03-2002, no. 2002-189986*).

Above all, the applicable law is governed by the principle of non-discrimination. Discrimination in general is defined in the Penal Code (Article 225-1). Article 225-2, 3° more precisely addresses discrimination in the workplace by criminalising the refusal to hire, to sanction, or dismiss a person on discriminatory grounds with a maximum sentence of three years' imprisonment and a fine of 45,000 euro.

The principle of non-discrimination is also entrenched in the Labour Code (Article L. 1132-1). Nevertheless, Article L. 1133-1, implementing EU directive

1 This preamble is now part of the preamble to the Constitution of 1958.

2000/78 allows difference in treatment where it 'constitutes a genuine and determining occupational requirement, provided that the objective is legitimate and the requirement is proportionate'. For example, the dismissal of a Muslim employee, whose clothing was held incompatible with the image of the company and regular contact with customers (in a women's fashion store), is justified (*Court of appeal of Saint-Denis de la Réunion, 09-09-1997, Société Milhac Nord v. Meraly, no. 1997-930234*). For an example of the opposite view see below case 1.

Finally, Article L. 1321-3 of the Labour Code prohibits unjustified restrictions on the rights and freedom of employees and discrimination in companies' internal regulations (for a justified dismissal for wearing an Islamic headscarf see below case 2).

Faith-based organisations benefit from adaptation of the principle of non-discrimination as their purpose demands the loyalty of their employees towards the religious object of the organisation. Such organisations are therefore allowed to impose conditions on their employees at the time of hiring, dismissal or during the course of their work contract which might otherwise amount to discrimination. The issue of faith-based organisations has recently been much discussed in the French context because the Baby Loup case (see below case 1) was interpreted as a *laïque* version of this kind of enterprise. It remains, however, that, apart from general provisions of Article L. 1133-1 of the Labour Code, there is no specific text regulating this kind of organisation. Case law is limited and proves to be unsettled as regards the exact applicable rules.[2]

Code du travail

Article L. 1121-1: Nul ne peut apporter aux droits des personnes et aux libertés individuelles et collectives de restrictions qui ne seraient pas justifiées par la nature de la tâche à accomplir ni proportionnées au but recherché.

Article L. 1132-1:[3] Aucune personne ne peut être écartée d'une procédure de recrutement ou de l'accès à un stage ou à une période de formation en entreprise, aucun salarié ne peut être sanctionné, licencié ou faire l'objet d'une

2 As an illustration likely to apply to Islam see below case 3. More generally on faith-based organisations in the French and European contexts see Marguénaud, Jean-Pierre and Mouly, Jean, 'Les droits de l'Homme salarié de l'entreprise identitaire (à propos des trois arrêts de la Cour EDH, *Obst* et *Schüth* du 23 septembre 2010 et *Siebenhaar* du 3 février 2011)', *Recueil Dalloz*, 2011, pp. 1637–1643.

3 Former Article L. 122-45 of the Labour Code.

mesure discriminatoire, directe ou indirecte, telle que définie à l'article 1er de la loi n° 2008-496 du 27 mai 2008 portant diverses dispositions d'adaptation au droit communautaire dans le domaine de la lutte contre les discriminations, notamment en matière de rémunération, au sens de l'article L. 3221-3, de mesures d'intéressement ou de distribution d'actions, de formation, de reclassement, d'affectation, de qualification, de classification, de promotion professionnelle, de mutation ou de renouvellement de contrat en raison de son origine, de son sexe, de ses mœurs, de son orientation ou identité sexuelle, de son âge, de sa situation de famille ou de sa grossesse, de ses caractéristiques génétiques, de son appartenance ou de sa non-appartenance, vraie ou supposée, à une ethnie, une nation ou une race, de ses opinions politiques, de ses activités syndicales ou mutualistes, de ses convictions religieuses, de son apparence physique, de son nom de famille, de son lieu de résidence ou en raison de son état de santé ou de son handicap.

Article L. 1132-4: Toute disposition ou tout acte pris à l'égard d'un salarié en méconnaissance des dispositions du présent chapitre est nul.

Article L. 1133-1: L'article L. 1132-1 ne fait pas obstacle aux différences de traitement, lorsqu'elles répondent à une exigence professionnelle essentielle et déterminante et pour autant que l'objectif soit légitime et l'exigence proportionnée.

Article L. 1321-3: Le règlement intérieur ne peut contenir:
1° Des dispositions contraires aux lois et règlements ainsi qu'aux stipulations des conventions et accords collectifs de travail applicables dans l'entreprise ou l'établissement;
2° Des dispositions apportant aux droits des personnes et aux libertés individuelles et collectives des restrictions qui ne seraient pas justifiées par la nature de la tâche à accomplir ni proportionnées au but recherché;
3° Des dispositions discriminant les salariés dans leur emploi ou leur travail, à capacité professionnelle égale, en raison de leur origine, de leur sexe, de leurs mœurs, de leur orientation ou identité sexuelle, de leur âge, de leur situation de famille ou de leur grossesse, de leurs caractéristiques génétiques, de leur appartenance ou de leur non-appartenance, vraie ou supposée, à une ethnie, une nation ou une race, de leurs opinions politiques, de leurs activités syndicales ou mutualistes, de leurs convictions religieuses, de leur apparence physique, de leur nom de famille ou en raison de leur état de santé ou de leur handicap.

Code pénal

Article 225-1: Constitue une discrimination toute distinction opérée entre les personnes physiques à raison de leur origine, de leur sexe, de leur situation de famille, de leur grossesse, de leur apparence physique, de leur patronyme, de leur lieu de résidence, de leur état de santé, de leur handicap, de leurs caractéristiques génétiques, de leurs mœurs, de leur orientation ou identité sexuelle, de leur âge, de leurs opinions politiques, de leurs activités syndicales, de leur appartenance ou de leur non-appartenance, vraie ou supposée, à une ethnie, une nation, une race ou une religion déterminée.
Constitue également une discrimination toute distinction opérée entre les personnes morales à raison de l'origine, du sexe, de la situation de famille, de l'apparence physique, du patronyme, du lieu de résidence, de l'état de santé, du handicap, des caractéristiques génétiques, des moeurs, de l'orientation ou identité sexuelle, de l'âge, des opinions politiques, des activités syndicales, de l'appartenance ou de la non-appartenance, vraie ou supposée, à une ethnie, une nation, une race ou une religion déterminée des membres ou de certains membres de ces personnes morales.

Article 225-2: La discrimination définie aux articles 225-1 et 225-1-1, commise à l'égard d'une personne physique ou morale, est punie de trois ans d'emprisonnement et de 45,000 euros d'amende lorsqu'elle consiste:
1° À refuser la fourniture d'un bien ou d'un service;
2° À entraver l'exercice normal d'une activité économique quelconque;
3° À refuser d'embaucher, à sanctionner ou à licencier une personne;
4° À subordonner la fourniture d'un bien ou d'un service à une condition fondée sur l'un des éléments visés à l'article 225-1 ou prévue à l'article 225-1-1;
5° À subordonner une offre d'emploi, une demande de stage ou une période de formation en entreprise à une condition fondée sur l'un des éléments visés à l'article 225-1 ou prévue à l'article 225-1-1;
6° À refuser d'accepter une personne à l'un des stages visés par le 2° de l'article L. 412-8 du code de la sécurité sociale.
Lorsque le refus discriminatoire prévu au 1° est commis dans un lieu accueillant du public ou aux fins d'en interdire l'accès, les peines sont portées à cinq ans d'emprisonnement et à 75,000 euros d'amende.

Case Law

Case 1: The Paris Court of Appeal decided to annul the dismissal of a telephone interviewer who refused to wear her veil tied as a hat because, on the one hand, she was already wearing it at the time of hiring and, on the other hand, she had not reported any problems in her contacts with customers.

In this case, the employer did not provide evidence of the existence of objective elements unrelated to any discrimination based on religious beliefs to justify the dismissal. He argued that the new conditions of work after the employee's transfer to another site justified the decision to prohibit the wearing of the headscarf. However the employee, a telephone-interviewer, had already been in contact with customers in her former position without any reported problem with them in connection with the headscarf (*Court of appeal of Paris, 19-06-2003, Société Téléperformance, no. S03/30212*).

Case 2: This decision is the final point—within the French legal system—of a very controversial and topical case about the dismissal of an employee of a private nursery who refused to remove her Islamic headscarf, in breach of the organisation's internal regulations.

The highest civil court eventually held that the general clause on *laïcité* and neutrality in the internal regulations of the Baby Loup Association limiting the employees' freedom of religion complied with the provisions of Article L. 1121-1 of the Labour Code. This limitation was justified owing to the small number of employees likely to be in contact with children and their parents. It is worth noting that the Court of Cassation rejected the reasoning of the Paris Court of Appeal—which issued its ruling of 27 November 2013—consisting in recognising the association as an '*entreprise de conviction*' (faith-based organisation), namely to making *laïcité* and neutrality the ethos of the association justifying the limitation of freedom of religion (*Court of cassation, 25-06-2014, Association Baby Loup, no. 13-28.369*).[4]

4 On this heated and debated case see, among many others: Calvès, Gwénaële, 'Devoir de réserve imposé aux salariés de la crèche Baby Loup. Quelle lecture européenne du problème?', *Revue de droit du travail*, 2014, pp. 94–100; Delvolvé, Pierre, 'Entreprise privée, laïcité, liberté religieuse L'affaire *Baby-Loup*', *Revue Française de Droit administratif*, 2014, pp. 954–964; Laronze, Fleur, 'Affaire *Baby Loup*: l'épuisement du droit dans sa recherche d'une vision apolitisée de la religion', *Droit social*, 2014, pp. 100–106; Mbongo, Pascal, 'Institutions privées, "entreprises de tendance" et droit au respect des croyances religieuses', *La Semaine Juridique, Edition Générale*, no. 26, 24-06-2013, no. 750; Mouton, Stéphane and Lamarche, Thierry, 'Affaire *Baby Loup*: suite et fin? Une décision en demi-teinte qui ne protège pas la neutralité nécessaire aux missions d'intérêt général', *Actualité Juridique. Droit administratif*, 2014, pp. 1842–1849.

Case 3: The defendant was the manager of a restaurant which provided kosher food. In order to guarantee that the food was prepared according to Jewish rites, he had hired a ritual supervisor, the applicant, who had subsequently been orally dismissed after he had been missing for twenty-five days to attend the burial of his son in Israel, when the law allows three days. The Beth-Din services had sent someone to replace him. The employer considered that he was the only person entitled to decide the length of such an absence. Before the court, the ritual supervisor claimed damages for unfair dismissal. The Court said that by providing kosher food and hiring a ritual supervisor, the employer intended to submit his restaurant to a strict respect of the Jewish law. Hence, the contractual relationships between the employer and the ritual supervisor assumed a mutual attachment to the Jewish law, beyond the mission of the employee. The employer could therefore not ignore the length of an absence due to a burial in Israel. The dismissal accordingly constituted an unfair dismissal (*Court of appeal of Paris, 25-05-1990, no. 36864/89*).

10.2 Employment in the Public Sector

10.2.1 *Employment in the Public Sector: Main Principles*[5]

Despite their various statuses and functions, all public officials have several principles in common, including religious neutrality, which derive from the principle of state neutrality in political, philosophical or religious matters. The principle of neutrality applies to civil servants but also to agents, who only have a fixed termed contract in public law with the state or local public authorities. This principle, deeply anchored in French political and administrative tradition, means that individuals turning to public services should expect to be treated equally and impartially. Surprisingly, despite the core importance of this principle of neutrality, no legislative text explicitly requires it. There is no mention of a duty of religious neutrality in Act no. 83-634 of 13 July 1983 on the rights and duties of civil servants. Actually, it is enshrined in case law and remains within the jurisdiction of the courts (see in particular cases 1 and 2 below). A clear reference to public hospital service neutrality (and civil servants) appears in the administrative circular of 2 February 2005 on *laïcité* in public hospitals. It is limited, however, to a reminder of the relevant case law. The bill on the ethics and the rights and obligations of civil servants of 17 July

5 For the dress code in the workplace see also below *12.2.1 Prohibition of religious dress for civil servants*.

2013 should be mentioned here, as its Article 1 is aimed at modifying Article 25 of the 1983 Act by including for the first time the duty of neutrality and compliance with the principle of *laïcité*.[6]

Nevertheless, the Act of 13 July 1983 on the rights and duties of civil servants protects civil servants' freedom of thought and the principle of equal access to public employment. This Act consequently prohibits distinctions based on, among others, religious opinion (see below *Council of State, 10-04-2009, El Haddioui, no. 311888*).

Constitution du 4 octobre 1958

Preambule:[7] Chacun a le devoir de travailler et le droit d'obtenir un emploi. Nul ne peut être lésé, dans son travail ou son emploi, en raison de ses origines, de ses opinions ou de ses croyances.

Article 1: La France est une République indivisible, *laïque*, démocratique et sociale. Elle assure l'égalité devant la loi de tous les citoyens sans distinction d'origine, de race ou de religion. Elle respecte toutes les croyances. Son organisation est décentralisée.
La loi favorise l'égal accès des femmes et des hommes aux mandats électoraux et fonctions électives, ainsi qu'aux responsabilités professionnelles et sociales.[8]

Loi n. 83-634 du 13 juillet 1983 modifiée portant droits et obligations des fonctionnaires

Article 6: La liberté d'opinion est garantie aux fonctionnaires.
Aucune distinction, directe ou indirecte, ne peut être faite entre les fonctionnaires en raison de leurs opinions politiques, syndicales, philosophiques ou religieuses, de leur origine, de leur orientation ou identité sexuelle, de leur âge, de leur patronyme, de leur état de santé, de leur apparence physique, de leur handicap ou de leur appartenance ou de leur non-appartenance, vraie ou supposée, à une ethnie ou une race.

6 See http://www.assemblee-nationale.fr/14/projets/pl1278.asp.

7 Including the preamble to the previous Constitution of 27 October 1946.

8 Translation available at http://www.conseil-constitutionnel.fr/conseil-constitutionnel/english/constitution/constitution-of-4-october-1958.25742.html#TitleI.

Article 18: Il ne peut être fait état dans le dossier d'un fonctionnaire, de même que dans tout document administratif, des opinions ou des activités politiques, syndicales, religieuses ou philosophiques de l'intéressé.

Circulaire DHOS/G n° 2005-57 du 2 février 2005 relative à la laïcité dans les établissements de santé (excerpt)

B.—Neutralité du service public hospitalier et des fonctionnaires et agents publics
L'obligation de neutralité est posée depuis plus d'un demi-siècle dans la jurisprudence (Conseil d'État 8 décembre 1948, Dlle Pasteau—3 mai 1950, Dlle Jamet).
Dans un arrêt en date du 27 novembre 2003 (Mlle Nadjet Ben Abdallah), la cour administrative d'appel de Lyon a considéré que: «Le port, par Mlle Ben Abdallah, détentrice de prérogatives de puissance publique, d'un foulard dont elle a expressément revendiqué le caractère religieux, et le refus réitéré d'obéir à l'ordre qui lui a été donné de le retirer, alors qu'elle était avertie de l'état non ambigu du droit applicable, a, dans les circonstances de l'espèce, constitué une faute grave de nature à justifier légalement la mesure de suspension dont elle a fait l'objet» (Mlle Ben Abdallah est contrôleur du travail).
[…] Ces principes s'appliquent à tous les fonctionnaires et agents publics, à l'exception des ministres des différents cultes mentionnés à l'article R. 1112-46 du code de la santé publique.[9] Il est rappelé que les agents publics sont des agents qui concourent à l'exécution du service public: contractuels, internes …

Case Law

Case 1: The applicant was a social worker with a fixed term contract. The Minister of Education had terminated her contract on religious grounds. The applicant had, however, never behaved in breach of her strict duty of neutrality, which applies to all public agents involved in public service activities. Hence, the Minister unlawfully intended generally to deny public officials having religious beliefs the ability to function as school and university health workers (*Council of State, 08-12-1948, Miss Pasteau, no. 91.406*).

9 Article R. 1112-46 of the Public Health Code deals with the right of hospital patients to practise their religion and to be visited by the religious leader of their choice.

Case 2: A temporary student monitor in a state school was dismissed by the regional chief education officer (*recteur d'Académie*). The administrative court in charge of the appeal requested an opinion from the Council of State. This opinion, which has since become a reference, is three-fold and answers the following points:

1. Should the requirements of the principle of *laïcité* be assessed according to the nature of the public services?
   The Council of State stated that the constitutional and legislative provisions mean that the principles of freedom of conscience and of *laïcité* of the state apply to all public services.
2. Within the public service of education, should a distinction be drawn between educational tasks and others, between the teaching functions and others? Following all civil servants, the members of the educational public service should not be discriminated against on religious grounds for entering the civil service, but the principle of *laïcité* prevents them from manifesting their religious beliefs within a public service. Within the educational public service, no distinction should be established among the various categories of personnel.
3. Should religious symbols be distinguished according to their nature or the level of their conspicuous character? A civil servant of the public education service manifesting his/her religious beliefs, particularly by displaying a symbol, is guilty of a breach of obligation. It is for the administration, under the control of the judge, to decide the consequences of this breach, considering the nature and the level of the conspicuous character of this sign (*Council of State, Opinion, 03-05-2000, Miss Marteaux, no. 217017*).

Case 3: The applicant had applied for a position as a police officer. During the interview, the panel asked questions about his national origin and his and his wife's religious practices.

These questions amounted to one of the distinctions prohibited by Article 6 of the 13 July 1983 Act on the rights and duties of civil servants and were in breach of the principle of equal access to public employment (*Council of State, 10-04-2009, El Haddioui, no. 311888*).

Case 4: The Court upheld the dismissal of a health-care technician who wore an Islamic veil on the ground that she worked for an organisation that provided a public service. The principles of neutrality and secularism of the public service are applicable to all public services and includes those provided by private bodies (*Court of cassation, 19-03-2013, Caisse primaire d'assurance maladie de Seine-Saint-Denis, no. 537*).

10.2.2 *Employment in the Public Sector: Working Time and Religious Duties*

As regards working time and religious duties, all civil servants are allowed authorised absences in order to celebrate the main religious holidays. This has been regulated by administrative circulars since the 1960s. The latest circular dates from 10 February 2012 and lists the main religious holidays. Unlike earlier circulars, it no longer determines the exact dates of religious holidays, so ending the need for annual updating. For these religious holidays and religious duties in general, it falls within the responsibility of the service head to assess whether a civil servant's absence is compatible with the proper functioning of the service. For example, a civil servant, a caretaker of social housing, could be refused temporary leave from his job to attend mosque every Friday afternoon, as his absence was not compatible with the proper functioning of the public service. The decision of the service head was not in breach of the applicant's freedom of religion (*Council of State, 16-02-2004, Benaissa, no. 264314*).

Circulaire du 10 février 2012, no. MFPF1202144C, relative aux autorisations d'absence pouvant être accordées à l'occasion des principales fêtes religieuses des différentes confessions

La circulaire FP n° 901 du 23 septembre 1967 a rappelé que les chefs de service peuvent accorder aux agents qui désirent participer aux cérémonies célébrées à l'occasion des principales fêtes propres à leur confession, les autorisations d'absence nécessaires.
Vous voudrez bien trouver ci-joint, à titre d'information, les cérémonies propres à certaines des principales confessions et pour lesquelles une autorisation d'absence peut être accordée.
Je vous serais obligé de rappeler aux chefs de service placés sous votre autorité qu'ils peuvent accorder à leurs agents une autorisation pour participer à une fête religieuse correspondant à leur confession dans la mesure où cette absence est compatible avec le fonctionnement normal du service.
[...] Fêtes musulmanes:
- Aïd El Adha.
- Al Mawlid Ennabi.
- Aïd El Fitr.

CHAPTER 11

Islamic Slaughter and Food Regulation

Although Islamic slaughter and food regulation are partly tied to practice, they need to be considered separately. While the first addresses a public health issue, the second falls within the responsibility of religious authorities only to define and assert what is *halal* food.

11.1 Islamic Slaughter

Ritual slaughter has been regulated mainly through administrative—and not legislative—texts since the 1960s, the trexts having been regularly updated since then. These provisions are today enshrined in the Rural and Maritime Fishing Code, whose provisions focus on the ritual slaughter process itself, slaughterhouses, and persons or bodies entitled to practise ritual slaughtering. Hence, Article R. 241-70 provides an exception to the obligation to stun animals before slaughter where stunning turns out to be incompatible with ritual slaughter requirements. Furthermore, Article R. 214-74 specifies that animals should be restrained during ritual slaughtering. In addition, Article R. 214-73 strictly forbids ritual slaughter outside an abattoir. Moreover, a slaughterhouse is authorised to host ritual slaughtering provided that it meets several strict conditions laid down in Article R. 214-70, such as the use of appropriate equipment, trained personnel, a satisfactory level of hygiene as well as ascertaining that ritual slaughter is required by commercial needs.

Finally, ritual slaughter must be carried out only by individuals duly authorised by religious authorities and previously approved by the Minister of Agriculture, upon suggestion of the Minister of Home Affairs. Where no religious authority has approved him, a person can be given an individual authorisation by the *préfet* of the *département* who is in charge of public order (Article 214-75, see case 2). Ministerial orders have listed religious bodies entitled to appoint ritual slaughterers: the Great Mosque of Paris in 1994, the Great Mosque of Lyon and the mosque of Évry in 1996.[1] Any infringement of these provisions is regu-

1 The ministerial approval granted to religious authorities resulted in the famous case Cha'are Shalom Ve Tsedek: a dissenting Jewish association was denied this approval, which had been granted instead to the Jewish consistorial association of Paris. The French court decision was

lated by Article R. 215-8 of the same Code (3). This was the case of a man who had sold sheep and made a plot available for ritual slaughter on the day of Aïd el Kebir and was charged with allowing ritual slaughter outside an abattoir (*Court of cassation, 31-05-2005, no. 04-87.708*).

Since January 2013, ritual slaughterers have been required to furthermore attend a specific training course to obtain a certificate of competence in 'Animal protection', which is delivered by the *département* directorate for animal protection after the applicant has attended the relevant training. This applies to all slaughterhouse personnel, irrespective of the nature of the slaughtering. The ministerial order of 31 July 2012 and above all the administrative circular of 23 August 2012[2] organise the training for and issuing of the certificate.

In addition, the question arose especially in 2011 of control over the destination of meat from animals not subject to prior stunning. It was argued that half the sheep would be slaughtered without prior stunning, thus exceeding the religious needs of religious groups in France and thus questioning the relevance of the exception entrenched in legislation.[3] In order to avoid abuses in slaughter without prior stunning, the decree of 28 December 2011 was adopted, which adds several conditions to Article R. 214-70 of the Rural Code. In particular, this decree requires that the abattoir maintain a registration system making it possible to check the correspondence between commercial orders and the implementation of the derogation on prior stunning.

Code rural et de la pêche maritime

Article R. 214-70: I.—L'étourdissement des animaux est obligatoire avant l'abattage ou la mise à mort, à l'exception des cas suivants:
1° Si cet étourdissement n'est pas compatible avec la pratique de l'abattage rituel
2° Lorsque le procédé utilisé pour la mise à mort du gibier d'élevage a été préalablement autorisé et entraîne la mort immédiate des animaux;

upheld by the European Court of Human Rights (*Cha'are Shalom Ve Tsedek v. France*, 27 June 2000, no. 27417/95).

2 Available at http://circulaires.legifrance.gouv.fr/index.php?action=afficherCirculaire&hit=1&r=35712.

3 Florence Bergeaud-Blackler, '*Halal*: d'une norme communautaire à une norme institutionnelle', *Journal des anthropologues*, 2006, pp. 106–107, available at http://jda.revues.org/1270. See also a parliamentary question on this point: http://www.senat.fr/leg/ppl09-711.html#fnref2.

3° En cas de mise à mort d'urgence.
II.—Les procédés d'étourdissement et de mise à mort mentionnés au I ainsi que les espèces auxquelles ils doivent être appliqués sont fixés par arrêté du ministre chargé de l'agriculture.
III.—Un abattoir ne peut mettre en œuvre la dérogation prévue au 1° du I que s'il y est préalablement autorisé.
L'autorisation est accordée aux abattoirs qui justifient de la présence d'un matériel adapté et d'un personnel dûment formé, de procédures garantissant des cadences et un niveau d'hygiène adaptés à cette technique d'abattage ainsi que d'un système d'enregistrements permettant de vérifier que l'usage de la dérogation correspond à des commandes commerciales qui le nécessitent.
La demande d'autorisation est adressée au préfet du département du lieu d'implantation de l'abattoir qui dispose d'un délai de trois mois à compter de la réception complète du dossier pour statuer sur la demande. L'autorisation est accordée par arrêté du préfet. Cet arrêté peut restreindre l'étendue de l'autorisation à certaines catégories d'animaux.
Le contenu du dossier de demande d'autorisation est précisé par arrêté du ministre chargé de l'agriculture.
Toute modification des éléments pris en compte pour l'octroi de l'autorisation initiale, de même que la cessation d'activité doivent être notifiées au préfet. Au vu des modifications constatées, celui-ci décide de la nécessité de renouveler ou modifier les conditions de l'autorisation.
L'autorisation peut être suspendue ou retirée à la demande de l'établissement, ou par le préfet en cas de méconnaissance des conditions de l'autorisation ou des dispositions du présent titre.

– Article R. 214-73: Il est interdit à toute personne de procéder ou de faire procéder à un abattage rituel en dehors d'un abattoir. La mise à disposition de locaux, terrains, installations, matériel ou équipement en vue de procéder à un abattage rituel en dehors d'un abattoir est interdite.

– Article R. 214-74: Avant l'abattage rituel, l'immobilisation par un procédé mécanique des animaux des espèces bovine, ovine et caprine est obligatoire. L'immobilisation doit être maintenue pendant la saignée.

– Article R. 214-75: Sous réserve des dispositions du troisième alinéa du présent article, l'abattage rituel ne peut être effectué que par des sacrificateurs habilités par les organismes religieux agréés, sur proposition du ministre de l'intérieur, par le ministre chargé de l'agriculture.

Les organismes agréés mentionnés à l'alinéa précédent doivent faire connaître au ministre chargé de l'agriculture le nom des personnes habilitées et de celles auxquelles l'habilitation a été retirée.
Si aucun organisme religieux n'a été agréé, le préfet du département dans lequel est situé l'abattoir utilisé pour l'abattage rituel peut accorder des autorisations individuelles sur demande motivée des intéressés.
Les sacrificateurs doivent être en mesure de justifier de cette habilitation aux agents mentionnés à l'article L. 221-5.

– Article R. 215-8: I.-Est puni de l'amende prévue pour les contraventions de la 5e classe le fait, de pratiquer l'abattage prévu au 1° du I de l'article R. 214-70 sans détenir l'autorisation mentionnée au III de l'article R. 214-70 ou de ne pas respecter les conditions de délivrance de cette autorisation;
II.-Est puni de l'amende prévue pour les contraventions de la 4e classe:
1° Le fait de ne pas se conformer aux prescriptions des articles R. 214-65 à R. 214-68;
2° Le fait d'utiliser des procédés d'immobilisation, d'étourdissement et de mise à mort non autorisés par arrêté, conformément aux articles R. 214-66, R. 214-72 et R. 214-74;
[...]
4° Le fait de ne pas immobiliser les animaux préalablement à leur étourdissement et, dans le cas de l'abattage rituel, préalablement et pendant la saignée;
[...]
6° Le fait, en dehors des cas prévus à l'article R. 214-70, de ne pas étourdir les animaux avant leur abattage ou leur mise à mort;
7° Le fait de mettre à disposition des locaux, terrains, installations, matériels ou équipements en vue d'effectuer ou de faire effectuer un abattage rituel en dehors d'un abattoir;
8° Le fait d'effectuer un abattage familial sans respecter les conditions prévues à l'article R. 214-77;
9° Le fait d'introduire un animal vivant dans un établissement d'équarrissage en dehors de l'exception prévue à l'article R. 214-79;
10° le fait de pratiquer un abattage rituel sans y avoir été habilité dans les conditions prévues à l'article R. 214-75.
III.-Est puni de l'amende prévue pour les contraventions de la 3e classe le fait, pour tout sacrificateur, de ne pas être en mesure de justifier de son habilitation.

Arrêté du 15 décembre 1994 relatif à l'agrément d'un organisme religieux habilitant des sacrificateurs rituels, NOR: AGRG9402382A[4]

Le ministre de l'agriculture et de la pêche,
Sur proposition du ministre d'État, ministre de l'intérieur et de l'aménagement du territoire,
Vu le code rural;
Vu le décret no. 80-791 du 1er octobre 1980 modifié pris pour l'application de l'article 276 du code rural;
Considérant qu'il est d'intérêt public d'organiser l'abattage rituel dans des conditions garantissant l'ordre et la santé publics, sous l'égide d'organismes religieux agréés; que la Grande Mosquée de Paris, de par son organisation et son rayonnement dans la communauté musulmane en France, est à même d'habiliter des sacrificateurs selon le rite musulman, sous réserve d'une extension éventuelle ultérieure à d'autres organismes, au vu de circonstances le justifiant par la mise en évidence de caractéristiques équivalentes;
Considérant que l'octroi d'autorisations individuelles par les préfets en vue de l'abattage rituel ne saurait être retenu à titre définitif, dès lors que de telles procédures ne sont prévues qu'à titre dérogatoire; que, toutefois, il y a lieu de prévoir une période transitoire tenant compte du régime dérogatoire précédemment pratiqué,
Arrête:

Art. 1er.—La Grande Mosquée de Paris relevant de la société des habous et lieux saints de l'Islam est agréée en tant qu'organisme religieux pour habiliter des sacrificateurs autorisés à pratiquer l'égorgement rituel.

Art. 2.—Une carte spéciale est délivrée à chaque sacrificateur par l'organisme religieux agréé, et doit comporter:
Au recto les rubriques suivantes nom, prénom, date et lieu de naissance, domicile, photographie, signature.
Au verso la mention ci-après « je certifie que ... » (nom et titre du responsable de l'organisme religieux agréé) a autorisé M ... à procéder à l'abattage rituel à ... (établissement d'abattage). Cette autorisation est valable jusqu'au ..., et renouvelable par tacite reconduction.

Art. 3.—Les autorisations individuelles accordées par les préfets conformément au dernier alinéa de l'article 10 du 1er octobre 1980 modifié susvisé

4 Available at http://www.legifrance.gouv.fr/affichTexte.do?cidTexte=JORFTEXT000000367964.

restent valables jusqu'au 30 octobre 1995. Après cette date, tous les sacrificateurs devront être habilités selon la procédure prévue à l'article 10, deuxième alinéa, par l'organisme religieux agréé.

Art. 4.—L'organisme religieux agréé communique aux préfets des départements où doivent intervenir les sacrificateurs habilités l'identité complète de ceux-ci, et les établissements dans lesquels ils exercent.

Art. 5.—Les préfets des départements sont chargés de l'exécution du présent arrêté, qui sera publié au Journal officiel de la République française.
Fait à Paris, le 15 décembre 1994.

Arrêté du 27 juin 1996 relatifs à l'agrément d'organismes religieux habilitant des sacrificateurs rituels

NOR: AGRG9601129A
Le ministre de l'agriculture, de la pêche et de l'alimentation,
Sur proposition du ministre de l'intérieur,
Vu le code rural;
Vu le décret no. 80-791 du 1er octobre 1980 modifié pris pour l'application de l'article 276 du code rural;
Vu la demande présentée le 30 octobre 1995 par l'Association culturelle des musulmans d'Ile-de-France;
Considérant qu'il est d'intérêt public d'organiser l'abattage rituel islamique dans des conditions garantissant l'ordre et la santé publics; que, par son rayonnement spirituel et culturel, sa représentativité dans la communauté musulmane de France et sa capacité à encadrer le marché de la viande rituellement abattue, le groupement suivant répond, sous réserve d'une éventuelle extension ultérieure à d'autres organismes religieux, aux conditions exigées par le décret du 1er octobre 1980 susvisé en vue de l'habilitation de sacrificateurs rituels, selon le rite musulman,
Arrête:

Art. 1er.—La mosquée d'Évry relevant de l'Association culturelle des musulmans d'Ile-de-France, maison de quartier du Parc-aux Lièvres, 91000 Évry, est agréée en tant qu'organisme religieux pour habiliter des sacrificateurs autorisés à pratiquer l'égorgement rituel.

Art. 2.—Une carte spéciale est délivrée à chaque sacrificateur par le représentant qualifié de l'organisme religieux agréé et doit comporter:

Au recto, les rubriques suivantes: nom, prénom, date et lieu de naissance, domicile, photographie, signature;
Au verso, la mention ci-après: «Je certifie que … (nom et titre du responsable de l'organisme religieux agréé) a autorisé M … à procéder à l'abattage rituel à … (établissement d'abattage). Cette autorisation est valable jusqu'au …, et renouvelable par tacite reconduction.»

Art. 3.—L'organisme religieux mentionné à l'article 1er du présent arrêté devra communiquer aux préfets des départements où doivent intervenir les sacrificateurs habilités l'identité complète de ceux-ci et les établissements dans lesquels ils exercent.

Art. 4.—Les préfets des départements sont chargés de l'exécution du présent arrêté, qui sera publié au Journal officiel de la République française.
Fait à Paris, le 27 juin 1996.

Arrêté du 27 juin 1996 relatif à l'agrément d'organismes religieux habilitant des sacrificateurs rituels, NOR: AGRG9601128A

Le ministre de l'agriculture, de la pêche et de l'alimentation,
Sur proposition du ministre de l'intérieur,
Vu le code rural;
Vu le décret no. 80-791 du 1er octobre 1980 modifié pris pour l'application de l'article 276 du code rural;
Vu la demande présentée le 27 décembre 1994 par l'Association rituelle de la grande mosquée de Lyon;
Considérant qu'il est d'intérêt public d'organiser l'abattage rituel islamique dans des conditions garantissant l'ordre et la santé publics; que, par son rayonnement spirituel et culturel, sa représentativité dans la communauté musulmane de France et sa capacité à encadrer le marché de la viande rituellement abattue, le groupement suivant répond, sous réserve d'une éventuelle extension ultérieure à d'autres organismes religieux, aux conditions exigées par le décret du 1er octobre 1980 susvisé en vue de l'habilitation de sacrificateurs rituels, selon le rite musulman,
Arrête:

Art. 1er.—La grande mosquée de Lyon relevant de l'Association rituelle de la grande mosquée de Lyon, 146, boulevard Pinel, 69008 Lyon, est agréée en tant qu'organisme religieux pour habiliter des sacrificateurs autorisés à pratiquer l'égorgement rituel.

Art. 2.—Une carte spéciale est délivrée à chaque sacrificateur par le représentant qualifié de l'organisme religieux agréé et doit comporter:
Au recto, les rubriques suivantes: nom, prénom, date et lieu de naissance, domicile, photographie, signature;
Au verso, la mention ci-après: «Je certifie que ... (nom et titre du responsable de l'organisme religieux agréé) a autorisé M. ... à procéder à l'abattage rituel à ... (établissement d'abattage). Cette autorisation est valable jusqu'au ..., et renouvelable par tacite reconduction.»

Art. 3.—L'organisme religieux mentionné à l'article 1er du présent arrêté devra communiquer aux préfets des départements où doivent intervenir les sacrificateurs habilités l'identité complète de ceux-ci et les établissements dans lesquels ils exercent.

Art. 4.—Les préfets des départements sont chargés de l'exécution du présent arrêté, qui sera publié au Journal officiel de la République française.
Fait à Paris, le 27 juin 1996.

Circulaire DGER/SDPOFE/C2012-2009, 23 août 2012, Ministère de l'agriculture, de l'agroalimentaire et de la forêt (excerpt)

II—1 Modules d'évaluation pour l'acquisition du certificat de compétence
Les candidats dont les profils sont décrits au paragraphe II-2-1 ci-dessous choisissent d'être évalués dans l'une des deux catégories "opérateur" ou "Responsable Protection animale".
Eu égard aux fonctions afférentes aux opérateurs et aux RPA, le niveau d'exigence pour un même module d'évaluation est plus élevé pour les RPA.
Chaque module d'évaluation est construit par l'association d'une catégorie d'animaux et d'une catégorie d'opération (et d'une catégorie de matériel d'étourdissement lorsque la catégorie d'animaux et d'opération le prévoit).
Exemple de module d'évaluation:
[Catégorie d'animaux—Catégorie d'opération—(Catégorie de matériel d'étourdissement)]
La formation et l'évaluation associée sont conçues pour permettre la délivrance de certificats de compétence "protection des animaux dans le cadre de leur mise à mort" mentionnant l'ensemble des modules d'évaluation acquis.
Le certificat de compétence mentionne la durée de validité de chacun des modules d'évaluation réussis.
L'habilitation peut concerner une ou plusieurs des huit catégories d'animaux ci-dessous.

II-1-1 Catégories d'animaux retenues:
Des catégories majeures
(1) Bovins/Équidés
(2) Ovins/Caprins
(3) Porcins
(4) Volailles
[...]
II-1-2 Trois catégories d'opérations retenues:
I) "Manipulation et soins aux animaux",
II) "Mise à mort",
III) "Complément abattage sans étourdissement" (pour certaines catégories d'animaux en référence à l'article R-214-70 du code rural et de la pêche maritime).
De même, les matériels pouvant être mentionnés sur le certificat de compétence appartiennent aux différentes catégories de matériels d'étourdissement utilisés dans le cadre de la mise à mort des animaux.
II-2 Formation à la protection animale
II-2-1 Public à former
Toutes les personnes des établissements d'abattage et des établissements d'élevage d'animaux à fourrure participant à la mise à mort des animaux et les opérations associées doivent être titulaires d'un certificat de compétence "protection des animaux dans le cadre de leur mise à mort". Les candidats au certificat de compétence présentent des profils variés. Leurs tâches et leurs fonctions sur les chaînes d'abattage et/ou de mise à mort des animaux étant diverses.
Pour la délivrance des certificats de compétence, cinq profils sont retenus. Ils sont décrits dans les paragraphes A et B ci-dessous:
A—Personnes affectées à un poste de travail, participant à la mise à mort et aux opérations annexes: opérateurs.
Ces personnes, dénommées "opérateurs" au sens de l'arrêté susvisé ont l'obligation d'acquérir le certificat de compétence attestant leur compétence sur leur poste de travail.
Quatre profils sont identifiables pour ces opérateurs:
1)—des opérateurs des établissements d'abattage participant à la manipulation et aux soins aux animaux (opérations telles que le déchargement, l'acheminement, l'hébergement, la contention ainsi que l'accrochage dans le cas des volailles),
2)—des opérateurs des établissements d'abattage participant à la mise à mort des animaux (l'immobilisation, l'étourdissement, l'affalage—accrochage, la saignée),

3)—des opérateurs des établissements d'abattage participant à l'abattage sans étourdissement des animaux (opérations telles que l'immobilisation, la saignée, l'affalage—accrochage), dans le cadre de la dérogation à l'obligation d'étourdissement prévue à l'article R. 214-70 du code rural et de la pêche maritime,
4)—des opérateurs des établissements d'élevage d'animaux à fourrure, effectuant la mise à mort et sa supervision pour les animaux à fourrure.

Case Law

Case 1: The applicant was an association aiming in general at protecting animals to be slaughtered. The association lodged an appeal against the provisions of Article R. 214-70 of the rural and maritime fishing code, which provides an exception to the obligation to stun animals before slaughter where stunning turns out to be incompatible with ritual slaughter requirements.

The Council of State held that this exception aims at reconciling health, public order and equal respect for belief and religious traditions. Moreover, the Council of State provided an interesting analysis of the principle of *laïcité* in that it implies not only equality of citizens regardless of their religious beliefs, but also the guarantee of religious practices. The Council thus concluded that the exception to stunning for ritual slaughter was not in breach of the principle of *laïcité* (*Council of State, 05-07-2013, Œuvre d'assistance aux bêtes d'abattoirs, no. 361441*).

Case 2: The applicant worked part-time for a company. This company wished to hire him for an indefinite term as *halal* slaughterer and therefore applied to the *préfet* of the county of Calvados for an authorisation. This authorisation was denied on the ground that the company had not considered other applications for this position. However, the Court held that the *préfet* did not take into account the fact that other applicants did not have the skills needed for halal slaughtering and had not been approved by religious authorities pursuant to Article R. 214-75 of the rural and maritime fishing code. Accordingly, the préfet committed a manifest error of assessment and should consider the application again (*Administrative Court of Appeal of Nantes, 4-10-2013, no. 12NT01233*).

11.2 Food Regulation

Outside the public sphere regulated by public authorities, there is no specific text applicable to Islamic food, in particular through labelling, which would exclusively fall within the scope of EU legislation.[5] Moreover, state neutrality makes it impossible for public authorities to define the criteria of *halal* food, which are established by religious groups themselves. However, using the *halal* label when the products do not comply with this definition amounts to misleading commercial practice in the sense of Article L. 121-1-1 of the Consumer Code.

The issue of Islamic food arises when it comes to providing meals in public institutions. Public authorities have to decide whether they have to abide by the claims of public service users on this point. Two categories of public services users are worth mentioning here: prisoners and students in state schools.

For prisoners, the Code of Criminal Procedure provides that, where possible, food should be made available which meets philosophical or religious requirements. The provisions pertaining to food for prisoners should be included in each prison's internal regulation (Article R. 57-6-18 of the Code of Criminal Procedure and the related Annex provided).

As regards catering in state schools, an administrative circular of 16 August 2011 refers to the main principles applicable. First, the principle of *laïcité* implies a balance between the neutrality of public services and religious claims, which should not impinge on the proper functioning of the services. Secondly, there is no constraint in providing meals compatible with religious requirements, since catering does not amount to a compulsory public service. This administrative circular results in varying practices, but state schools generally meet such religiously-based claims by providing replacement meals not containing pork.[6]

Code de la consommation

Article L. 121-1: I.-Une pratique commerciale est trompeuse si elle est commise dans l'une des circonstances suivantes:
1° Lorsqu'elle crée une confusion avec un autre bien ou service, une marque, un nom commercial, ou un autre signe distinctif d'un concurrent;
2° Lorsqu'elle repose sur des allégations, indications ou présentations fausses ou de nature à induire en erreur et portant sur l'un ou plusieurs des éléments suivants:

5 On this point see the ministerial response to a parliamentary question of 22 November 2012, available at http://www.senat.fr/questions/base/2012/qSEQ121103157.html.

6 In an official report issued in March 2013 on state schools catering in general, it was stated that religious claims relating to food do not amount to a priority issue. Report of the *Défenseur des droits*, available at http://www.defenseurdesdroits.fr/sites/default/files/atoms/files/ddd_r_20130328_cantine.pdf, p. 14.

a) L'existence, la disponibilité ou la nature du bien ou du service;
b) Les caractéristiques essentielles du bien ou du service, à savoir: ses qualités substantielles, sa composition, ses accessoires, son origine, sa quantité, son mode et sa date de fabrication, les conditions de son utilisation et son aptitude à l'usage, ses propriétés et les résultats attendus de son utilisation, ainsi que les résultats et les principales caractéristiques des tests et contrôles effectués sur le bien ou le service;
c) Le prix ou le mode de calcul du prix, le caractère promotionnel du prix et les conditions de vente, de paiement et de livraison du bien ou du service;
d) Le service après-vente, la nécessité d'un service, d'une pièce détachée, d'un remplacement ou d'une réparation;
e) La portée des engagements de l'annonceur, la nature, le procédé ou le motif de la vente ou de la prestation de services;
f) L'identité, les qualités, les aptitudes et les droits du professionnel;
g) Le traitement des réclamations et les droits du consommateur;
3° Lorsque la personne pour le compte de laquelle elle est mise en oeuvre n'est pas clairement identifiable.
II.-Une pratique commerciale est également trompeuse si, compte tenu des limites propres au moyen de communication utilisé et des circonstances qui l'entourent, elle omet, dissimule ou fournit de façon inintelligible, ambiguë ou à contretemps une information substantielle ou lorsqu'elle n'indique pas sa véritable intention commerciale dès lors que celle-ci ne ressort pas déjà du contexte.
Lorsque le moyen de communication utilisé impose des limites d'espace ou de temps, il y a lieu, pour apprécier si des informations substantielles ont été omises, de tenir compte de ces limites ainsi que de toute mesure prise par le professionnel pour mettre ces informations à la disposition du consommateur par d'autres moyens.
Dans toute communication commerciale constituant une invitation à l'achat et destinée au consommateur mentionnant le prix et les caractéristiques du bien ou du service proposé, sont considérées comme substantielles les informations suivantes:
1° Les caractéristiques principales du bien ou du service;
2° L'adresse et l'identité du professionnel;
3° Le prix toutes taxes comprises et les frais de livraison à la charge du consommateur, ou leur mode de calcul, s'ils ne peuvent être établis à l'avance;
4° Les modalités de paiement, de livraison, d'exécution et de traitement des réclamations des consommateurs, dès lors qu'elles sont différentes de celles habituellement pratiquées dans le domaine d'activité professionnelle concerné;

5° L'existence d'un droit de rétractation, si ce dernier est prévu par la loi.
III.-Le I est applicable aux pratiques qui visent les professionnels.

Code de procédure pénale

Article R. 57-6-18: Le règlement intérieur type pour le fonctionnement de chacune des catégories d'établissements pénitentiaires, comprenant des dispositions communes et des dispositions spécifiques à chaque catégorie, est annexé au présent titre.

Article Annexe à l'article R. 57-6-18 (règlement intérieur type des établissements pénitentiaires) [excerpt]

Article 9
L'alimentation
Chaque personne détenue reçoit une alimentation variée, bien préparée et présentée, répondant tant en ce qui concerne la qualité que la quantité aux règles de la diététique et de l'hygiène, compte tenu de son âge, de son état de santé, de la nature de son travail et, dans toute la mesure du possible, de ses convictions philosophiques ou religieuses.
Le régime alimentaire comporte trois distributions par jour. Les deux principaux repas sont espacés d'au moins six heures.
La personne détenue malade bénéficie du régime alimentaire qui lui est médicalement prescrit.

Circulaire du 16 août 2011 relative au rappel des règles afférentes au principe de laïcité—Demandes de régimes alimentaires particuliers dans les services de restauration collective du service public, NOR: IOCK1110778C[7]

Le ministre de l'intérieur, de l'outre-mer, des collectivités territoriales et de l'immigration à Mesdames et Messieurs les préfets.
Des événements récents conduisent à rappeler les règles afférentes au principe de laïcité dans certains services publics. Cette circulaire rappelle le régime juridique applicable en matière de restauration collective du service public.
La République française est laïque, comme l'affirme solennellement l'article 1er de la Constitution. Dans son arrêt SNES du 6 avril 2001, le Conseil d'État

7 Available at http://www.interieur.gouv.fr/Publications/Textes-officiels/Bulletin-officiel-du-ministere-de-l-interieur/N-2011-08-Aout-2011.

a réaffirmé que le principe de laïcité de l'État est un principe fondamental reconnu par les lois de la République, de valeur constitutionnelle.
La laïcité n'est ni le reniement ni le cantonnement des religions. Elle est la condition du respect des choix personnels dans une société ouverte où histoire et patrimoine ont été souvent forgés par les grandes traditions spirituelles ou religieuses.
La laïcité de l'État implique donc une neutralité des services publics à l'égard de toutes les croyances ou pratiques religieuses.
Pour les usagers du service public, la neutralité implique que la prise en compte des différences de situation fondées sur les convictions religieuses ne peut remettre en cause le fonctionnement normal du service (Conseil d'État, 14 avril 1995, Consistoire central des israélites de France, no. 125148). Des demandes particulières, fondées sur des motifs religieux, ne peuvent donc justifier une adaptation du service public. La circulaire du Premier ministre no. 5209/SG du 13 avril 2007 relative à la charte de la laïcité dans les services publics a ainsi rappelé que «les usagers du service public ne peuvent exiger une adaptation du fonctionnement d'un service public ou d'un équipement public. Cependant, le service s'efforce de prendre en compte les convictions des usagers dans le respect des règles auquel il est soumis et de son bon fonctionnement».
Ces règles s'appliquent aussi en matière de restauration collective fournie aux usagers dans certains services publics comme les établissements d'enseignement ou les hôpitaux.
Dans chacun des services offrant une prestation de restauration collective, la neutralité est la règle, même si l'organisation de chaque service obéit à des dispositions particulières.
Il m'est apparu opportun de rappeler les règles fondamentales de ces régimes.
1. Dans l'enseignement public
Les questions relatives à la laïcité dans l'enseignement public trouvent leur fondement dans l'article L. 141-2 du code de l'éducation, selon lequel « suivant les principes définis dans la Constitution, l'État assure aux enfants et adolescents dans les établissements publics d'enseignement la possibilité de recevoir un enseignement conforme à leurs aptitudes dans un égal respect de toutes les croyances. L'État prend toutes dispositions utiles pour assurer aux élèves de l'enseignement public la liberté des cultes et de l'instruction religieuse».
La loi du 13 août 2004 relative aux libertés et responsabilités locales transfère aux collectivités locales la responsabilité de la restauration scolaire. La cantine scolaire est alors un service public facultatif proposé par elles. En l'absence de réglementation nationale précise, il appartient à chaque organe

délibérant compétent (conseil municipal pour l'enseignement primaire, conseil général pour les collèges et conseil régional pour les lycées) de poser des règles en la matière.

Ainsi, la circulaire NOR: LRLB0410074C du 10 septembre 2004 prévoit que « les termes de la loi autoriseront ainsi les collectivités locales ... à pratiquer des prix différents en fonction de la prestation servie (repas bio, repas spécifiques pour les régimes particuliers, etc.) », régimes conformes aux exigences des différents cultes compris.

Pour autant, les collectivités locales disposent d'une grande liberté dans l'établissement des menus et le fait de prévoir des menus en raison de pratiques confessionnelles ne constitue ni un droit pour les usagers ni une obligation pour les collectivités (cf. TA Marseille, 1er octobre 1996, no. 96-3523, no. 96-3524). Ainsi, le Conseil d'État a jugé, dans une ordonnance du 25 octobre 2002, Mme Renault (no. 251161), que la circonstance qu'une commune serve du poisson le vendredi dans ses cantines scolaires mais refuse de tenir compte des prescriptions alimentaires en vigueur dans les autres cultes ne constituait pas une atteinte aux droits fondamentaux.

Il n'en reste pas moins qu'en pratique la plupart des cantines proposent depuis longtemps des substituts au porc et servent du poisson le vendredi, permettant ainsi le respect de certaines prescriptions ou recommandations religieuses.

En ce qui concerne la possible fourniture de paniers-repas aux enfants par leurs parents, celle-ci est appréciée au cas par cas conformément aux dispositions de la circulaire interministérielle no. 2001-118 du 25 juin 2001 (Bulletin officiel de l'éducation nationale spécial no. 9 du 28 juin 2001), dans le cadre d'un projet d'accueil individualisé à destination des élèves ayant besoin d'un aménagement de scolarité (art. D. 351-9 du code de l'éducation). En tout état de cause, les croyances religieuses des élèves et de leurs familles ne sauraient, en elles-mêmes, être invoquées pour justifier la fourniture d'un panier-repas.

[...]

Note NOR/JUSK1440001N du 16 juillet 2014 relative à la pratique du culte en détention[8]

[...]

5—L'accès aux nourritures confessionnelles

a—La distribution de repas

8 Available at http://circulaires.legifrance.gouv.fr/pdf/2014/08/cir_38686.pdf.

L'article 9 du décret nº 2013-368 du 30 avril 2013 relatif aux règlements intérieurs types des établissements pénitentiaires dispose que « les détenus doivent recevoir une alimentation variée, bien préparée et présentée, répondant tant en ce qui concerne la qualité et la quantité aux règles de la diététique et de l'hygiène, compte tenu de leur âge, de leur état de santé, de la nature de leur travail et, dans toute la mesure du possible, de leurs convictions philosophiques ou religieuses ». Lors des « entretiens arrivants », il est demandé aux personnes détenues de choisir parmi les trois types de menus proposés: classique, sans viande et sans porc.

Un changement de régime alimentaire en cours de détention est toujours possible.

À l'occasion de temps forts du calendrier religieux impliquant le respect de certains rites, des aménagements dans les modalités de distribution des repas peuvent être nécessaires. Des notes de la direction de l'administration pénitentiaire, élaborées en lien avec l'aumônier national concerné, précisent les mesures qu'il convient de prendre.

L'administration pénitentiaire ne propose pas de menus confessionnels. Toutefois, les personnes détenues ont la possibilité d'acheter des produits confessionnels ou d'en recevoir à l'occasion des principales fêtes religieuses.

b—Les cantines

Le dispositif des cantines permet aux détenus d'améliorer l'ordinaire en achetant divers produits, notamment des aliments destinés à compléter les repas proposés gratuitement par l'administration pénitentiaire. Les personnes détenues peuvent, si elles le souhaitent, avoir accès à des nourritures confessionnelles par l'achat de ces produits en cantine.

Chaque établissement pénitentiaire, qu'il soit en gestion publique ou en gestion déléguée, est tenu d'organiser cette offre de produits confessionnels. Au besoin, les établissements se rapprochent de la direction interrégionale et de l'aumônier compétent pour obtenir les coordonnées de fournisseurs et déterminer quels produits intégrer dans le catalogue des cantines.

En cas d'absence de stock, l'établissement accomplit toutes les diligences utiles dès qu'une personne détenue déclare son intention de s'alimenter selon les préceptes de sa religion.

c—Les colis rituels

La remise de colis rituels par les aumôniers agréés est ponctuellement autorisée par notes de la direction de l'administration pénitentiaire lors de fêtes religieuses.

Par ailleurs, les aumôniers sont autorisés à apporter des nourritures confessionnelles aux arrivants lorsque la cantine de l'établissement n'en propose pas, le temps que les démarches nécessaires à l'approvisionnement soient

> accomplies. Cette dérogation au principe d'interdiction des colis alimentaires est limitée dans le temps; elle cesse dès lors que des produits confessionnels sont proposés dans le cadre des cantines.

Case Law

Case 1: A prisoner appealed against the decision of the head of a prison refusing to make a menu including *halal* meat available for Muslim prisoners. The Council of State held that due to the cost of such a measure, the head of the prison was entitled to refuse. Moreover, such a measure was likely to amount to a breach of the principle of *laïcité* (*Council of State, 16-07-2014, Garde des Sceaux, Ministre de la justice c/. M. B., no. 377145*).

CHAPTER 12

Islamic Dress

Like other religious dress codes, Islamic dress regulation closely depends on a combination of considerations of activities and premises in which these religious practices take place. The strictly private sphere is marked by the ability to dress freely, but the challenge underpinning the issue lies elsewhere. Outside the strictly private sphere of the home, the regulation of religious dress ranges from limitations in the workplace (12.3) to prohibitions in public functions. Regarding the latter, and though it is generally agreed that the principle of *laïcité* applies only to civil servants and governs public services in general, there is no clear-cut divide between public and private on certain issues (12.2). The issue of Islamic dress has above all been marked by the debate on face-covering in public (12.1).

12.1 Dress Code in Public Space

Although it was handled and publicised as 'the burqa ban', the link between the Act of 11 October 2010 banning face-covering in public and Islamic dress does not appear in the text.[1] Actually, the legal impossibility of opting for a blanket ban on the Islamic full veil within the context of applicable legal norms and principles explains the shift to covering the face in public.[2] Hence, Article 1 of the 2010 Act provides only that 'No-one shall, in public space, wear clothing designed to conceal one's face'. In addition, Article 2 defines public space, which is 'composed of public streets and places open to the public or dedicated to a public service'. Article 2 further attaches a number of exceptions to the ban in Article 1 as it does not apply 'if the garment is required or permitted by law or regulations, if it is justified for health or professional reasons, or if it is part of sporting practices, festivals or artistic or traditional events'. Finally, Article 4 adds some new provisions to the Penal Code (Article 225-4-10) creating a criminal offence of concealment of the face or coercion of a person to hide his face.

1 On this issue see Anne Fornerod, 'The Burqa affair in France', in A. Ferrari and S. Pastorelli (eds), *The burqa affairs across Europe*, Farnham: Ashgate, 2013, pp. 59–76.

2 See Conseil d'État, *Étude relative aux possibilités juridiques d'interdiction du port du voile intégral*, available at http://www.conseil-etat.fr/cde/media/document/avis/etude_vi_30032010.pdf.

The issue of the Islamic full veil was, however, present during the whole political and legislative process and remains largely perceptible after the Act was passed, justifying the present focus in this section. As an example, the explanatory memorandum to the bill of 19 May 2010 included the idea that the concealment of the face, and wearing of the full veil in particular, is detrimental to the values which 'guarantee the cohesion of the Nation' and constitute 'a manifestation of a rejection by a community of Republican values'.[3] The return, in one way, to the initial object of the ban—full veil—is also observable in the administrative circular of 2 March 2011 enacted by the Prime Minister and providing details on the scope of the Act and how it should apply. Indeed, this circular recalls that 'concealing one's face amounts to undermining the minimum requirements of social life'. According to this circular of March 2011, banned 'garments used to conceal the face' should be understood as those 'that make it impossible to identify the person', which include the 'full veil (burqa, niqab ...)'.[4] The list of exceptions is longer and covers clothes worn for professional reasons, referring to Article L. 4122-1 of the Labour Code on safety garments in situations of risk at work. The circular adds that religious processions are included in the exceptions to the ban as they fall within the category of 'sporting practices, festivals or artistic or traditional events'. A detailed list follows of places which should be understood as 'public space'. Thus, places like beaches, public gardens and promenades, entertainment facilities, shops, banks, stations, airports, public transport, and so on, are to be considered as 'public space'. In other words, only the private home and private vehicles can be excluded from the ban. Regarding the latter, the administrative circular of 2 March 2011 provides that face concealment in a car falls outside the scope of the 2010 Act but is likely to be covered by the provisions of the Highway Code, and especially Article R. 412-6 which obliges drivers not to allow themselves to be hindered in their manoeuvres.

It is worth noting that in March and April 2011, besides the above-mentioned circular of 2 March 2011, no fewer than four other administrative circulars were issued pertaining to the application of the Act in courtrooms (13 April 2011),[5]

---

3 Available at http://www.assemblee-nationale.fr/13/projets/pl2520.asp.

4 Specifically addressed are 'the wearing of hoods, full veils (burqa, niqab ...), masks or any clothing or accessory that has the effect, whether alone or combined with others, of concealing the face'.

5 Circulaire NOR/JUSD1110366C du 13 avril 2011 relative à la mise en œuvre de la loi du 11 octobre 2010 interdisant la dissimulation du visage dans l'espace public—Application de la loi dans les juridictions.

to fines for concealing one's face (11 March 2011),[6] to border controls (8 April 2011),[7] and to the implementation of the Act (31 March 2011).[8]

Loi n° 2010-1192 du 11 octobre 2010 interdisant de dissimuler son visage dans l'espace public

Article 1: Nul ne peut, dans l'espace public, porter une tenue destinée à dissimuler son visage.

Article 2: I.—Pour l'application de l'article 1er, l'espace public est constitué des voies publiques ainsi que des lieux ouverts au public ou affectés à un service public.
II.—L'interdiction prévue à l'article 1er ne s'applique pas si la tenue est prescrite ou autorisée par des dispositions législatives ou réglementaires, si elle est justifiée par des raisons de santé ou des motifs professionnels, ou si elle s'inscrit dans le cadre de pratiques sportives, de fêtes ou de manifestations artistiques ou traditionnelles.

Article 3: La méconnaissance de l'interdiction édictée à l'article 1er est punie de l'amende prévue pour les contraventions de la deuxième classe.
L'obligation d'accomplir le stage de citoyenneté mentionné au 8° de l'article 131-16 du code pénal peut être prononcée en même temps ou à la place de la peine d'amende.
[...]

Article 5: Les articles 1er à 3 entrent en vigueur à l'expiration d'un délai de six mois à compter de la promulgation de la présente loi.

Article 6: La présente loi s'applique sur l'ensemble du territoire de la République.

Article 7: Le Gouvernement remet au Parlement un rapport sur l'application de la présente loi dix-huit mois après sa promulgation. Ce rapport dresse un

6 Circulaire NOR/JUSD1107187C du 11 mars 2011 relative à la présentation des dispositions relatives à la contravention de dissimulation du visage dans l'espace public.

7 Circulaire NOR/IOCC1128755J du 8 avril 2011. Interdiction de la dissimulation du visage sur le territoire et lors des contrôles transfrontières.

8 Circulaire NOR/IOCD1109134C du 31 mars 2011 d'application de la loi n° 2010-1192 du 11 octobre 2010 posant le principe de l'interdiction de la dissimulation du visage dans l'espace public.

bilan de la mise en œuvre de la présente loi, des mesures d'accompagnement élaborées par les pouvoirs publics et des difficultés rencontrées.

Code pénal

Article 225-4-10: Le fait pour toute personne d'imposer à une ou plusieurs autres personnes de dissimuler leur visage par menace, violence, contrainte, abus d'autorité ou abus de pouvoir, en raison de leur sexe, est puni d'un an d'emprisonnement et de 30,000 € d'amende.
Lorsque le fait est commis au préjudice d'un mineur, les peines sont portées à deux ans d'emprisonnement et à 60,000 € d'amende.

Code du travail

Article L. 4122-1 (excerpt): Les instructions de l'employeur précisent, en particulier lorsque la nature des risques le justifie, les conditions d'utilisation des équipements de travail, des moyens de protection, des substances et préparations dangereuses. Elles sont adaptées à la nature des tâches à accomplir.

Circulaire du 2 mars 2011 relative à la mise en œuvre de la loi n° 2010-1192 du 11 octobre 2010 interdisant la dissimulation du visage dans l'espace public, NOR: PRMC1106214C[9]

La loi n° 2010-1192 du 11 octobre 2010 interdisant la dissimulation du visage dans l'espace public marque la volonté de la représentation nationale de réaffirmer solennellement les valeurs de la République et les exigences du vivre ensemble.
Se dissimuler le visage, c'est porter atteinte aux exigences minimales de la vie en société. Cela place en outre les personnes concernées dans une situation d'exclusion et d'infériorité incompatible avec les principes de liberté, d'égalité et de dignité humaine affirmés par la République française.
La République se vit à visage découvert. Parce qu'elle est fondée sur le rassemblement autour de valeurs communes et sur la construction d'un destin partagé, elle ne peut accepter les pratiques d'exclusion et de rejet, quels qu'en soient les prétextes ou les modalités.
La loi interdisant la dissimulation du visage dans l'espace public a été publiée au Journal officiel du 12 octobre 2010, après avoir été soumise au contrôle du Conseil constitutionnel.

---

9 Available at http://www.legifrance.gouv.fr/eli/circulaire/2011/3/2/PRMC1106214C/jo/texte.

Elle pose le principe d'une interdiction générale de la dissimulation du visage dans l'espace public, son article 1er énonçant à cet effet que «nul ne peut, dans l'espace public, porter une tenue destinée à dissimuler son visage». La loi sanctionne également le fait de contraindre un tiers à dissimuler son visage.

Si cette dernière sanction est entrée en vigueur immédiatement, la loi a prévu que la mesure d'interdiction générale de la dissimulation du visage ne serait applicable qu'à l'expiration d'un délai de six mois à compter de sa promulgation.

Cette interdiction prendra donc effet à partir du 11 avril 2011. Il vous appartiendra de veiller à ce qu'elle soit pleinement respectée dans l'ensemble des services relevant de votre autorité ou placés sous votre tutelle.

La période de six mois prévue avant l'entrée en vigueur de l'interdiction générale a été mise à profit, dans le respect de la volonté du législateur, pour préparer les éléments d'information et de communication nécessaires à la sensibilisation du public, plus particulièrement l'information des personnes directement concernées par des pratiques de dissimulation du visage.

Dans le respect de vos attributions respectives et en vous appuyant sur les réseaux de proximité de vos administrations, il vous appartient de mettre en œuvre les campagnes d'information adaptées, afin de contribuer efficacement à la bonne compréhension de la loi du 11 octobre 2010 et à son application effective.

La présente circulaire présente à cet effet les dispositions de la loi et ses modalités d'application.

I.—Le champ d'application de la loi

1. Les éléments constitutifs de la dissimulation du visage dans l'espace public

La dissimulation du visage dans l'espace public est interdite à compter du 11 avril 2011 sur l'ensemble du territoire de la République, en métropole comme en outre-mer. Cette infraction est constituée dès lors qu'une personne porte une tenue destinée à dissimuler son visage et qu'elle se trouve dans l'espace public; ces deux conditions sont nécessaires et suffisantes.

a) La dissimulation du visage

La portée de l'interdiction

Les tenues destinées à dissimuler le visage sont celles qui rendent impossible l'identification de la personne. Il n'est pas nécessaire, à cet effet, que le visage soit intégralement dissimulé.

Sont notamment interdits, sans prétendre à l'exhaustivité, le port de cagoules, de voiles intégraux (burqa, niqab ...), de masques ou de tout autre accessoire ou vêtement ayant pour effet, pris isolément ou associé avec d'autres, de dissimuler le visage. Dès lors que l'infraction est une contravention, l'existence d'une intention est indifférente: il suffit que la tenue soit destinée à dissimuler le visage.

Les exceptions légales

L'article 2 de la loi prévoit plusieurs exceptions à l'interdiction de la dissimulation du visage.

En premier lieu, l'interdiction ne s'applique pas « si la tenue est prescrite ou autorisée par des dispositions législatives ou réglementaires». Il s'agit par exemple de l'article L. 431-1 du code de la route qui impose le port du casque aux conducteurs de deux-roues à moteur.

En deuxième lieu, l'interdiction ne s'applique pas « si la tenue est justifiée par des raisons de santé ou des motifs professionnels». Les motifs professionnels concernent notamment le champ couvert par l'article L. 4122-1 du code du travail aux termes duquel « les instructions de l'employeur précisent, en particulier lorsque la nature des risques le justifie, les conditions d'utilisation des équipements de travail, des moyens de protection, des substances et préparations dangereuses. Elles sont adaptées à la nature des tâches à accomplir».

Enfin, l'interdiction ne s'applique pas « si elle s'inscrit dans le cadre de pratiques sportives, de fêtes ou de manifestations artistiques ou traditionnelles». Ainsi les processions religieuses, dès lors qu'elles présentent un caractère traditionnel, entrent dans le champ des exceptions à l'interdiction posée par l'article 1er. Au titre des pratiques sportives figurent les protections du visage prévues dans plusieurs disciplines.

Les dispositions de la loi du 11 octobre 2010 s'appliquent sans préjudice des dispositions qui interdisent ou réglementent, par ailleurs, le port de tenues dans certains services publics et qui demeurent en vigueur.

Il en est ainsi de la loi n° 2004-228 du 15 mars 2004 encadrant, en application du principe de laïcité, le port de signes ou de tenues manifestant une appartenance religieuse dans les écoles, collèges et lycées publics (article L. 141-5-1 du code de l'éducation nationale et circulaire d'application du 18 mai 2004). Demeurent également applicables la charte du patient hospitalisé, annexée à la circulaire du 2 mars 2006 relative aux droits des patients hospitalisés, et la circulaire du 2 février 2005 relative à la laïcité dans les établissements de santé.

b) La définition de l'espace public

L'article 2 de la loi précise que « l'espace public est constitué des voies publiques ainsi que des lieux ouverts au public ou affectés à un service public».

La notion de voies publiques n'appelle pas de commentaire. Il convient de préciser qu'à l'exception de ceux affectés aux transports en commun les véhicules qui empruntent les voies publiques sont considérés comme des lieux privés. La dissimulation du visage, par une personne se trouvant à bord d'une voiture particulière, n'est donc pas constitutive de la contravention prévue par la loi. Elle peut en revanche tomber sous le coup des dispositions du code de la route prévoyant que la conduite du véhicule ne doit pas présenter de risque pour la sécurité publique.
Constituent des lieux ouverts au public les lieux dont l'accès est libre (plages, jardins publics, promenades publiques …) ainsi que les lieux dont l'accès est possible, même sous condition, dans la mesure où toute personne qui le souhaite peut remplir cette condition (paiement d'une place de cinéma ou de théâtre par exemple). Les commerces (cafés, restaurants, magasins), les établissements bancaires, les gares, les aéroports et les différents modes de transport en commun sont ainsi des espaces publics.
Les lieux affectés à un service public désignent les implantations de l'ensemble des institutions, juridictions et administrations publiques ainsi que des organismes chargés d'une mission de service public. Sont notamment concernés les diverses administrations et établissements publics de l'État, les collectivités territoriales et leurs établissements publics, les mairies, les tribunaux, les préfectures, les hôpitaux, les bureaux de poste, les établissements d'enseignement (écoles, collèges, lycées et universités), les caisses d'allocations familiales, les caisses primaires d'assurance maladie, les services de Pôle emploi, les musées et les bibliothèques.

2. L'absence de restriction à l'exercice de la liberté religieuse dans les lieux de culte
Lorsqu'ils sont ouverts au public, les lieux de culte entrent dans le champ d'application de la loi. Le Conseil constitutionnel a toutefois précisé que « l'interdiction de dissimuler son visage dans l'espace public ne saurait, sans porter une atteinte excessive à l'article 10 de la Déclaration de 1789, restreindre l'exercice de la liberté religieuse dans les lieux de culte ouverts au public ».

3. La sanction de la dissimulation du visage
L'article 3 de la loi prévoit que la méconnaissance de l'interdiction de la dissimulation du visage dans l'espace public est punie de l'amende prévue pour les contraventions de la deuxième classe (d'un montant maximal de 150 euros). Le prononcé de cette amende relève de la compétence des juridictions de proximité.

L'obligation d'accomplir un stage de citoyenneté peut également être prononcée par les mêmes juridictions, à titre de peine alternative ou de peine complémentaire. Le stage de citoyenneté, adapté à la nature de l'infraction commise, doit notamment permettre de rappeler aux personnes concernées les valeurs républicaines d'égalité et de respect de la dignité humaine.

4. La sanction de l'exercice d'une contrainte
La dissimulation du visage constatée dans l'espace public peut résulter d'une contrainte exercée contre la personne concernée et révéler la commission par un tiers du délit de dissimulation forcée du visage.
Ce délit, prévu à l'article 4 de la loi (créant un nouvel article 225-4-10 du code pénal), est puni d'un an d'emprisonnement et de 30,000 euros d'amende. Lorsque le fait est commis au préjudice d'une personne mineure, les peines sont portées à deux ans d'emprisonnement et à 60,000 euros d'amende.
La répression de ces agissements participe de la volonté des pouvoirs publics de lutter vigoureusement contre toutes les formes de discriminations et de violences envers les femmes, qui constituent autant d'atteintes inacceptables au principe d'égalité entre les sexes.

II.—La conduite à tenir dans les services publics
a) Le rôle du chef de service
Dans le cadre des pouvoirs qu'il détient pour assurer le bon fonctionnement de son administration, le chef de service est responsable du respect des dispositions de la loi du 11 octobre 2010 et des mesures mises en œuvre, en particulier l'actualisation des règlements intérieurs, pour assurer son application. Il lui appartient de présenter et d'expliquer l'esprit et l'économie de la loi aux agents placés sous son autorité, afin que ces derniers se conforment à ses dispositions et puissent veiller, dans les meilleures conditions, à son respect par les usagers du service public.
Il lui appartient également de veiller à ce que l'information adéquate prévue par le Gouvernement sous la forme d'affiches et de dépliants soit mise en place dans les locaux accueillant du public ou ouverts au public.

b) Le contrôle de l'accès aux lieux affectés au service public
À compter du 11 avril 2011, les agents chargés d'un service public, qui pouvaient déjà être conduits à demander à une personne de se découvrir ponctuellement pour justifier de son identité, seront fondés à refuser l'accès au service à toute personne dont le visage est dissimulé.
Dans le cas où la personne dont le visage est dissimulé serait déjà entrée dans les locaux, il est recommandé aux agents de lui rappeler la réglementation

applicable et de l'inviter au respect de la loi, en se découvrant ou en quittant les lieux. La dissimulation du visage fait obstacle à la délivrance des prestations du service public.
En revanche, la loi ne confère en aucun cas à un agent le pouvoir de contraindre une personne à se découvrir ou à sortir. L'exercice d'une telle contrainte constituerait une voie de fait et exposerait son auteur à des poursuites pénales. Elle est donc absolument proscrite.
En face d'un refus d'obtempérer, l'agent ou son chef de service doit faire appel aux forces de la police ou de la gendarmerie nationales, qui peuvent seules constater l'infraction, en dresser procès-verbal et procéder, le cas échéant, à la vérification de l'identité de la personne concernée. Des instructions particulières sont adressées à cet effet par le ministre de l'intérieur aux agents de la force publique.
Le refus d'accès au service ne pourra faire l'objet d'aménagements que pour tenir compte de situations particulières d'urgence, notamment médicales.
[...]

Code de la route

Article R. 412-6: I.-Tout véhicule en mouvement ou tout ensemble de véhicules en mouvement doit avoir un conducteur. Celui-ci doit, à tout moment, adopter un comportement prudent et respectueux envers les autres usagers des voies ouvertes à la circulation. Il doit notamment faire preuve d'une prudence accrue à l'égard des usagers les plus vulnérables.
II.-Tout conducteur doit se tenir constamment en état et en position d'exécuter commodément et sans délai toutes les manœuvres qui lui incombent. Ses possibilités de mouvement et son champ de vision ne doivent pas être réduits par le nombre ou la position des passagers, par les objets transportés ou par l'apposition d'objets non transparents sur les vitres.
III.-Le fait, pour tout conducteur, de contrevenir aux dispositions du II ci-dessus est puni de l'amende prévue pour les contraventions de la deuxième classe.
IV.-En cas d'infraction aux dispositions du II ci-dessus, l'immobilisation du véhicule peut être prescrite dans les conditions prévues aux articles L. 325-1 à L. 325-3.

Case Law

Case 1: A woman wearing a full veil was arrested while demonstrating with other people wearing masks in front of the Élysée Palace, the residence of the

President of the Republic. She was taken to a police station but still refused to remove her veil and show her face. She argued that she had acted in the exercise of her religious beliefs and that the 2010 Act was in breach of Article 9 ECHR. The Court of Cassation first recalled that limitations on freedom of religion are possible only so long as they are necessary in a democratic society for public safety, the protection of public order, health and morals or the rights and freedoms of others. Then, the Court decided that the Act prohibiting the full concealment of the face in public was in accordance with that principle in that it aims at protecting public order and safety by requiring anyone moving in public space to show their face (*Court of cassation, 05-03-2013, no. 12-80.891*).

12.2 Islamic Dress and Public Service

Like other expression of religious beliefs in public services, Islamic dress regulation depends on the principle of state neutrality which results in the ban on religious dress for civil servants, while users of public services are free to dress according to their religious beliefs provided such dress is compatible with the proper function of the public service.

12.2.1 *Prohibition of Religious Dress for Civil Servants*

All public officials should abide by religious neutrality, which derives from the principle of state neutrality in political, philosophical, or religious matters (see also above 10.2 *Employment in public sector*). The principle of neutrality constitutes a limit to public officials' freedom of religion, specifically as regards their dress code. No religious clothing is allowed.[10]

Case Law

Case 1: The applicant worked as a labour inspector and was supervised by the Ministry of Employment. She repeatedly refused to remove the Islamic headscarf she wore at work. As a result her employer—the ministry—first took a decision to send her home and then to exclude her temporarily for two weeks, deeming that her refusal amounted to an infringement of the principle of *laïcité* of the state and the neutrality of the public services.

---

10 On this issue see Hana van Ooijen, *Religious Symbols in Public Functions: Unveiling State Neutrality: A Comparative Analysis of Dutch, English and French Justifications for Limiting the Freedom of Public Officials to Display*, 2012, Intersentia Ltd, School of Human Rights Research Series, vol. 58.

The court referred to the Council of State's advice of 3 May 2000 dealing with the importance of abiding by the principle of *laïcité* of the state, and held that the disciplinary decisions rely on the importance of this principle for a civil servant. In addition, the Court held that the civil servant conspicuously manifesting her religious beliefs while working and refusing to obey the orders of her managers constituted gross misconduct (*Administrative court of Lyon, 27-11-2003, no. 03LY01392*).

Case 2: The Court upheld the dismissal of a health-care technician who wore an Islamic veil on the ground that she worked for an organisation that provided a public service. The principles of neutrality and secularism of the public service are applicable to all public services and include those provided by private bodies (*Court of cassation, 19-03-2013, Caisse primaire d'assurance maladie de Seine-Saint-Denis, no. 537*).

12.2.2 *Prohibition of Religious Dress for Pupils*

Unlike civil servants, public service users are free to dress according to their religious beliefs, unless it otherwise required for the proper functioning of the service.[11] Accordingly, the Council of State annulled the expulsion of pupils based on the regulations of the school which had imposed a general prohibition on religious clothing. In the same case, the Council held that the freedom of religion deriving from the principle of *laïcité* entails for pupils the right to express and manifest their religious beliefs (Council of State, 02-11-1992, no. 130394, *Kherouaa*). Later and as an exception, the prohibition on wearing religious dress and symbols applicable to civil servants was extended to pupils in public schools by Act no. 2004-228 of 15 March 2004 governing, pursuant to the principle of *laïcité*, the wearing in public schools of symbols or clothing denoting religious adherence (whose provisions are now entrenched in Article L. 141-5-1 of the Education Code). The adoption of this Act followed a wide public debate on Islam in society and its compatibility with *laïcité*, whose most significant expression took the form of the report issued by the Stasi Commission in 2003.[12] The focus on the Islamic headscarf was due to the perception that it

---

11 On this point see the analysis issued by the Council of State on 19 December 2013, especially p. 30: http://www.defenseurdesdroits.fr/sites/default/files/atoms/files/ddd_avis_20130909_laicite.pdf.

12 The creation of the commission was later adjudged to be a component of a broader mechanism designed to provide an opinion in favour of the outlawing of the headscarf in public schools: see Françoise Lorcerie, 'La "loi sur le voile": une entreprise politique', *Droit et société*, 2008/1, no. 68, pp. 53–74.

embodied the failure of integration and the slow progress towards sex equality. It follows that the wearing of the Islamic headscarf appears incompatible with Republican values, and school constitutes the traditionally most appropriate place to restore respect for these values.[13] The administrative circular of 18 May 2004 reflects this narrow link between school and the Republican principle of *laïcité*, which is conceived as the basis of national unity beyond particular belongings.

The administrative circular of 18 May 2004 provides many details on how the Act should be implemented. More precisely this order specifies the interpretation to be given to 'symbols or clothing denoting religious belonging': they are those 'whose wearing leads one to be immediately recognised by religious affiliation, such as the Islamic veil, whatever name it is given, the kippah, or a cross of manifestly excessive dimension'. Moreover, according to this administrative circular, the Act is applicable to all religions and is likely to cover new symbols or any attempts to circumvent its provisions (point II, 2.1). This gives room for interpretation of the signs worn by pupils in that these do not need to be directly and in themselves religious to be prohibited. In this regard, two rulings are worth mentioning which upheld the decisions of the expulsion of pupils who respectively wore a bandana-like headscarf (*Council of State, 5-12-2007, no. 295671*)[14] and a long skirt (*Council of State, 19-03-2013, no. 366749*)[15] but interpreted like religious clothing and then falling within the scope of the prohibition contained in Article L. 141-5-1 of the Education Code.

In addition, the administrative circular of May 2004 transcends the scope of the 2004 Act it is supposed only to clarify. Point 2.4 recalls some of the rules governing the expression of religious beliefs by pupils. More precisely, it provides that pupils are not entitled to challenge teachings—and female teachers—which they consider contrary to their religious beliefs, nor can they challenge the obligation to attend classes or examination for religious reasons.

The judicial application of the 2004 Act deserves attention, at both European and national levels. As regards the former, the European Court of Human Rights upheld the 2004 Act in 2008 and 2009 through a range of cases involving public

13 See Bernard Stasi, *Commission de réflexion sur l'application du principe de laïcité dans la République: rapport au Président de la République*, Paris: La documentation française, December 2003, especially pp. 45 and ff.

14 See the ruling at http://www.legifrance.gouv.fr/affichJuriAdmin.do?idTexte=CETATEXT000018007973.

15 Available at http://www.legifrance.gouv.fr/affichJuriAdmin.do?oldAction=rechJuriAdmin&idTexte=CETATEXT000027201089&fastReqId=232757717&fastPos=1.

secondary school pupils wearing the Islamic headscarf[16] as well as pupils refusing to remove their Sikh turbans.[17] The French Court of Cassation extended the implementation of the 2004 Act to private schools, which normally do not fall within the scope of the Act (see below, case 1). Finally, it is worth noting that the equality body—the HALDE—has had to recall several times that the 2004 Act applies only to pupils in state schools and not outside this scope: a hotel manager,[18] a private training centre,[19] and a university professor cannot deny access to their premises to women wearing Islamic headscarves.[20] Finally, the Court of Cassation held that the 2004 Act is applicable to private schools (see below case 1).

The question has arisen whether all these rules apply to the specific situation of pupils' mothers wearing the Islamic headscarf while taking part in educational activities like school trips. Mothers have been excluded from such activities because of their wearing of the Islamic headscarf. The administrative circular of 18 May 2004 clearly states that the 2004 Act does not apply to pupils' parents. Moreover, the above mentioned equality body, the HALDE, issued a deliberation on this issue in 2007, concluding that such a refusal to pupils' mothers was likely to amount to a religion-based discriminatory denial of access to a volunteer activity.[21] However, a ruling of the Montreuil administrative court of 22 November 2011 (no. 1012015) held that the constitutional principles of neutrality and of *laïcité* of public services applies to pupils' parents who, by accompanying school trips, take part in the provision of public educational services. Several months later, administrative circular no. 2012-056 of 25 March 2012 provided that the principles of *laïcité* and of neutrality prevent pupils' parents from expressing their religious, political or philosophical beliefs

16 *Aktas v. France*, no. 43563/08; *Bayrak v. France*, no. 14308/08; *Gamaleddyn v. France*, no. 18527/08; *Ghazal v. France*, no. 29134/08. Cases *Dogru v. France* (no. 27058/05) and *Kervanci v. France* (no. 31645/04) had been introduced before the passing of the 2004 Act.

17 *J. Singh v. France*, no. 25463/08; *R. Singh v. France*, no. 27561/08.

18 Discriminatory refusal of a hotel manager to rent a room to a customer on the ground that she wore a veil: HALDE, deliberation no. 2006-133 of 5 June 2006, available at http://www.halde.fr/IMG/pdf/halde_rapport_annuel_2007.pdf, p. 41.

19 HALDE, deliberation no. 2011-34 of 21 March 2011, available at http://www.halde.fr/Deliberation-relative-a-un-refus-d,14841c8b7.html?page=article_domaine&id_mot=3.

20 The HALDE recalled that the 2004 Act does not apply at university in its deliberation no. 2008-194 of 29-09-2008, available at http://www.halde.fr/Deliberation-relative-a-un-refus-d,12612.html.

21 HALDE, *Délibération relative à l'exclusion de mères d'élèves de la participation à des activités éducatives et/ou de l'encadrement de sorties scolaires en raison du port du foulard*, no. 2007-117, 14-05-2007, available at http://www.halde.fr/IMG/alexandrie/2798.PDF.

through their speech or clothing. This issue is, however, still being debated. Indeed, in December 2013, the Council of State provided an opinion supporting the idea that the principle of neutrality does not apply to pupils' parents,[22] and a ruling of the Nice administrative court of 9 June 2015 (nº 1305386) adopted the same solution.

Code de l'éducation

Article L. 141-5-1: Dans les écoles, les collèges et les lycées publics, le port de signes ou tenues par lesquels les élèves manifestent ostensiblement une appartenance religieuse est interdit.
Le règlement intérieur rappelle que la mise en œuvre d'une procédure disciplinaire est précédée d'un dialogue avec l'élève.

Circulaire du 18 mai 2004 relative à la mise en œuvre de la loi nº 2004-228 du 15 mars 2004 encadrant, en application du principe de laïcité, le port de signes ou de tenues manifestant une appartenance religieuse dans les écoles, collèges et lycées publics, NOR: MENG0401138C[23]

La présente circulaire précise les modalités d'application de la loi du 15 mars 2004. Elle abroge et remplace la circulaire du 12 décembre 1989 relative à la laïcité, au port de signes religieux par les élèves et au caractère obligatoire des enseignements, la circulaire du 26 octobre 1993 sur le respect de la laïcité, et la circulaire du 20 septembre 1994 relative au port de signes ostentatoires dans les établissements scolaires.

I.—Les principes
La loi du 15 mars 2004 est prise en application du principe constitutionnel de laïcité qui est un des fondements de l'école publique. Ce principe, fruit d'une longue histoire, repose sur le respect de la liberté de conscience et sur l'affirmation de valeurs communes qui fondent l'unité nationale par-delà les appartenances particulières.
L'école a pour mission de transmettre les valeurs de la République parmi lesquelles l'égale dignité de tous les êtres humains, l'égalité entre les hommes et les femmes et la liberté de chacun y compris dans le choix de son mode

22 This opinion is available at http://www.defenseurdesdroits.fr/sites/default/files/atoms/files/ddd_avis_20130909_laicite.pdf.

23 Text available at http://www.legifrance.gouv.fr/eli/circulaire/2004/5/18/MENG0401138C/jo/texte.

de vie. Il appartient à l'école de faire vivre ces valeurs, de développer et de conforter le libre arbitre de chacun, de garantir l'égalité entre les élèves et de promouvoir une fraternité ouverte à tous. En protégeant l'école des revendications communautaires, la loi conforte son rôle en faveur d'un vouloir-vivre-ensemble. Elle doit le faire de manière d'autant plus exigeante qu'y sont accueillis principalement des enfants.

L'État est le protecteur de l'exercice individuel et collectif de la liberté de conscience. La neutralité du service public est à cet égard un gage d'égalité et de respect de l'identité de chacun.

En préservant les écoles, les collèges et les lycées publics, qui ont vocation à accueillir tous les enfants, qu'ils soient croyants ou non croyants et quelles que soient leurs convictions religieuses ou philosophiques, des pressions qui peuvent résulter des manifestations ostensibles des appartenances religieuses, la loi garantit la liberté de conscience de chacun. Elle ne remet pas en cause les textes qui permettent de concilier, conformément aux articles L. 141-2, L. 141-3 et L. 141-4 du code de l'éducation, l'obligation scolaire avec le droit des parents de faire donner, s'ils le souhaitent, une instruction religieuse à leurs enfants.

Parce qu'elle repose sur le respect des personnes et de leurs convictions, la laïcité ne se conçoit pas sans une lutte déterminée contre toutes les formes de discrimination. Les agents du service public de l'éducation nationale doivent faire preuve de la plus grande vigilance et de la plus grande fermeté à l'égard de toutes les formes de racisme ou de sexisme, de toutes les formes de violence faite à un individu en raison de son appartenance réelle ou supposée à un groupe ethnique ou religieux. Tout propos, tout comportement qui réduit l'autre à une appartenance religieuse ou ethnique, à une nationalité (actuelle ou d'origine), à une apparence physique, appelle une réponse. Selon les cas, cette réponse relève de l'action pédagogique, disciplinaire, voire pénale. Elle doit être ferme et résolue dans tous les cas où un élève ou un autre membre de la communauté éducative est victime d'une agression (qu'elle soit physique ou verbale) en raison de son appartenance réelle ou supposée à un groupe donné.

Parce que l'intolérance et les préjugés se nourrissent de l'ignorance, la laïcité suppose également une meilleure connaissance réciproque y compris en matière de religion. À cet égard, les enseignements dispensés peuvent tous contribuer à consolider les assises d'une telle connaissance. De même, les activités de « vivre ensemble » à l'école primaire, l'éducation civique au collège ou l'éducation civique, juridique et sociale au lycée constituent des moments privilégiés pour faire progresser la tolérance et le respect de l'autre. Plus spécifiquement, les faits religieux, notamment quand ils sont des éléments explicites des programmes, comme c'est le cas en français et en histoire, doivent être utilisés au mieux dans les enseignements pour apporter aux élèves les éléments de culture indispensables à la compréhension du monde contemporain.

II.—Le champ d'application de la loi

Aux termes du premier alinéa de l'article L. 141-5-1 du code de l'éducation, « dans les écoles, les collèges et les lycées publics, le port de signes ou tenues par lesquels les élèves manifestent ostensiblement une appartenance religieuse est interdit ».

2.1. La loi interdit les signes et les tenues qui manifestent ostensiblement une appartenance religieuse

Les signes et tenues qui sont interdits sont ceux dont le port conduit à se faire immédiatement reconnaître par son appartenance religieuse tels que le voile islamique, quel que soit le nom qu'on lui donne, la kippa ou une croix de dimension manifestement excessive. La loi est rédigée de manière à pouvoir s'appliquer à toutes les religions et de manière à répondre à l'apparition de nouveaux signes, voire à d'éventuelles tentatives de contournement de la loi.

La loi ne remet pas en cause le droit des élèves de porter des signes religieux discrets.

Elle n'interdit pas les accessoires et les tenues qui sont portés communément par des élèves en dehors de toute signification religieuse. En revanche, la loi interdit à un élève de se prévaloir du caractère religieux qu'il y attacherait, par exemple, pour refuser de se conformer aux règles applicables à la tenue des élèves dans l'établissement.

2.2. La loi s'applique aux écoles, aux collèges et aux lycées publics

La loi s'applique à l'ensemble des écoles et des établissements d'enseignement scolaire publics. Dans les lycées, la loi s'applique à l'ensemble des élèves, y compris ceux qui sont inscrits dans des formations post-baccalauréat (classes préparatoires aux grandes écoles, sections de technicien supérieur).

La loi s'applique à l'intérieur des écoles et des établissements et plus généralement à toutes les activités placées sous la responsabilité des établissements ou des enseignants y compris celles qui se déroulent en dehors de l'enceinte de l'établissement (sortie scolaire, cours d'éducation physique et sportive ...).

2.3. La loi ne modifie pas les règles applicables
aux agents du service public et aux parents d'élèves

Les agents contribuant au service public de l'éducation, quels que soient leur fonction et leur statut, sont soumis à un strict devoir de neutralité qui leur interdit le port de tout signe d'appartenance religieuse, même discret. Ils doivent également s'abstenir de toute attitude qui pourrait être interprétée comme une marque d'adhésion ou au contraire comme une critique à l'égard d'une croyance particulière. Ces règles sont connues et doivent être respectées.

La loi ne concerne pas les parents d'élèves. Elle ne s'applique pas non plus aux candidats qui viennent passer les épreuves d'un examen ou d'un concours dans les locaux d'un établissement public d'enseignement et qui ne deviennent pas de ce seul fait des élèves de l'enseignement public. Ceux-ci doivent toutefois se soumettre aux règles d'organisation de l'examen qui visent notamment à garantir le respect de l'ordre et de la sécurité, à permettre la vérification de l'identité des candidats ou à prévenir les risques de fraudes.

2.4. Les obligations qui découlent, pour les élèves, du respect du principe de laïcité ne se résument pas à la question des signes d'appartenance religieuse

La loi du 15 mars 2004 complète sur la question du port des signes d'appartenance religieuse le corpus des règles qui garantissent le respect du principe de laïcité dans les écoles, collèges et lycées publics.

Les convictions religieuses des élèves ne leur donnent pas le droit de s'opposer à un enseignement. On ne peut admettre par exemple que certains élèves prétendent, au nom de considérations religieuses ou autres, contester le droit d'un professeur, parce que c'est un homme ou une femme, d'enseigner certaines matières ou le droit d'une personne n'appartenant pas à leur confession de faire une présentation de tel ou tel fait historique ou religieux. Par ailleurs, si certains sujets appellent de la prudence dans la manière de les aborder, il convient d'être ferme sur le principe selon lequel aucune question n'est exclue a priori du questionnement scientifique et pédagogique.

Les convictions religieuses ne sauraient non plus être opposées à l'obligation d'assiduité ni aux modalités d'un examen. Les élèves doivent assister à l'ensemble des cours inscrits à leur emploi du temps sans pouvoir refuser les matières qui leur paraîtraient contraires à leurs convictions. C'est une obligation légale. Les convictions religieuses ne peuvent justifier un absentéisme sélectif par exemple en éducation physique et sportive ou sciences de la vie et de la Terre. Les consignes d'hygiène et de sécurité ne sauraient non plus être aménagées pour ce motif.

Des autorisations d'absence doivent pouvoir être accordées aux élèves pour les grandes fêtes religieuses qui ne coïncident pas avec un jour de congé et dont les dates sont rappelées chaque année par une instruction publiée au Bulletin officiel de l'éducation nationale. En revanche, les demandes d'absence systématique ou prolongée doivent être refusées dès lors qu'elles sont incompatibles avec l'organisation de la scolarité. L'institution scolaire et universitaire, de son côté, doit prendre les dispositions nécessaires pour qu'aucun examen ni aucune épreuve importante ne soient organisés le jour de ces grandes fêtes religieuses.

III.—Le dialogue

Aux termes du second alinéa de l'article L. 141-5-1 du code de l'éducation tel qu'il résulte de la loi du 15 mars 2004, « le règlement intérieur rappelle que la mise en œuvre d'une procédure disciplinaire est précédée d'un dialogue avec l'élève ».

3.1. La mise en œuvre de la loi passe d'abord par le dialogue

Le second alinéa de l'article L. 141-5-1 illustre la volonté du législateur de faire en sorte que la loi soit appliquée dans le souci de convaincre les élèves de l'importance du respect du principe de laïcité. Il souligne que la priorité doit être donnée au dialogue et à la pédagogie.

Ce dialogue n'est pas une négociation et ne saurait bien sûr justifier de dérogation à la loi.

3.2. L'organisation du dialogue relève de la responsabilité du chef d'établissement

Lorsqu'un élève inscrit dans l'établissement se présente avec un signe ou une tenue susceptible de tomber sous le coup de l'interdiction, il importe d'engager immédiatement le dialogue avec lui.

Le chef d'établissement conduit le dialogue en liaison avec l'équipe de direction et les équipes éducatives en faisant notamment appel aux enseignants qui connaissent l'élève concerné et pourront apporter leur contribution à la résolution du problème. Mais cette priorité n'est en rien exclusive de tout autre choix que le chef d'établissement pourrait au cas par cas juger opportun.

Pendant la phase de dialogue, le chef d'établissement veille, en concertation avec l'équipe éducative, aux conditions dans lesquelles l'élève est scolarisé dans l'établissement.

Dans les écoles primaires, l'organisation du dialogue est soumise en tant que de besoin à l'examen de l'équipe éducative prévue à l'article 21 du décret n° 90-788 du 6 septembre 1990.

Le dialogue doit permettre d'expliquer à l'élève et à ses parents que le respect de la loi n'est pas un renoncement à leurs convictions. Il doit également être l'occasion d'une réflexion commune sur l'avenir de l'élève pour le mettre en garde contre les conséquences de son attitude et pour l'aider à construire un projet personnel.

Pendant le dialogue, l'institution doit veiller avec un soin particulier à ne pas heurter les convictions religieuses de l'élève ou de ses parents. Le principe de laïcité s'oppose évidemment à ce que l'État ou ses agents prennent parti sur l'interprétation de pratiques ou de commandements religieux.

3.3. En l'absence d'issue favorable au dialogue
Le dialogue devra être poursuivi le temps utile pour garantir que la procédure disciplinaire n'est utilisée que pour sanctionner un refus délibéré de l'élève de se conformer à la loi.
Si le conseil de discipline prononce une décision d'exclusion de l'élève, il appartiendra à l'autorité académique d'examiner avec l'élève et ses parents les conditions dans lesquelles l'élève poursuivra sa scolarité.

IV.—Le règlement intérieur
La loi du 15 mars 2004 s'applique à compter de la rentrée scolaire prochaine. Même si l'interdiction posée par le premier alinéa de l'article L. 141-5-1 est d'application directe, il est utile de la rappeler dans les règlements intérieurs et de veiller à ce que ceux-ci ne comportent plus de référence à la notion de signes ostentatoires qui s'appuyait sur la jurisprudence du Conseil d'État à laquelle la loi nouvelle se substitue.
Les règlements intérieurs doivent rappeler, conformément aux prescriptions du second alinéa de l'article L. 141-5-1, que la mise en œuvre d'une procédure disciplinaire est précédée d'un dialogue avec l'élève.
Les chefs d'établissement sont invités à soumettre aux conseils d'administration les clauses jointes en annexe.

Circulaire n° 2012-056 du 27-3-2012, Orientations et instructions pour la préparation de la rentrée 2012, NOR: MENE1209011C (excerpt)[24]

Garantir la laïcité
La laïcité est un principe constitutionnel de la République: elle donne le cadre qui, au-delà des appartenances particulières, permet de vivre ensemble. Elle est accueillante, à la fois idéal d'une société ouverte et moyen de la liberté de chacun. L'école met en pratique la laïcité et apprend aux élèves à distinguer savoir et croire. Facteur de cohésion sociale, la laïcité s'impose à tous dans l'espace et le temps scolaires. Chacun, à sa place, est le garant de son application et de son respect.
Il est recommandé de rappeler dans le règlement intérieur que les principes de laïcité de l'enseignement et de neutralité du service public sont pleinement applicables au sein des établissements scolaires publics. Ces principes permettent notamment d'empêcher que les parents d'élèves ou tout autre

24 Available at http://circulaires.legifrance.gouv.fr/index.php?action=afficherCirculaire&hit=1&r=34967.

intervenant manifestent, par leur tenue ou leurs propos, leurs convictions religieuses, politiques ou philosophiques lorsqu'ils accompagnent les élèves lors des sorties et voyages scolaires.

Case Law

Case 1: A pupil was allowed to attend a private Catholic school provided that she abided by the internal ruling banning the wearing of her headscarf inside the school. Her parents lodged an appeal against this restriction imposed by the association running the school. They argued that this condition would infringe the commitment of this type of school to provide teaching respectful of freedom of conscience and to welcome all pupils without distinction of origin, opinion, or belief. The Court of Cassation nevertheless held that the prohibition on wearing the headscarf was not contrary to the Act of 31 December 1959 relating to private education institutions, given that it affected neither the neutrality of the education provided nor the pupils' freedom of conscience. It only addressed a simple means of conspicuous expression of those beliefs and was related to the management of the school and its educational project. It did not infringe its obligation to welcome the children without any distinction of origin, opinion and belief. Finally, the Court deemed that the right freely to manifest one's religion, entrenched in Article 9 of the European Convention of Human Rights, is not absolute and must be reconciled with other imperatives (*Court of cassation, 21-06-2005, no. 02-19831*).

12.3 Religious Dress in the Workplace

Labour law does not address the issue of Islamic dress as such, but rather provides a general framework on which limitations to the dress code can be based. Thus, pursuant to Article L. 1121-1 of the Labour Code, no restriction can be imposed on the rights and freedoms of individuals in the workplace, unless it is 'justified by the nature of the task' or 'proportionate to the aim pursued'. In this regard, the Court of Cassation held in 2003 that freedom to dress as one wishes during working time and at the workplace does not fall within the scope of fundamental freedoms.[25]

25 Court of cassation, 28-05-2003, no. 02-40.273: the case involved an employee who was sanctioned for wearing Bermuda shorts and ignoring his employer's requiring trousers.

As stated above, freedom to dress can be limited in the workplace for safety reasons and is in this case regulated by Article L. 4122-1 of the Labour Code on safety garments in situations of risk at work. Case law provides a certain number of cases involving women wearing the Islamic headscarf in the workplace (see also above *10.1. Employment and social law in the private sector*).

Code du travail

Article L. 1121-1: Nul ne peut apporter aux droits des personnes et aux libertés individuelles et collectives de restrictions qui ne seraient pas justifiées par la nature de la tâche à accomplir ni proportionnées au but recherché.

Article L. 4122-1: Les instructions de l'employeur précisent, en particulier lorsque la nature des risques le justifie, les conditions d'utilisation des équipements de travail, des moyens de protection, des substances et préparations dangereuses. Elles sont adaptées à la nature des tâches à accomplir.

CHAPTER 13

Criminal Law

The relationship between criminal law and religion can be understood in two ways: either by dealing with cases in which religious beliefs are liable to conflict with the law in that they lead to religiously-driven behaviours amounting to criminal offences,[1] or through offences aimed at protecting religious beliefs and practices. Both aspects of the relationship between criminal law and religion are addressed in French law, which covers a large range of offences likely to be committed with a religious element. Religious practices likely to be criminalised range—by way of example—from refusing vaccination (and in general claims for religious-based exceptions to medical treatment) to deprivation of food or care to the point of endangering the health of a minor under fifteen years of age (article 227-15 of the Penal Code), fraudulent abuse of a person's ignorance or weakness (Article 223-15-2 et seq. of the Penal Code),[2] or failure by the parents of a child to register him in an educational institution without a valid reason (Article 227-17-1 of the Penal Code), and wilful offences against the physical integrity of the person, like acts of violence causing mutilation or permanent disability (Article 222-9 et seq. of the Penal Code). Criminal law applied to religious practices was characterised in the 1990s by the fight against cults. At first sight 'neutral' criminal offences have in reality been enacted in response to the religious practices of those movements giving cause for concern.

Criminal law is called on here as a way of protecting religious beliefs (13.1) and practices (13.2).

13.1 Protection of Religious Beliefs

First, religious beliefs are protected through the fight against discrimination. In labour law, this derives from the implementation of European Union directives,

1 Article 111-1 of the Penal Code provides for the fundamental distinction among criminal offences according to their seriousness between felonies, misdemeanours and petty offences. Unless otherwise specified, criminal offences referred to in this section are misdemeanours (*délits*).

2 This offence, introduced in the Penal Code in 2001, was designed for fighting certain acts of sectarian movements (see Act no. 2001-504 of 12 June 2001 to reinforce the prevention and repression of sectarian movements affecting human rights and fundamental freedoms).

whereas the criminal dimension of discrimination has roots in the fight against racism. The Act of 1 July 1972 on the fight against racism introduced into the Penal Code not only the offence of racial discrimination, but more broadly of discrimination based on 'membership or non-membership, true or supposed, of a given ethnic group, nation, race or religion' (Article 225-1 of the Penal Code). Moreover, five specific behaviours lead to discrimination, like refusing to provide goods or services (Article 225-2, 1°) or refusing to recruit, penalise or dismiss a person (Article 225-2, 3°). Discrimination carries a sentence of up to five years' imprisonment and a fine of 75,000 Euros (Article 225-2, 6°). This is the case notably where discrimination is committed by a person holding public authority or carrying out a public service mission and consists of refusing the benefit of a right conferred by law (Article 432-7).

The French equality body created in 2004—replaced by the Defender of Rights in 2009—played a key role in the fight against discrimination.[3]

Secondly, religious beliefs are protected in that it is an aggravating circumstance when the offence is committed because of the victim's actual or supposed membership or non-membership of a given ethnic group, nation, race or religion (Article 132-76 of the Penal Code). Such an aggravating circumstance, however, applies only to offences for which it is expressly provided by law.[4] The offence of blasphemy no longer exists in French criminal law except in local law applicable in Alsace-Moselle in the Local Penal Code (Article 166).

Code pénal

Article 132-76: Dans les cas prévus par la loi, les peines encourues pour un crime ou un délit sont aggravées lorsque l'infraction est commise à raison de l'appartenance ou de la non-appartenance, vraie ou supposée, de la victime à une ethnie, une nation, une race ou une religion déterminée.
La circonstance aggravante définie au premier alinéa est constituée lorsque l'infraction est précédée, accompagnée ou suivie de propos, écrits, images, objets ou actes de toute nature portant atteinte à l'honneur ou à la considé-

3 This equality body was the High Authority for Fighting Discriminations and for Equality (HALDE-*Haute Autorité de Lutte contre les Discriminations et pour l'Egalité*).

4 It is so for murder (Article 221-4, 6°), torture or acts of barbarity (Article 222-3, 5° bis), violence (Articles 222-8, 222-10, 222-12 et 222-13, 5° bis), destroying, defacing, or damaging property (Article 322-2), destroying, defacing, or damaging property dangerous for persons (Article 322-8, 3°), threats (Article 222-18-1), theft (Article 311-4, 9°), extortion (Article 312-2, 3°), violation or desecration of tombs, burials grounds, or monuments erected to the memory of the dead (Article 225-18), non-public defamation, and insult (Articles R. 624-3 and 624-4).

ration de la victime ou d'un groupe de personnes dont fait partie la victime à raison de leur appartenance ou de leur non-appartenance, vraie ou supposée, à une ethnie, une nation, une race ou une religion déterminée.

Article 225-1: Constitue une discrimination toute distinction opérée entre les personnes physiques à raison de leur origine, de leur sexe, de leur situation de famille, de leur grossesse, de leur apparence physique, de leur patronyme, de leur lieu de résidence, de leur état de santé, de leur handicap, de leurs caractéristiques génétiques, de leurs mœurs, de leur orientation ou identité sexuelle, de leur âge, de leurs opinions politiques, de leurs activités syndicales, de leur appartenance ou de leur non-appartenance, vraie ou supposée, à une ethnie, une nation, une race ou une religion déterminée.
Constitue également une discrimination toute distinction opérée entre les personnes morales à raison de l'origine, du sexe, de la situation de famille, de l'apparence physique, du patronyme, du lieu de résidence, de l'état de santé, du handicap, des caractéristiques génétiques, des mœurs, de l'orientation ou identité sexuelle, de l'âge, des opinions politiques, des activités syndicales, de l'appartenance ou de la non-appartenance, vraie ou supposée, à une ethnie, une nation, une race ou une religion déterminée des membres ou de certains membres de ces personnes morales.

Article 225-2: La discrimination définie aux articles 225-1 et 225-1-1, commise à l'égard d'une personne physique ou morale, est punie de trois ans d'emprisonnement et de 45,000 euros d'amende lorsqu'elle consiste:
1° À refuser la fourniture d'un bien ou d'un service;
2° À entraver l'exercice normal d'une activité économique quelconque;
3° À refuser d'embaucher, à sanctionner ou à licencier une personne;
4° À subordonner la fourniture d'un bien ou d'un service à une condition fondée sur l'un des éléments visés à l'article 225-1 ou prévue à l'article 225-1-1;
5° À subordonner une offre d'emploi, une demande de stage ou une période de formation en entreprise à une condition fondée sur l'un des éléments visés à l'article 225-1 ou prévue à l'article 225-1-1;
6° À refuser d'accepter une personne à l'un des stages visés par le 2° de l'article L. 412-8 du code de la sécurité sociale.
Lorsque le refus discriminatoire prévu au 1° est commis dans un lieu accueillant du public ou aux fins d'en interdire l'accès, les peines sont portées à cinq ans d'emprisonnement et à 75,000 euros d'amende.

Article 432-7: La discrimination définie aux articles 225-1 et 225-1-1, commise à l'égard d'une personne physique ou morale par une personne déposi-

taire de l'autorité publique ou chargée d'une mission de service public, dans l'exercice ou à l'occasion de l'exercice de ses fonctions ou de sa mission, est punie de cinq ans d'emprisonnement et de 75,000 euros d'amende lorsqu'elle consiste:
1° À refuser le bénéfice d'un droit accordé par la loi;
2° À entraver l'exercice normal d'une activité économique quelconque

Code pénal local (Alsace-Moselle)

Article 166: Celui qui aura causé un scandale en blasphémant publiquement contre Dieu par des propos outrageants, ou aura publiquement outragé un des cultes chrétiens ou une communauté religieuse établie sur le territoire de la Confédération et reconnue comme corporation, ou les institutions ou cérémonies de ces cultes ou qui, dans une église ou un autre lieu consacré à des assemblées religieuses, aura commis des actes injurieux et scandaleux sera puni d'un emprisonnement de trois ans au plus.

Case Law

Case 1: An association in partnership with a professional training centre had adopted an internal ruling prohibiting the wearing of religious symbols. The applicant was denied participation in courses because of her wearing of the Islamic headscarf. The Court held that the applicant was exercising her freedom of religion and that refusal of access to a service (in this case, courses in a training centre) amounted to discrimination within the meaning of Article 225-1 of the Penal Code (*Appeal Court of Paris, 08-06-2010, no. 08/08286*).

Case 2: The manager of a driving-school had refused to give lessons to a woman because of her wearing of the Islamic headscarf. However, this refusal was based on security concerns and not on the intention to discriminate. As a result, the intentional element of the offence required in Article 225-2, 1° of the Penal Code was lacking (*Appeal Court of Nîmes, 08-11-2007, no. 07/00864*).

13.2 Offences against Religious Beliefs

This section addresses various criminal offences like incitement to religious discrimination or religious hatred or violence, defamation of religions and insult. All three are regulated by the ancient but still in force Freedom of the Press Act of 29 July 1881, which has been regularly revised and updated by introducing new offences, like denying crimes against humanity. All revolve today around the limits likely to be imposed on freedom of speech set out in Article 10 of the European Convention on Human Rights. The title of the 1881 Act is partly misleading as Article 23 provides for a wide range of media, which offences are based on, such as 'written or printed text, drawing, engraving, painting, emblem, image, or any other written, spoken or pictorial item sold or handed out' and also electronic media (Article 23).

Incitement to discrimination, hatred or violence against a person or group of people because of their origin or their belonging or non-belonging to an ethnic group, nation, race or religion is criminalised by Article 24 of the 1881 Act.

Besides targeting a person or a group due to their racial, ethnic or religious belonging, the offence of incitement to discrimination or hatred requires a positive act, like exhortation or incitement to these actions, attitudes, or feelings. Publications, videos or cartoons raising indignation are not enough to constitute this offence. Provisions of the Act of 29 July 1881 regularly give rise to case law and involve all main religious groups. Although courts often retain the racial ground, it is proving difficult to distinguish between religious and racial discrimination or hate or violence (see below cases 1 and 2).

Defamation is defined by Article 29 of the 1881 Act as 'any allegation or attribution of a fact that damages the honour or reputation of the person or entity to which the fact is attributed'. Courts repeatedly affirm that such allegation or attribution should be based on precise and coherent facts likely to be evidenced and the object of a debate. Otherwise, the allegation or attribution should be characterised as insult, which is an offence defined by Article 29 of the 1881 Act too. Insult consists of 'any offensive remark or expression of contempt or invective which does not contain a specific allegation' (see below case 3).

Case Law

Case 1: A newspaper article denounced the conditions of the ritual slaughter of sheep during Aïd-El-kebir and made a link with a Muslim faith group. The court held that denouncing such practice falls within acceptable criticism. However, the offence of incitement to racial hatred had been committed as the Muslim faith group had been compared to the German invasions during the two world wars, and the article implicitly called for a new fight (*Appeal Court of Paris, 09-10-1997, no. 1458-97*).

Case 2: Following the decision of the regional council of Alsace to fund a mosque, two regional councillors had distributed leaflets entitled 'no cathedral in Mecca, no mosque in Strasbourg'. They were eventually not charged with the offence of incitement to religious discrimination as the message of the leaflets was political and did not exceed the limits of freedom of speech. The criticism concerned the decision to fund a place of worship but was not intended to stigmatise those who practised that faith and to subject them to hatred by others (*Court of cassation, 30-05-2007, no. 06-84.328*).

Case 3: The weekly newspaper *Charlie Hebdo* had published several cartoons representing Muhammad, among which was a cartoon of the Prophet with a bomb in his turban.[5] Several associations decided to sue the newspaper on the basis of Article 33 of the Penal Code (public insult). The Court eventually held that in spite of the shocking or offensive character of this cartoon to the sensitivity of Muslims, the context and the circumstances of its publication in the newspaper appeared to be without any deliberate intention directly and gratuitously to offend all Muslims. The publication remained within the admissible limits of freedom of speech. The cartoon did not constitute an insult justifying, in a democratic society, a limitation of the free exercise of freedom of speech (*First Instance Court of Paris, 22-03-2007, no. 2007-327959*).[6]

Loi du 29 juillet 1881 modifiée sur la liberté de la presse

Article 23: Seront punis comme complices d'une action qualifiée crime ou délit ceux qui, soit par des discours, cris ou menaces proférés dans des lieux ou réunions publics, soit par des écrits, imprimés, dessins, gravures, peintures, emblèmes, images ou tout autre support de l'écrit, de la parole ou de l'image vendus ou distribués, mis en vente ou exposés dans des lieux ou réunions publics, soit par des placards ou des affiches exposés au regard du public, soit par tout moyen de communication au public par voie électronique, auront directement provoqué l'auteur ou les auteurs à commettre ladite action, si la provocation a été suivie d'effet.
Cette disposition sera également applicable lorsque la provocation n'aura été suivie que d'une tentative de crime prévue par l'article 2 du code pénal.

Article 24: Seront punis de cinq ans d'emprisonnement et de 45,000 euros d'amende ceux qui, par l'un des moyens énoncés à l'article précédent, auront directement provoqué, dans le cas où cette provocation n'aurait pas été suivie d'effet, à commettre l'une des infractions suivantes:

5 This was a reproduction of the cartoons published on 30 September 2005 by the Danish newspaper JyllandsPosten.

6 This ruling was upheld by the court of Paris in March 2008.

1° Les atteintes volontaires à la vie, les atteintes volontaires à l'intégrité de la personne et les agressions sexuelles, définies par le livre II du code pénal;
2° Les vols, les extorsions et les destructions, dégradations et détériorations volontaires dangereuses pour les personnes, définis par le livre III du code pénal.
Ceux qui, par les mêmes moyens, auront directement provoqué à l'un des crimes et délits portant atteinte aux intérêts fondamentaux de la nation prévus par le titre Ier du livre IV du code pénal, seront punis des mêmes peines.
Seront punis de la même peine ceux qui, par l'un des moyens énoncés en l'article 23, auront fait l'apologie des crimes visés au premier alinéa, des crimes de guerre, des crimes contre l'humanité ou des crimes et délits de collaboration avec l'ennemi.
Tous cris ou chants séditieux proférés dans les lieux ou réunions publics seront punis de l'amende prévue pour les contraventions de la 5° classe.
Ceux qui, par l'un des moyens énoncés à l'article 23, auront provoqué à la discrimination, à la haine ou à la violence à l'égard d'une personne ou d'un groupe de personnes à raison de leur origine ou de leur appartenance ou de leur non-appartenance à une ethnie, une nation, une race ou une religion déterminée, seront punis d'un an d'emprisonnement et de 45,000 euros d'amende ou de l'une de ces deux peines seulement.
Seront punis des peines prévues à l'alinéa précédent ceux qui, par ces mêmes moyens, auront provoqué à la haine ou à la violence à l'égard d'une personne ou d'un groupe de personnes à raison de leur sexe, de leur orientation ou identité sexuelle ou de leur handicap ou auront provoqué, à l'égard des mêmes personnes, aux discriminations prévues par les articles 225-2 et 432-7 du code pénal.
En cas de condamnation pour l'un des faits prévus par les deux alinéas précédents, le tribunal pourra en outre ordonner:
1° Sauf lorsque la responsabilité de l'auteur de l'infraction est retenue sur le fondement de l'article 42 et du premier alinéa de l'article 43 de la présente loi ou des trois premiers alinéas de l'article 93-3 de la loi n° 82-652 du 29 juillet 1982 sur la communication audiovisuelle, la privation des droits énumérés aux 2° et 3° de l'article 131-26 du code pénal pour une durée de cinq ans au plus;
2° L'affichage ou la diffusion de la décision prononcée dans les conditions prévues par l'article 131-35 du code pénal.

Article 24 bis: Seront punis des peines prévues par le sixième alinéa de l'article 24 ceux qui auront contesté, par un des moyens énoncés à l'article 23, l'existence d'un ou plusieurs crimes contre l'humanité tels qu'ils sont définis par

l'article 6 du statut du tribunal militaire international annexé à l'accord de Londres du 8 août 1945 et qui ont été commis soit par les membres d'une organisation déclarée criminelle en application de l'article 9 dudit statut, soit par une personne reconnue coupable de tels crimes par une juridiction française ou internationale.
Le tribunal pourra en outre ordonner:
1° L'affichage ou la diffusion de la décision prononcée dans les conditions prévues par l'article 131-35 du code pénal.

Article 29: Toute allégation ou imputation d'un fait qui porte atteinte à l'honneur ou à la considération de la personne ou du corps auquel le fait est imputé est une diffamation. La publication directe ou par voie de reproduction de cette allégation ou de cette imputation est punissable, même si elle est faite sous forme dubitative ou si elle vise une personne ou un corps non expressément nommés, mais dont l'identification est rendue possible par les termes des discours, cris, menaces, écrits ou imprimés, placards ou affiches incriminés.
Toute expression outrageante, termes de mépris ou invective qui ne renferme l'imputation d'aucun fait est une injure.

Article 32: La diffamation commise envers les particuliers par l'un des moyens énoncés en l'article 23 sera punie d'une amende de 12,000 euros.
La diffamation commise par les mêmes moyens envers une personne ou un groupe de personnes à raison de leur origine ou de leur appartenance ou de leur non-appartenance à une ethnie, une nation, une race ou une religion déterminée sera punie d'un an d'emprisonnement et de 45,000 euros d'amende ou de l'une de ces deux peines seulement.
Sera punie des peines prévues à l'alinéa précédent la diffamation commise par les mêmes moyens envers une personne ou un groupe de personnes à raison de leur sexe, de leur orientation ou identité sexuelle ou de leur handicap.
En cas de condamnation pour l'un des faits prévus par les deux alinéas précédents, le tribunal pourra en outre ordonner:
1° L'affichage ou la diffusion de la décision prononcée dans les conditions prévues par l'article 131-35 du code pénal.
Article 33: L'injure commise par les mêmes moyens envers les corps ou les personnes désignés par les articles 30 et 31 de la présente loi sera punie d'une amende de 12,000 euros.
L'injure commise de la même manière envers les particuliers, lorsqu'elle n'aura pas été précédée de provocations, sera punie d'une amende de 12,000 euros.

> Sera punie de six mois d'emprisonnement et de 22,500 euros d'amende l'injure commise, dans les conditions prévues à l'alinéa précédent, envers une personne ou un groupe de personnes à raison de leur origine ou de leur appartenance ou de leur non-appartenance à une ethnie, une nation, une race ou une religion déterminée.
> Sera punie des peines prévues à l'alinéa précédent l'injure commise dans les mêmes conditions envers une personne ou un groupe de personnes à raison de leur sexe, de leur orientation ou identité sexuelle ou de leur handicap.
> En cas de condamnation pour l'un des faits prévus par les deux alinéas précédents, le tribunal pourra en outre ordonner:
> 1° L'affichage ou la diffusion de la décision prononcée dans les conditions prévues par l'article 131-35 du code pénal.

13.3 Offences against Religious Practices

There are several other offences designed to protect acts of worship of various kinds, including places of worship themselves.

First, Article 31 of the 1905 Act punishes those who have forced an individual to exercise or to refrain from practising a religion, either by assault, violence or threats against an individual, or by making him fear the loss of his job or the exposure of his person, his family or his property to harm. These provisions are only rarely applied. A case is worth mentioning which involved a Muslim employee who had been obliged by his employer to swear on the Qur'an, and during the prayer to clear himself of starting a fight at work which could lead to his dismissal. The elements of the crime were however not met (*Court of appeal of Bourges, 21-03-1985, no. 1985-041416*). Secondly, Article 32 of the 9 December 1905 Act addresses more specifically acts taking place in places of worship by punishing those who have prevented, delayed or interrupted worship by causing disorder, or disorder caused in premises dedicated to worship. There has been no significant application of these provisions.

The protection by criminal law of places of worship themselves is recent. Indeed, places of worship, as such, have not benefited from any specific protection so far. The aggravating circumstance relating to the status of place of worship for the offence of destroying, defacing or damaging property belonging to other persons was introduced in 2003 (Article 322-3-1 of the Penal Code). This offence is punishable by seven years' imprisonment and a fine of 100,000 Euros.[7]

7 As an illustration of the application of these provisions see Court of Appeal of Montpellier, 22-09-2005, no. 05/00743, involving a man who had damaged the door of a mosque.

The data in a parliamentary report on the policy of prevention and fight against desecration of places of worship and cemeteries of 2011 show that all main religious denominations are concerned, although Catholic buildings come first.[8]

Finally, cemeteries are also protected through Article 225-17 of the Penal Code which criminalises the violation or desecration of tombs, burials grounds or monuments to the memory of the dead. The same provisions apply to any violation of the integrity of a corpse. It is an aggravating circumstance to commit this offence on the ground of membership or non-membership, true or supposed, of a given ethnic group, nation, race or religion (Article 225-18).[9]

Loi du 9 décembre 1905 concernant la séparation des Églises et de l'État

Article 31: Sont punis de la peine d'amende prévue pour les contraventions de la 5ème classe et d'un emprisonnement de six jours à deux mois ou de l'une de ces deux peines seulement ceux qui, soit par voies de fait, violences ou menaces contre un individu, soit en lui faisant craindre de perdre son emploi ou d'exposer à un dommage sa personne, sa famille ou sa fortune, l'auront déterminé à exercer ou à s'abstenir d'exercer un culte, à faire partie ou à cesser de faire partie d'une association cultuelle, à contribuer ou à s'abstenir de contribuer aux frais d'un culte.

Article 32: Seront punis des mêmes peines ceux qui auront empêché, retardé ou interrompu les exercices d'un culte par des troubles ou désordres causés dans le local servant à ces exercices.

Article 33: Les dispositions des deux articles précédents ne s'appliquent qu'aux troubles, outrages ou voies de fait, dont la nature ou les circonstances ne donneront pas lieu à de plus fortes peines d'après les dispositions du Code pénal.

8 Report available at http://www.jpmaurer.info/dossier%20JPM/rapport_profanation.pdf. In 2010, out of 621 acts of degradation of places of worship, 57 concerned Muslim buildings.

9 These provisions on aggravating circumstances were introduced into the new Penal Code of 1994, as the parliamentary debates were still marked by particularly serious acts of vandalism committed in the Jewish section of the cemetery of Carpentras consisting, in addition to the destruction of a large number of headstones, in the mutilation of a corpse.

Code pénal local

Article 167: Celui qui, par voie de fait ou menaces aura empêché une personne d'exercer le culte d'une communauté religieuse établie dans l'État, ou qui, dans une église ou dans un autre lieu destiné à des assemblées religieuses, aura par tapage ou désordre volontairement empêché ou troublé le culte ou certaines cérémonies du culte d'une communauté religieuse établie dans l'État, sera puni d'un emprisonnement de trois ans au plus.

Code pénal

Article 225-17: Toute atteinte à l'intégrité du cadavre, par quelque moyen que ce soit, est punie d'un an d'emprisonnement et de 15,000 euros d'amende.
La violation ou la profanation, par quelque moyen que ce soit, de tombeaux, de sépultures, d'urnes cinéraires ou de monuments édifiés à la mémoire des morts est punie d'un an d'emprisonnement et de 15,000 euros d'amende.
La peine est portée à deux ans d'emprisonnement et à 30,000 euros d'amende lorsque les infractions définies à l'alinéa précédent ont été accompagnées d'atteinte à l'intégrité du cadavre.

Article 225-18: Lorsque les infractions définies à l'article précédent ont été commises à raison de l'appartenance ou de la non-appartenance, vraie ou supposée, des personnes décédées à une ethnie, une nation, une race ou une religion déterminée, les peines sont portées à trois ans d'emprisonnement et à 45,000 euros d'amende pour les infractions définies aux deux premiers alinéas de l'article 225-17 et à cinq ans d'emprisonnement et à 75,000 euros d'amende pour celle définie au dernier alinéa de cet article.

Article 322-1: La destruction, la dégradation ou la détérioration d'un bien appartenant à autrui est punie de deux ans d'emprisonnement et de 30,000 euros d'amende, sauf s'il n'en est résulté qu'un dommage léger.
Le fait de tracer des inscriptions, des signes ou des dessins, sans autorisation préalable, sur les façades, les véhicules, les voies publiques ou le mobilier urbain est puni de 3,750 euros d'amende et d'une peine de travail d'intérêt général lorsqu'il n'en est résulté qu'un dommage léger.

Article 322-3-1: La destruction, la dégradation ou la détérioration est punie de sept ans d'emprisonnement et de 100,000 € d'amende lorsqu'elle porte sur:
1° Un immeuble ou objet mobilier classé ou inscrit en application des dispositions du code du patrimoine ou un document d'archives privées classé en application des dispositions du même code;

2° Une découverte archéologique faite au cours de fouilles ou fortuitement, un terrain sur lequel se déroulent des opérations archéologiques ou un édifice affecté au culte;
3° Un bien culturel qui relève du domaine public mobilier ou qui est exposé, conservé ou déposé, même de façon temporaire, soit dans un musée de France, une bibliothèque, une médiathèque ou un service d'archives, soit dans un lieu dépendant d'une personne publique ou d'une personne privée assurant une mission d'intérêt général, soit dans un édifice affecté au culte.
Les peines sont portées à dix ans d'emprisonnement et 150,000 € d'amende lorsque l'infraction prévue au présent article est commise avec la circonstance prévue au 1° de l'article 322-3.
Les peines d'amende mentionnées au présent article peuvent être élevées jusqu'à la moitié de la valeur du bien détruit, dégradé ou détérioré.

CHAPTER 14

Family Law

Religious beliefs and practices have a limited impact on family law as on private law in general. Their influence is much more tangible when it comes to private international law in this field. Indeed, courts have to rule on applications involving religiously-based personal law.

14.1 Marriage and Divorce

Unlike international law, French domestic law does not expressly confirm the right to marry. Courts, however, have enshrined the freedom to marry as a component of individual freedom (Constitutional Council, 20-11-2003, no. 2003-484 DC) or as a fundamental freedom (Council of State, 9-07-2014, no. 382145).

Only civil marriage is regulated in French law, which has long refused to recognise any legal effect to religious marriage. Marriage has been secularised since the 1791 Constitution, and the Civil Code in force since 1802 has brought no change to this conception of marriage. In addition, a civil marriage must be celebrated before a religious union. The Act of 17 May 2013 (see Article 143 of the Civil Code) on same-sex marriage has even increased the civil dimension of marriage by adding to Article 165—which provides that marriage is celebrated in public by an officer of the civil registrar—that marriage is celebrated in a republican ceremony.

Article 433-21 of the Penal Code punishes religious leaders who celebrate a religious marriage before a civil one with six months' imprisonment and a fine of 7,500 euros. Although these provisions were designed in a Catholic environment, they still apply to all religions without distinction and regardless of the form that the religious ceremony may take, since the Penal Code does not provide any definition for it.[1] This rule of anteriority of civil marriage is at first sight surprising in a system of separation between Church and state. In fact, it would be justified by the significant legal effects of marriage with regard to both the situation of children of the marriage and the relations of spouses with third parties. In other words, the aim pursued through this rule of anteriority is legal

1 Ministerial response to parliamentary question no. 111, *Journal Officiel-Sénat*, 04/10/2007, p. 1782.

protection.[2] All this does not mean that religious marriage has no influence at all in the legal field, in that religious beliefs are likely to be taken into account when it comes to implementing legal conditions pertaining to marriage such as its annulment (see below case 1).

Bigamy is prohibited by Article 147 of the Civil Code, which makes it impossible to marry again before a first marriage is dissolved.

Finally, married life is based on the respective duties and rights of the spouses and governed, among others, by Article 212 of the Civil Code, which provides that spouses owe each other respect, fidelity, support and assistance. The duty of respect is likely to provide the legal basis for the freedom of religion of each spouse. In the case of a spouse who converted to a Jehovah's Witness, this amounts to exercising her freedom of religion; her previous commitment to abide by Catholic requirements including the education of children has no legal effect (*Appeal court of Montpellier, 29-06-1992, no. 1992-034435*). The limit to freedom of religion in married life lies in its compatibility with the marriage related duties and should not make it unbearable. A breach of these duties is a ground for divorce (Article 242 of the Civil Code).

The Civil Code provides for four grounds for divorce (Article 229): by mutual consent when both spouses agree to a divorce (Article 230); by acceptance of the principle of the breakdown of the marriage when one spouse takes the initiative to divorce (Article 233); by definitive alteration of the bond of marriage where the community life has ceased (Articles 237 and 238); for fault when renewed violation of the duties and obligations of marriage are ascribable to the other spouse, making the community life unbearable (Article 242). The influence of religious beliefs and belonging on divorce issue should be considered with regard to the latter grounds, as excessive zeal regarding the practice of religion might lead to unbearable community life and then to divorce. It should be noted, nevertheless, that excessive religious practices rarely constitute an issue in case law.

Over the last four decades, the issue of divorce has been marked by a progressive easing of divorce conditions, mainly taking the form of constantly further distancing the population from the Catholic view of marriage. While a religiously driven opposition to divorce by a spouse could previously—at least to a certain extent—rely on law, consideration for religious belonging seems today to be limited to the awarding of damages pursuant to Article 266 of the Civil Code. This provides that, in general, such damages may be awarded to a spouse

2 Ministerial response to parliamentary question no. 52843, *Journal Officiel-Assemblée nationale*, 24/09/1984, p. 4267.

in reparation for the consequences of particular gravity he suffers because of the dissolution of the marriage.[3] As an example, damages for non-pecuniary harm were granted to a spouse of a Protestant given her religious beliefs, as part of a religious marriage that resulted in a confession of faith signed by both spouses (the divorce was pronounced after the Catholic husband's adultery).[4]

Code civil

Article 143: Le mariage est contracté par deux personnes de sexe différent ou de même sexe.

Article 146: Il n'y a pas de mariage lorsqu'il n'y a point de consentement.

Article 147: On ne peut contracter un second mariage avant la dissolution du premier.

Article 165: Le mariage sera célébré publiquement lors d'une cérémonie républicaine par l'officier de l'état civil de la commune dans laquelle l'un des époux, ou l'un de leurs parents, aura son domicile ou sa résidence à la date de la publication prévue par l'article 63, et, en cas de dispense de publication, à la date de la dispense prévue à l'article 169 ci-après.

Article 180: Le mariage qui a été contracté sans le consentement libre des deux époux, ou de l'un d'eux, ne peut être attaqué que par les époux, ou par celui des deux dont le consentement n'a pas été libre, ou par le ministère public. L'exercice d'une contrainte sur les époux ou l'un d'eux, y compris par crainte révérencielle envers un ascendant, constitue un cas de nullité du mariage.
S'il y a eu erreur dans la personne, ou sur des qualités essentielles de la personne, l'autre époux peut demander la nullité du mariage.

Article 212: Les époux se doivent mutuellement respect, fidélité, secours, assistance.

Article 213: Les époux assurent ensemble la direction morale et matérielle de la famille. Ils pourvoient à l'éducation des enfants et préparent leur avenir.

3 See *Traité de droit français des religions*, pp. 1016 et seq.
4 Court of Appeal of Bordeaux, 24-11-2009, no. 2009-015123.

Article 229: Le divorce peut être prononcé en cas:
– soit de consentement mutuel;
– soit d'acceptation du principe de la rupture du mariage;
– soit d'altération définitive du lien conjugal;
– soit de faute.

Article 242: Le divorce peut être demandé par l'un des époux lorsque des faits constitutifs d'une violation grave ou renouvelée des devoirs et obligations du mariage sont imputables à son conjoint et rendent intolérable le maintien de la vie commune.

Article 266: Sans préjudice de l'application de l'article 270, des dommages et intérêts peuvent être accordés à un époux en réparation des conséquences d'une particulière gravité qu'il subit du fait de la dissolution du mariage soit lorsqu'il était défendeur à un divorce prononcé pour altération définitive du lien conjugal et qu'il n'avait lui-même formé aucune demande en divorce, soit lorsque le divorce est prononcé aux torts exclusifs de son conjoint.
Cette demande ne peut être formée qu'à l'occasion de l'action en divorce.

Code pénal

Article 433-21: Tout ministre d'un culte qui procédera, de manière habituelle, aux cérémonies religieuses de mariage sans que ne lui ait été justifié l'acte de mariage préalablement reçu par les officiers de l'état civil sera puni de six mois d'emprisonnement et de 7,500 euros d'amende.

Case Law

Case 1: Both spouses were of the Muslim faith, implying that civil marriage must be followed by religious marriage, until the celebration of which spouses do not live together and the marriage is not consummated. The husband, however, refused to marry religiously after the civil marriage. Accordingly, the wife sought annulment of the marriage. Indeed, the refusal of one of the spouses to submit to religious marriage constitutes a delict on the other essential qualities likely to justify the annulment of the marriage on the basis of Article 180 of the Civil Code (*Appeal Court of Aix-en-Provence, 15-11-2005, no. 2005-293158*).

Case 2: A man sought the annulment of his marriage, arguing that his wife had lied about her past love life and was no longer a virgin. The court held, however, that a lie not pertaining to an essential quality cannot be a basis for annulment. Indeed, virginity is not an essential quality, as its absence does not affect married life (*Appeal Court of Douai, 17-11-2008, no. 2008-371528*).

Case 3: A wife applied for divorce for fault on the ground that her husband's religious practices made community life unbearable. The excessive religious practices consisted in regular conspicuous prayers in his workplace, refusal to take part in family meals, and excessive religious practices amounting to fundamentalism. The Court held that even if the practice of religion is not in itself objectionable, excesses in practice may be a basis for complaints. In the case at hand, the divorce was granted based on the fault of the husband alone (*Appeal Court of Rennes, 27-03-2012, no. 10/07958*).

14.2 Children

The sole legislative reference to the religion of children in family law is in Article 1200 of the Civil Procedure Code, which states that while implementing educational assistance measures decided by the judge in charge of children's affairs, the religious or philosophical convictions of the minor or of his family must be taken into consideration. In general, Article 213 of the Civil Code vests the spouses with the moral and material direction of the family, including education of the children.

A child's religion falls within parental authority, which covers the rights and duties of parents—or holders of parental authority—and whose aim is the interests of the child (Article 371-1 of the Civil Code). The concept of 'best interests of the child' was set out in law by the Act of 4 March 2002 on parental authority which governs the applicable law here. The issue of the religious belonging and beliefs of children is likely to be raised in these general legal provisions. It is constantly held in courts that, besides health, leaving the national territory, school or leisure activities, religion plays a part in all important decisions regarding the child's life and deriving from parental authority. Moreover, courts occasionally refer to Article 14 of the Convention on the Rights of the Child, which specifically confirms the right of the child to freedom of thought, conscience and religion.

Conflicts pertaining to the religious education of children generally arise when parents divorce and disagree with choices made by one of them. Case law, however, overwhelmingly involves parents—and children—belonging to a Christian faith and, above all, to cults. As regards applications with respect to persons of Islamic faith, a father who had imposed circumcision on his children in conditions likely to threaten their balance was therefore deprived of his visitation right and right to overnight stays by the child. Moreover, the mother could legitimately fear that the exercising of these rights would be an opportunity for the father to remove the children from her authority (*Court of Cassation, 26-01-1994, no. 92-10.838*). In another case, the father's visitation right was suspended due to the pressure exercised on his young daughters, by his imposing on them the wearing of the Islamic veil and forbidding them to go to public swimming pools (*Court of Cassation, 24-10-2000, no. 98-14.386*).

Convention relative aux droits de l'enfant du 26 janvier 1990

Article 14: 1. Les États parties respectent le droit de l'enfant à la liberté de pensée, de conscience et de religion.
2. Les États parties respectent le droit et le devoir des parents ou, le cas échéant, des représentants légaux de l'enfant, de guider celui-ci dans l'exercice du droit susmentionné d'une manière qui corresponde au développement de ses capacités.
3. La liberté de manifester sa religion ou ses convictions ne peut être soumise qu'aux seules restrictions qui sont prescrites par la loi et qui sont nécessaires pour préserver la sûreté publique, l'ordre public, la santé et la moralité publiques, ou les libertés et droits fondamentaux d'autrui.

Code civil

Article 213: Les époux assurent ensemble la direction morale et matérielle de la famille. Ils pourvoient à l'éducation des enfants et préparent leur avenir.

Article 371-1: L'autorité parentale est un ensemble de droits et de devoirs ayant pour finalité l'intérêt de l'enfant.
Elle appartient aux parents jusqu'à la majorité ou l'émancipation de l'enfant pour le protéger dans sa sécurité, sa santé et sa moralité, pour assurer son éducation et permettre son développement, dans le respect dû à sa personne.
Les parents associent l'enfant aux décisions qui le concernent, selon son âge et son degré de maturité.

Code de procédure civile

Article 1200: Dans l'application de l'assistance éducative, il doit être tenu compte des convictions religieuses ou philosophiques du mineur et de sa famille.

14.3 Private International Law

Private international law tries to determine which law, foreign (called 'personal law') or French, should apply to a wide range of situations involving an international element. Foreign legislation relying on religious personal status will have effects in the domestic legal order, provided that it does not run counter to the national *ordre public*. In this regard, it is noticeable that Article 4 of the French-Moroccan convention on the status of persons and family explicitly states that the law of one of the states may be set aside only if it is incompatible with *ordre public*. Marriage, divorce and children will be addressed successively.

Marriages between foreigners—or between a foreigner and a French national—celebrated in France are governed by Articles 202-1 and 202-2 of the Civil Code which lay down the principle of each spouse's personal law's applicability as regards required qualities and conditions.[5] The strict implementation of these provisions would lead to taking into account foreign law requirements which make a binding marriage depend on a religious ceremony. Legal mechanisms, like *ordre public*, however, considerably limit the room left for foreign law. As regards the religious ceremony required by some foreign legislation, it appears that the religious or secular nature of marriage is regarded as a formal and not substantive rule, justifying the application of the ancient legal custom *locus regit actum*. As a result a civil marriage of foreigners contracted in France is valid, provided that it abides by French formal rules, irrespective of the foreign law requirements regarding religious marriage. This was sanctioned by the *Caraslanis* case, which is still valid, in which the husband was Greek orthodox (*Court of Cassation, 22-06-1955*).

Substantive legal rules on marriage (like age or consent to marriage) are, however, determined pursuant to Article 202-1 of the Civil Code, provided that foreign law in this field does not contradict French *ordre public*. Thus, the Tunisian personal status code was applied to a Tunisian who had married a French national with a view to obtaining a residence permit and not to start a family. Pursuant to previous Article 3 of the French Civil Code and the Tunisian Code, this could be read as pursuing an aim contrary to the essence of marriage (*Court of cassation, 01-06-2011, no. 09-67.805*).

The issue of polygamy is twofold. On the one hand, polygamous marriage involving a French national contradicts *ordre public* and cannot be recognised

5 Article 3 of the Civil Code was applicable before the passing of the Act of 19 May 2013 allowing same-sex couples to marry.

in the French legal order. Polygamous marriages celebrated abroad are valid provided that they are authorised by the personal law of both spouses. However, as soon as one of the spouses is French, the marriage is no longer binding (see below case 1). On the other hand, the applicability of some effects of a polygamous marriage is admitted under French law in that Article 201 of the Civil Code gives effect to marriage contracted in good faith. As an example, the deceased husband had married twice. The second marriage was declared void but putative as regards the second spouse pursuant to Article 201 of the Civil Code. Accordingly, she could benefit from the survivor's pension (*Court of cassation, 16-09-2003, no. 02-30.224*).

Like marriage, divorce follows conflict of laws rules in cases with an international element. In addition to Article 3 of the Civil Code, Article 309 specifically addresses divorce and legal separation (separation from bed and board) and provides that they are governed by French law where both spouses are French nationals, where they live in France or where they are not governed by foreign law. The issue of divorce in private international law leads to the addressing of the question of repudiation, which is considered as contrary to *ordre public*. Most of the cases relevant here involve Algerian or Moroccan nationals. As an example, an Algerian spouse had applied for a divorce before a French court. As her husband argued that a divorce had previously been granted by an Algerian court, the Court of Cassation held that the Algerian court only observed the unilateral repudiation by the husband without giving effect to the possible opposition of the wife, leaving to the French jurisdiction the sole opportunity to arrange the financial aspects of the divorce. Thus, it was contrary to the equality of rights of the spouses during the marriage dissolution, entrenched in the additional protocol no. 7 to the European Convention on Human Rights (Article 5). It was also contrary to international *ordre public*, entrenched in Article 1st d of the French-Algerian Convention of 1964 (*Court of Cassation, 17-02-2004, no. 01-11549*). Similarly, the firm position of the Court of Cassation consists in refusing to give effect in France to Moroccan judgments recognising repudiation, as it considers that the wife is deprived of a right equivalent to the husband's right to dissolve the marriage. Despite the reform of the Moroccan family law of 3 February 2004 giving similar rights to the wife during the proceedings, it seems that the Court of Cassation has not changed its position (*Court of cassation, 04-11-2009, no. 08-20.574*).

Litigation also arises when spouses seek recognition of their divorce in the French legal order. Thus, a divorce between two Moroccan nationals granted in Morocco could be lawfully transcribed into the French registry of births, marriages and deaths as the divorce was a divorce for discord under article 97 of the Moroccan Civil Code and the spouses had been living separately for three years. The Moroccan judgment granting the divorce did not amount to the recognition of unilateral repudiation (*Court of cassation, 23-02-2011, no. 10-14.760*).

As regards children, private international law rules do not in principle rule out the application of foreign law, provided that it abides by the French conception of *ordre public*. The recognition of *kafala* constitutes the main relevant issue here.[6] In French law, it is called the legal placement of children in families and defined as a commitment to take care of a minor child without creating parentage. Its link to adoption is ruled by Articles 370-3 to 370-5 of the Civil Code. These provisions were added to the Civil Code in 2001 with a view to taking into account foreign legislation such as Algerian and Moroccan laws. According to regular case law, though, *kafala* does not legally constitute adoption; it allows the child to benefit from protection meeting the requirements entrenched in Article 20 of the Convention on the Rights of the Child, that is, for a child deprived of his or her family environment, the competent state should ensure alternative care including 'kafalah of Islamic law' (see among others *Court of Cassation, 15-12-2015, no. 09-10.439*).[7]

According to Article 370-3, adoption is impossible when it is prohibited by foreign law, unless the child was born and lives in France. In addition, the administrative circular of the Ministry of Justice on the legal effects of the legal placement of children of 22 October 2014, which aims at making the legal status of *kafala* clearer, provides that a *kafala* lawfully granted abroad directly enters the French legal order.

Case Law

Case 1: Mr A. had married Mrs M. according to the Christian Maronite rite. Later he became a Sunni Muslim and married Mrs C., a French national, in Egypt. The first marriage had not been dissolved and Mr A. was accordingly bigamous. The public prosecutor of the French court of Nanterre applied for annulment of the second marriage. The Court of Cassation deemed that a marriage formed abroad with a bigamous status for one of the spouses is not necessarily void in France, provided that the domestic law of each spouse permits the bigamy.

---

6 A ministerial response to a parliamentary question of 4 February 2014 indicates that approximately 300–400 long-stay visas are issued each year for children placed in the care of French or foreign couples within a *kafala*. Available at http://questions.assemblee-nationale.fr/q14/14-43409QE.htm.

7 In *Harroudji c/ France* of 4 October 2012, no. 43631/09, the European Court of Human Rights held that this case law abides by the rights guaranteed by the European Convention.

Considering, however, that Mrs. M. has been a French national since 1985 and that she was subject to Article 147 of the Civil Code, the marriage was void (*Court of Cassation, 24-09-2002, no. 00-15.789*).

Case 2: The public prosecutor opposed a marriage between a French national and a Moroccan national, both men and living in France. He invoked Article 5 of the French-Moroccan Convention of 10 August 1981 on the status of persons and the family and on judicial cooperation, Article 5 of which states that substantive legal rules on marriage—such as age or consent—are governed by the law of one or both states of which he is a national. The Court of Cassation, however, held that Article 4 of the same Convention allows the setting aside of the law of one or both countries if it is obviously incompatible with *ordre public*. Such is the case with the relevant Moroccan law opposing same-sex marriage (*Court of Cassation, 28-01-2015, no. 13-50.059*).

Case 3: Both applicants were Algerian nationals who married in Algeria. The husband obtained a divorce before a court in Algeria in 1995. In 1996 he asked the court of Colmar to make this judgment enforceable in France. The TGI and the court of appeal of Colmar both dismissed the husband's appeal. He argued before the Court of Cassation that by having ignored whether the financial compensation entrenched in Moroccan law could ensure equality between the spouses during the divorce process, the judgment was not legally founded with regard to the European Convention of Human Rights and the French-Algerian Convention of 1964.

The Court of Cassation held that the Algerian court only observed the unilateral repudiation by the husband without giving effect to the possible opposition of the wife, leaving to the French jurisdiction alone the opportunity to arrange the financial aspects of the divorce. Thus, it was contrary to the equality of rights of the spouses during the marriage dissolution, entrenched in additional Protocol no. 7 to the European Convention on Human Rights (Article 5). It was also contrary to international *ordre public*, which lay in the French-Algerian Convention of 1964. The husband's appeal was accordingly dismissed (*Court of cassation, 17-02-2004, no. 01-11549*).

Convention relative aux droits de l'enfant du 26 janvier 1990

Article 20

1. Tout enfant qui est temporairement ou définitivement privé de son milieu familial, ou qui dans son propre intérêt ne peut être laissé dans ce milieu, a droit à une protection et une aide spéciale de l'État.

2. Les États parties prévoient pour cet enfant une protection de remplacement conforme à leur législation nationale.
3. Cette protection de remplacement peut notamment avoir la forme du placement dans une famille, de la kafalah de droit islamique, de l'adoption ou, en cas de nécessité, du placement dans un établissement pour enfants approprié. Dans le choix entre ces solutions, il est dûment tenu compte de la nécessité d'une certaine continuité dans l'éducation de l'enfant, ainsi que de son origine ethnique, religieuse, culturelle et linguistique.

Code civil

Article 3: Les lois de police et de sûreté obligent tous ceux qui habitent le territoire.
Les immeubles, même ceux possédés par des étrangers, sont régis par la loi française.
Les lois concernant l'état et la capacité des personnes régissent les Français, même résidant en pays étranger.

Article 171-1: Le mariage contracté en pays étranger entre Français, ou entre un Français et un étranger, est valable s'il a été célébré dans les formes usitées dans le pays de célébration et pourvu que le ou les Français n'aient point contrevenu aux dispositions contenues au chapitre Ier du présent titre.
Il en est de même du mariage célébré par les autorités diplomatiques ou consulaires françaises, conformément aux lois françaises.
Toutefois, ces autorités ne peuvent procéder à la célébration du mariage entre un Français et un étranger que dans les pays qui sont désignés par décret.

Article 201: Le mariage qui a été déclaré nul produit, néanmoins, ses effets à l'égard des époux, lorsqu'il a été contracté de bonne foi.
Si la bonne foi n'existe que de la part de l'un des époux, le mariage ne produit ses effets qu'en faveur de cet époux.

Article 202-1: Les qualités et conditions requises pour pouvoir contracter mariage sont régies, pour chacun des époux, par sa loi personnelle. Quelle que soit la loi personnelle applicable, le mariage requiert le consentement des époux, au sens de l'article 146 et du premier alinéa de l'article 180.
Deux personnes de même sexe peuvent contracter mariage lorsque, pour au moins l'une d'elles, soit sa loi personnelle, soit la loi de l'État sur le territoire duquel elle a son domicile ou sa résidence le permet.

Article 202-2: Le mariage est valablement célébré s'il l'a été conformément aux formalités prévues par la loi de l'État sur le territoire duquel la célébration a eu lieu.

Article 309: Le divorce et la séparation de corps sont régis par la loi française:
– lorsque l'un et l'autre époux sont de nationalité française;
– lorsque les époux ont, l'un et l'autre, leur domicile sur le territoire français;
– lorsque aucune loi étrangère ne se reconnaît compétence, alors que les tribunaux français sont compétents pour connaître du divorce ou de la séparation de corps.

Chapitre III: Du conflit des lois relatives à la filiation adoptive et de l'effet en France des adoptions prononcées à l'étranger
Article 370-3: Les conditions de l'adoption sont soumises à la loi nationale de l'adoptant ou, en cas d'adoption par deux époux, par la loi qui régit les effets de leur union. L'adoption ne peut toutefois être prononcée si la loi nationale de l'un et l'autre époux la prohibe.
L'adoption d'un mineur étranger ne peut être prononcée si sa loi personnelle prohibe cette institution, sauf si ce mineur est né et réside habituellement en France.
Quelle que soit la loi applicable, l'adoption requiert le consentement du représentant légal de l'enfant. Le consentement doit être libre, obtenu sans aucune contrepartie, après la naissance de l'enfant et éclairé sur les conséquences de l'adoption, en particulier, s'il est donné en vue d'une adoption plénière, sur le caractère complet et irrévocable de la rupture du lien de filiation préexistant.

Article 370-4: Les effets de l'adoption prononcée en France sont ceux de la loi française.

Article 370-5: L'adoption régulièrement prononcée à l'étranger produit en France les effets de l'adoption plénière si elle rompt de manière complète et irrévocable le lien de filiation préexistant. À défaut, elle produit les effets de l'adoption simple. Elle peut être convertie en adoption plénière si les consentements requis ont été donnés expressément en connaissance de cause.

Convention entre la République Française et le Royaume du Maroc relative au statut des personnes et de la famille et à la coopération judiciaire, 10 août 1981 (excerpt)

Article 1er
L'état et la capacité des personnes physiques sont régis par la loi de celui des deux États dont ces personnes ont la nationalité.
Le domicile d'une personne est le lieu où elle a sa résidence habituelle effective.

Article 4
La loi de l'un des deux États désignés par la présente Convention ne peut être écartée par les juridictions de l'autre État que si elle est manifestement incompatible avec l'ordre public.

Article 5
Les conditions du fond du mariage tels que l'âge matrimonial et le consentement de même que les empêchements, notamment ceux résultant des liens de parenté ou d'alliance, sont régies pour chacun des futurs époux par la loi de celui des deux États dont il a la nationalité.

Article 6
Les conditions de forme du mariage sont régies par la loi de celui des deux États dont l'autorité célèbre le mariage.
Chaque État peut décider que le mariage dans l'autre État entre des époux qui possèdent tous deux sa nationalité sera célébré par ses fonctionnaires consulaires.
Le mariage sur le territoire français entre un époux de nationalité marocaine et un époux de nationalité française doit être célébré par un officier de l'état civil compétent selon la loi française. Pour la validité de cette union au regard de la loi marocaine, les fonctionnaires consulaires marocains compétents procèdent, après justification de la célébration, à l'enregistrement de ce mariage.
Le mariage sur le territoire marocain d'un époux de nationalité marocaine et d'un époux de nationalité française ne peut être célébré par les adouls que sur présentation par l'époux français du certificat de capacité matrimoniale, délivré par les fonctionnaires consulaires français. Les adouls célèbrent le mariage selon les formes prescrites par le statut personnel du futur époux de nationalité marocaine. Lorsque l'épouse française n'a pas désigné de personne pouvant jouer le rôle de wali, ce rôle est rempli par le magistrat qui homologue le mariage. Dans tous les cas, le magistrat avise immédiatement du mariage les fonctionnaires consulaires français compétents.

Les effets personnels du mariage sont régis par la loi de celui des deux États dont les époux ont la nationalité.
Si l'un des époux a la nationalité de l'un des deux États et le second celle de l'autre, les effets personnels du mariage sont régis par la loi de celui des deux États sur le territoire duquel les époux ont leur domicile commun ou avaient leur dernier domicile commun.
Les obligations alimentaires entre époux sont réglées conformément aux dispositions du chapitre III de la présente Convention.

Article 9
La dissolution du mariage est prononcée selon la loi de celui des deux États dont les époux ont tous deux la nationalité à la date de la présentation de la demande.
Si à la date de la présentation de la demande, l'un des époux a la nationalité de l'un des deux États et le second celle de l'autre, la dissolution du mariage est prononcée selon la loi de l'État sur le territoire duquel les époux ont leur domicile commun ou avaient leur dernier domicile commun.

Article 10
Les règles de conflit de lois définies à l'article précédent s'appliquent aux effets personnels qui découlent de la dissolution du mariage.
Les effets relatifs à la garde des enfants et aux pensions alimentaires qui leur sont dues relèvent des dispositions du chapitre III de la présente Convention.

Article 11
Au sens de l'alinéa a) de l'article 16 de la Convention d'aide mutuelle judiciaire et d'exequatur des jugements du 5 octobre 1957, la dissolution du mariage peut être prononcée par les juridictions de celui des deux États sur le territoire duquel les époux ont leur domicile commun ou avaient leur dernier domicile commun.
Toutefois, au cas où les époux ont tous deux la nationalité de l'un des deux États, les juridictions de cet État peuvent être également compétentes, quel que soit le domicile des époux au moment de l'introduction de l'action judiciaire.
Si une action judiciaire a été introduite devant une juridiction de l'un des deux États, et si une nouvelle action entre les mêmes parties et ayant le même objet est portée devant le tribunal de l'autre État, la juridiction saisie en second lieu doit surseoir à statuer.

Article 12
Les règles définies aux articles 9, 10 et 11 de la présente Convention s'appliquent à la séparation de corps lorsque celle-ci est prévue par la loi compétente de l'un des deux États.

Article 13
Les actes constatant la dissolution du lien conjugal homologués par un juge au Maroc entre conjoints de nationalité marocaine dans les formes prévues par leur loi nationale produisent effet en France dans les mêmes conditions que les jugements de divorce prononcés à l'étranger.
Lorsqu'ils sont devenus irrévocables, les actes constatant la dissolution du lien conjugal selon la loi marocaine entre un mari de nationalité marocaine et son épouse de nationalité française, dressés et homologués par un juge au Maroc, produisent effet en France à la demande de la femme dans les mêmes conditions que les jugements de divorce.

Article 14
Par l'exception à l'article 17 de la Convention d'aide mutuelle judiciaire et d'exequatur des jugements du 5 octobre 1957, en matière d'état des personnes les décisions en force de chose jugée peuvent être publiées ou transcrites sans exequatur sur les registres de l'état civil.

Convention entre le Gouvernement de la République algérienne démocratique et populaire et la République française relative à l'exequatur et à l'extradition, signée à Paris le 29 août 1964.

Le Gouvernement de la République algérienne démocratique et populaire et le Gouvernement de la République française, désirant renforcer la coopération qui s'est instaurée en matière judiciaire entre la France et l'Algérie et en attendant la conclusion d'une convention judiciaire générale, sont convenus des dispositions suivantes:

Titre Ier de l'exequatur.
Article 1er.
En matière civile et commerciale, les décisions contentieuses et gracieuses rendues par les juridictions siégeant en France ou en Algérie, ont de plein droit l'autorité de la chose jugée sur le territoire de l'autre État si elles réunissent les conditions suivantes:
a. La décision émane d'une juridiction compétente selon les règles concernant les conflits de compétence admises dans l'État où la décision doit être exécutée;

b. Les parties ont étaient légalement citées, représentées ou déclarées défaillantes, selon la loi de l'État où la décision a été rendue;
c. La décision est, d'après la loi de l'État où elle a été rendue, passée en force de chose jugée et susceptible d'exécution;
d. La décision ne contient rien de contraire à l'ordre public de l'État où elle est invoquée ou aux principes de droit public applicables dans cet État. Elle ne doit pas non plus être contraire à une décision judiciaire prononcée dans cet État et possédant à son égard l'autorité de la chose jugée.

Article 2.
Les décisions visées à l'article précédent ne peuvent donner lieu à aucune exécution forcée par les autorités de l'autre État ni faire l'objet de la part de ces autorités d'aucune formalité publique, telle que l'inscription, la transcription ou la rectification sur les registres publics qu'après avoir été déclarées exécutoires sur le territoire de l'État requis.

Article 3.
L'exequatur est accordé à la demande de toute partie intéressée, par l'autorité compétente d'après la loi de l'État où il est requis.
La procédure de la demande en exequatur est régie par la loi de l'État dans lequel l'exécution est demandée.

Circulaire du 22 octobre 2014 relative aux effets juridiques du recueil légal en France, NOR: JUSC1416688C[8] (excerpt)

L'attention de la Chancellerie a été appelée sur la nécessité de clarifier la situation juridique en France des enfants ayant fait l'objet d'une mesure de « kafala » dans leur pays d'origine, dénommée en droit français sous le terme de « recueil légal ».
En effet, il apparaît que les personnes qui ont recueilli un enfant selon cette modalité rencontrent des difficultés administratives. Or, celles-ci pourraient être, pour certaines, surmontées par une meilleure connaissance de la mesure étrangère et par une meilleure prise en compte des effets de celle-ci dans notre ordre juridique interne.
Aussi, la présente circulaire a pour objet de présenter les contours du recueil légal dans les pays d'origine, d'en préciser les effets en France et de rappeler les conditions dans lesquelles un enfant ayant fait l'objet d'un recueil légal et devenu français peut être adopté.

---

8 Available at http://circulaires.legifrance.gouv.fr/pdf/2014/11/cir_38976.pdf.

1—Les contours du recueil légal dans les pays d'origine
Le recueil légal est une institution étrangère qui permet le recueil d'un enfant par une personne ou un couple dont l'un au moins des conjoints est de confession musulmane (1.1). Les enfants ainsi recueillis et résidant en France sont principalement d'origine marocaine et algérienne (2.2).
1.1 Le recueil d'un enfant dans les pays de droit musulman
Le droit musulman, prohibant l'adoption, connaît une institution, la «kafala», qui permet de confier un enfant, durant sa minorité, à une personne ou un couple dont l'un des conjoints au moins est de confession musulmane (le «kafil») afin qu'il assure bénévolement sa protection, son éducation et son entretien.
Le recueil légal peut concerner des enfants abandonnés ou délaissés mais aussi des enfants ayant des parents qui ne peuvent matériellement ou moralement les élever.
Le recueil légal est une mesure de protection pour des enfants mineurs. Elle cesse de produire effet à la majorité de l'enfant (en Algérie, à 19 ans et au Maroc, à 18 ans ou pour les filles jusqu'à leur mariage ou leur autonomie financière) ou sur décision de l'autorité qui a prononcé la mesure. [...]
2—Effets juridiques du recueil légal en France
2.1 Reconnaissance de la décision judiciaire de recueil légal
2.1.1 Le principe: la reconnaissance de plein droit
La décision judiciaire de recueil légal est, comme toute décision relative à l'état des personnes, reconnue de plein droit sur le territoire français, sans formalité particulière, dès lors que sa régularité internationale n'est pas contestée.
La convention franco-marocaine d'aide mutuelle judiciaire, d'exequatur des jugements et d'extradition du 5 octobre 1957 et la convention franco-algérienne relative à l'exequatur et à l'extradition du 27 août 1964 énoncent que pour avoir de plein droit l'autorité de la chose jugée en France, les décisions contentieuses ou gracieuses rendues par une juridiction siégeant au Maroc ou en Algérie doivent réunir les conditions de compétence internationale de la juridiction, de régularité de la citation ou de la comparution des parties, du caractère exécutoire de la décision et de l'absence de contrariété de celle-ci à l'ordre public français ou à une décision rendue en France.
Il n'est donc en principe pas nécessaire de solliciter l'exequatur de la décision judiciaire prononçant le recueil légal.

Bibliography

Béraud, Céline, de Galembert, Claire, and Rostaing, Corinne, *Des hommes et des dieux en prison* (Paris: Mission de recherche Droit et Justice, 2013).

Béraud, Céline and Claire de Galembert, 'Des hommes et des dieux en prison' (2014), avaliable at http://www.gip-recherche-justice.fr/wp-content/uploads/2014/05/Entretien_hommes-dieux-en-prison.pdf

Bergeaud-Blackler, Florence, '*Halal*: d'une norme communautaire à une norme institutionnelle', *Journal des anthropologues*, 106–107 (2006), available at http://jda.revues.org/1270.

Boyer, Alain, *Le droit des religions en France* (Paris: Presses Universitaires de France, 1993).

Conseil d'État, *Rapport public 2004. Un siècle de laïcité* (Paris: La documentation française, 2004).

Fornerod, Anne, 'The places of worship in France and the public/private divide', in Ferrari, Silvio, and Pastorelli, Sabrina (eds), *Religion in public spaces* (Farnham: Ashgate, 2012), pp. 323–336.

Fornerod, Anne, 'Religion et acquisition de la nationalité française', *Revue du droit public et de la science politique en France et à l'étranger*, 3/2009, pp. 715–741.

Godard, Bernard and Taussig, Sylvie, *Les musulmans en France. Courants, institutions, communautés: un état des lieux* (Paris: Hachette Littératures, 2007).

Hafiz, Chems-Eddine and Devers, Gilles, *Droit et religion musulmane* (Paris: Dalloz, 2005).

Haquet, Arnaud, 'L'enseignement privé musulman dans une République laïque', *Revue Française de Droit Administratif*, 2009, pp. 515–524.

Khosrokhavar, Farhad, *L'Islam dans les prisons* (Paris: Balland, 2004).

Khosrokhavar, Farhad, 'Radicalization in Prison: The French Case', *Politics, Religion & Ideology*, vol. 14, issue 2 (2013), pp. 284–306.

Koussens, David, 'Expertise publique sous influence?', *Archives de sciences sociales des religions*, 155 (juillet-septembre 2011), available at http://assr.revues.org/23306.

Le Bras, Gabriel, *La police religieuse dans l'ancienne France. Cours d'histoire du droit public de 1940–1941* (handout: 1941).

Lecerf, Jean-René, *Avis présenté au nom de la commission des lois constitutionnelles, de législation, du suffrage universel, du Règlement et d'administration générale sur le projet de loi de finances pour 2015*, Tome VIII, Administration Pénitentiaire, no. 114 (20 November 2014), Senate, p. 53. Available at http://www.senat.fr/rap/a14-114-8/a14-114-81.pdf

Long, Marceau (ed.), *Être français aujourd'hui et demain. Rapport remis au Premier ministre* (Paris: La documentation française, 1988, tome 2).

Lorcerie, Françoise, 'La 'loi sur le voile': une entreprise politique', *Droit et société*, 2008/1, no. 68, pp. 53–74.

Machelon, Jean-Pierre, *Les relations des cultes avec les pouvoirs publics: rapport au ministre de l'Intérieur* (Paris: La Documentation française, 2006).

Marguénaud, Jean-Pierre and Mouly, Jean, 'Les droits de l'Homme salarié de l'entreprise identitaire (à propos des trois arrêts de la Cour EDH, *Obst* et *Schüth* du 23 septembre 2010 et *Siebenhaar* du 3 février 2011)', *Recueil Dalloz*, 2011 pp. 1637–1643.

Maurey, Hervé, *Les collectivités territoriales et le financement des lieux de culte. Rapport d'information n° 345* (Paris: Sénat, 2014–2015), Available at http://www.senat.fr/rap/r14-345/r14-345.html.

Messner, Francis, Prélot, Pierre-Henri, and Woehrling, Jean-Marie, *Traité de droit français des religions* (Paris: LexisNexis, 2013).

Ponty, Janine, 'Les étrangers et le droit d'association au XXe siècle', *Matériaux pour l'histoire de notre temps*, 2003, no. 69, pp. 24–25.

Senate, *Local public authorities and the funding of places of worship*, 17 March 2015, available at http://www.senat.fr/rap/r14-345/r14-345.html.

Van Ooijen, Hana, *Religious Symbols in Public Functions: Unveiling State Neutrality: A Comparative Analysis of Dutch, English and French Justifications for Limiting the Freedom of Public Officials to Display* (Antwerp: Intersentia, School of Human Rights Research Series, vol. 58, 2012).

Zeghal, Malika, 'La constitution du Conseil Français du Culte Musulman: reconnaissance politique d'un Islam français?', *Archives de sciences sociales des religions*, 129, (2005), pp. 97–113, available at http://assr.revues.org/1113.

Index